ROMANS REVIEWED

OUR STORYBOOK FAIRY-TALE REALITY OF THE KINGDOM OF GOD

LAURIE KAY RODRIGUEZ

WESTBOW
PRESS®
A DIVISION OF THOMAS NELSON
& ZONDERVAN

WestBow Press books may be ordered through booksellers or by contacting:

WestBow Press
A Division of Thomas Nelson & Zondervan
1663 Liberty Drive
Bloomington, IN 47403
www.westbowpress.com
844-714-3454

ISBN: 978-1-6642-4924-0 (sc)
ISBN: 978-1-6642-4923-3 (e)

Library of Congress Control Number: 2021922834

Print information available on the last page.

WestBow Press rev. date: 06/28/2022

Unless You, Lord, build, guide and inspire
I labor in vain.

To God, my Father
Jesus, my Savior
Holy Spirit, my Guide
Thank You,
You know what I mean!

DEDICATION

My First Book, Family!

I dedicate this book to Sam, My Love,
My Best Friend, I am so grateful to be your wife.
To my children Natasha, Ashley, and Sammy,
Angel, Michael, and Chandler,
Alex Lee, Alfredo and Magz!
I wrote this book for you
to encourage you to continue to walk
in what is most important in life.
I love each of you more than you know.

To my grandchildren,
Tatiana, Josiah, Elijah, and Isabella,
Penelope and Giselle,
Baby-girl Rodriguez
(and those to come),
I did not know I could love anyone more
than your Papa, and your parents,
But then you came along and showed me
A different "Ama-kind of love."
This book is for you for your future.

And to my Forever Friends
Bev, Laurinda, Becky,
Gerianne, Aida, and Martha,
Who walked with me through this
Journey, thank you for your prayers,
Your support and always asking me,
"When is your book going to be finished?"
It's finished!

Special Dedication

This book would not have been accomplished without
two very important, generous friends.
Apolonio Garcia graciously and obediently surprised
me by giving me his MacBook when he heard that
I was writing Romans Reviewed. Words will never
express my gratitude to such a selfless act.
Karen Cruz has been with me editing my manual with
so much love and care as if it were hers. I am forever in
her debt for such long hours laboring to get it right.
Thank you, my friends!

EPIGRAPH

"Romans is our play-by-play book of how to transform our lives of sin into an abundant life full of His Spirit!"

I am the Door. If anyone enters by Me, he will be saved, and will go in and out and find pasture. The thief does not come except to steal, and to kill, and to destroy. I have come that they may have life, and that they may have it more abundantly (John 10:9, 10).

FOREWORD BY SAMMY RODRIGUEZ

The author of this book has been a person who has impacted me my whole life! That tends to happen when the author is your mother. Besides that point, I get the privilege of talking with you a bit about her book. Before we jump into the book, I believe we must look into a window of time and at the author to get the whole picture of all the passion, hard work, prayer, and excellence invested into this book.

Flashback to a time when I was around ten years old; as many other young boys do, they have hang-time and sleepovers with the bros. Back in my day (I will be 33 soon), we would play basketball until you could not see the ball, then run in and play some Nintendo 64 (yes, best game console ever).

If you have not been to a sleepover, you should, but one of the rules is the first to fall asleep gets messed with by the boys who are awake! It turned out my bro's younger brother was the victim. Now, as he was fast asleep on the top bunk in my buddy's room, we decided to go to the fridge and grab whatever we could! He will remember never to fall asleep first again. As we enter the room and gingerly climb up the ladder, we start to put butter, toothpaste, and a few other condiments on him. The one I remember most was the Aunt Jemima syrup! After our amazing victory (or so we thought), we headed back to the front room to play a few more games before going to sleep.

I remember being forcefully woken up by my buddy's Mom, who said my Mom was on the phone and wanted to talk with me, now! On a Saturday, you do not want to be getting up at 7 am. What happened was, his younger brother woke up and went to his Mom, who told my Mom, and now I was in big trouble. I remember distinctly my mother telling me to "get home right now!" I knew that it would be a long week, so I decided to take the long way home on my baller razor scooter. I walked in and met my mother in the kitchen, where she had a look on her face, which made me know she was not to be messed with. She asked if I thought it was funny, and to my response, I just told her, "If I could go back, I would." The next moment is what forever stays in my head. As I respond, she asks me, "Do you think that was funny?" And then disappears into our walk-in pantry. She comes back out with a massive tub of Log Cabin Syrup (oh yeah, we shopped at Costco, the big kind). She pops the lid open and again asks me," Do you think that was funny?" Then she proceeds to dump half the bottle on my head. The syrup is going down my face and clothes and onto the floor. At this moment, we both can't help but laugh, and she tells me to get in the shower. This moment, though extreme, forever sticks (no pun intended) with me. I believe that because my mama decided to make this point known, I didn't have to guess with her and that her audacious acts forever convinced me never to do that again. Although more than that, she could truly communicate and fight for love, truth, and honesty!

I tell you this story because all of the truth from this Romans Reviewed book is written by my wild mama, who dumped half a bottle of syrup on my head to drive home the truth of the matter that has never left me. I can share so many other stories, but the last one I will share is remembering how we had gone through the entire Bible eight times before I was in the 8th grade. My passion for the Word, and without a doubt, my direction in ministry, is directly correlated to her ability to keep our family in the Word and prioritizing the Word in our lives!

Throughout the book, a common phrase you will hear is the *"Storybook Fairy-Tale Reality of the Kingdom of God."* I love that phrase because the truth is the **Storybook** of the gospel, which seems too good to be true, but is, in fact, the truth that will set us free. Not a freedom to just quote words or live good lives but to truly live out our **Fairy-Tale** (supernatural) lives with Jesus, seeing the sick healed, seeing the lost saved, and seeing those in bondage find freedom. In this supernatural walk, we genuinely get to stand in the **Reality of the Kingdom of God!** I believe that my mama hits on this with such clarity and real insight. I know that my favorite books are those in which I know the author has done their work, and as for Romans Reviewed, I can say this is entirely true.

You will read others' thoughts of the scriptures in many other commentaries, and I love that; I love reading many of them. The difference in this book is that it gives you the author's thought and an application of this thought, as well as stirring our hearts to search out more of what Jesus is speaking through Paul. Now personally, *Romans* is one of my favorite books in the Bible. It is the most complete explanation of the gospel from Paul. I believe that in a day and age when it can be easy not to have depth or clarity in the Word, this book, Romans Reviewed, is completely in season with what we all need.

Lastly, I believe that this book encourages us all, the everyday believer, to move from inaction to action. My final encouragement would be to buckle up and step into every chapter and every verse with an open heart and allow Jesus to move in you. This book will confront and disrupt your life, so please, if you want to stay the same, I would recommend stopping right now.

With so much love and appreciation for the author, I say this, "Mother, you have given your guts to this book, and I know that there will be countless amounts of peoples' lives changed because of your obedience in writing this. I am excited that this is your first but not your last! I love you."

Sammy Rodriguez

PREFACE

Isaiah 50:4 (NIV) "The Sovereign Lord has given me a well-instructed tongue, to know the word that sustains the weary. He wakens me morning by morning, wakens my ear to listen like one being instructed."

One summer morning in 2011, just before I woke up, I heard, "Write *Romans*," I had a clear understanding of what to do. I got up, went down to our local library to use their computer (my laptop had seen its final days), and wrote *Roman's* first chapter as a commentary. I understood what it was to look like, and the first chapter came easy. I knew I could not use the internet or any commentaries, just what I had learned through reading *Romans* and studying it and living it and listening to it preached about in my 54 years of life. After the project was complete, I went back to set in references and look up scripture.

It has taken me years to complete this work. I let it lay in a drawer for what seemed years to marinate, as I prayed and fasted over it. God's timing is perfect, I was not in a hurry to publish Romans Reviewed until He opened all the doors and said to my heart that it is ready! This book is His idea. He inspired me and helped me write this book. Why *Romans*? Simply, because God told me to. The Bible is God's manifesto of His standards for us to live here on earth, and into eternity. *Romans* instructs us how to navigate through this life, abundantly. The Bible is the most misunderstood and unread book by the millennials and generations that follow, which means that most of our younger generations do not know how to live a fulfilled life! These generations are the most unchurched generations. I passionately desire to inspire these generations to know who our Father God and Jesus really are (https://www.barna.com/research/millennials-and-the-bible-3-surprising-insights/).

The *Romans'* book is the road to our purpose, salvation, fulfillment, faith, maturity, transformation, love, obedience, mystery, and many great theological understandings. Paul, our brother who wrote most of the New Testament, wrote the book, *Romans*, to the new converts in Rome. Not having a Jewish degree, the Romans could not quite understand the whole picture of salvation without knowing the Jewish culture. Today, we too, need an understanding of Paul's book to know:

why we are here,

what our purpose is and

where we are going.

Jesus says, "I know where I came from and where I am going."
John 8:14 NIV

I pray this book falls into the hands of an army of courageous young world changers.

ACKNOWLEDGMENT

I would like to acknowledge, in deep appreciation, the Pastors that preached the Word of God passionately all my years in the church community, I have learned much. I want to call out three people who especially bred into me the importance of the Word and the application of the Word.

In Heaven now with my Mom, June Rae Nelson, is My Dad, Fred M. Nelson, both are living out the reality of Heaven. My Dad instilled in my siblings and me the duty of reading the Word of God in morning Bible reading throughout our lives in our home. We went through the Bible more times than I can count. I thank my Dad and Mom for raising me in the standard of the Word of God. In their later years, my Mom and Dad would read three chapters of the Word each in the morning and the evening, that's 12 chapters a day. They read through the Bible many times. When my Dad died in 2003, my Mom continued to read her Word morning and night. Mom took on both of their readings (12 chapters a day) until she went to Heaven in 2009. Reading the Word was a discipline they taught me, and I was full of the knowledge of God. Thank you, Mom and Dad, for being great influencers in my life.

The other significant influencer in my life is Pastor Jon Courson of Applegate Christian Fellowship, a mentor since 1983, more by his teachings and commentaries than in person. He expounded the Word in such a palatable way and opened my eyes to understanding exponentially. He broke down the Old and New Testament in ways I had never heard before. I was mesmerized and fell in love with Jesus all over again. He made Jesus so personable and attractive, so attainable and not afar off. He spoke in ways opening my heart to wanting more of Jesus and His Word. Every service there was an application for that week, how to live out in practical ways the Word of God. Thanks to Pastor Jon, I discovered in my late 20s that reading the Word was not enough. He truly challenged me to change my dutiful reading of the Bible into a daily delight of searching out the scriptures to see what God, our Father, had to say to me.

Jeremiah 33:3 'Call to Me, and I will answer you, and show you great and mighty things, which you do not know.'

If you want a growing personal relationship with Jesus other than just knowing about Him, I encourage you to go to his YouTube channel, Jon Courson or joncourson.com.

Thank you, Pastor Jon, for being so dedicated to teaching and living out the Word of God for so many years.

INTRODUCTION

Never has there been a book written that so many biblical scholars have deemed it their favorite, as the book of *Romans*. There have been so many commentaries written about *Romans*. Unlike any other *Romans* analysis, this book is for the millennials and anyone else who would like to see *Romans* from a down to earth perspective. *Romans* Reviewed is written from a lived out, enjoyed viewpoint. There were times I was troubled and misunderstood what God was saying. I have read and reread the book of *Romans*. I had asked hard questions to God, why He has to be so harsh in some areas of life, why He had already picked my destiny before I was born, and why is it so difficult to follow some of His ways? I have joyfully found the answers to these questions and so many more as Paul's teachings became clear through the insight of the Holy Spirit.

Abundant life (*John 10:10*) is possible! I call it the *Storybook Fairy-Tale Reality of the Kingdom of God*. Let me explain: **The Storybook** (the Bible, our life's manual, we step into God's Kingdom through His Word and live by different standards than the world's standards) **Fairy-Tale** (supernatural: God's super to our natural, *"I tell you this timeless truth: The person who follows Me in faith, believing in Me, will do the same mighty miracles that I do–even greater miracles than these because I go to be with my Father! John 14:12 TPT*) **Reality of the Kingdom of God** (*be in the world but not of the world, "For they no longer belong to this world any more than I do." John 17:16 and John 18:36 Jesus answered, "My kingdom is not of this world. If My kingdom were of this world, then My servants would fight, that I would not be handed over to the Jews. But my kingdom is not from here."*). You will read that phrase throughout Romans Reviewed. Abundant life is promised us in *John 10:10*, and I always questioned it. Why am I not living in abundant life? Questions are good because if you are questioning, then you are searching. God wants us to search for Him ourselves. Ask, He will answer you! Seek, you will find Him! Knock, He will open the door of abundant life for you! I ask you lots of questions throughout Romans Reviewed to get you to think for yourself, to look for the truth and initiate more questions. I don't answer all the questions for you, that's your job, you have a lifetime to find them while building your relationship with Jesus!

The *Storybook Fairy-Tale Reality of the Kingdom of God* is living *Romans 12*, truly understanding we are body, soul, and spirit. Our soul (mind and heart) connected wholly to our spirit brings us to the understanding of what abundant life is all about. Your soul (thoughts and emotions) is a force to be reckoned with, and it takes courage to quiet your soul and give in to following the Spirit of God. Our soul determines how strong our spirit will be. We will live a life of self-decision that doesn't work out well, or we will live a life of self-discipline, allowing the Spirit of God to determine our ways and days.

What is an abundant life? The perfect example is Jesus. He said I did not come to speak my thoughts. I came to speak the words of My Father. I did not come seeking to be served but to serve. I did not come for my own plan, but I came to accomplish My Father's will. Abundant life is transferring our purpose, agenda, and destiny to God. Giving our will over to the Spirit of God. What does that look like anyway? It looks like waking up, acknowledging your dependency on the Spirit of God, living every day with purpose, pleasing God, and being led every day by the Spirit.

How you ask? Good question. A soldier did not make general in a day. He listened and learned and acted in the ways his officers told him. He went through trial and errors and many years of training to eventually become a general. We, too, need to be trained in the workmanship of the Christian life; we must separate ourselves from the world and still occupy. Abundant life comes when we surrender, so the quicker you surrender your soul to Jesus, the faster you live in the *Storybook Fairy-Tale Reality of the Kingdom of God*. We are placed here in this world to completely obey what the Word and the Spirit say. We are to train diligently becoming trustworthy soldiers, and then we are to enter the battle understanding our foes and those we are to rescue (save souls and set the captives free). We do not fight the way the world does; we do not fight against flesh and blood (people); we fight against the principalities and the dark forces of this world. Our position is in the heavenly realms with Jesus (Ephesians 2:6). We are His kings (leaders) and priests (intercessors) distributed throughout the world (Revelation 1:6). We are God's agents of war and love. We are dispatched daily to do God's bidding. When we are at that level, we are living in the *Storybook Fairy-Tale Reality of the Kingdom of God* or Abundant Life!

I believe Romans Reviewed will take you on a path to discover your potential and purpose. You will learn to live an abundant life if you are courageous enough to lay down your life (will and desires) and pick up the purpose of your Eternal Father who loves you more than you can think or imagine. He has a destiny for us that far outweighs our imagination. He has set you in a kingdom with villains, not of this world. God has made you more significant than today's fairy-tale characters and superheroes. You and I are destined for greatness in the *Storybook Fairy-Tale Reality of the Kingdom of God* as we become less, and He becomes more.

Romans Reviewed comes with a warning. It is not for the faint of heart or the whiny. It takes a real man or woman of God to be willing to step into a new realm of reality. It's not what we see with our eyes but what we see with our spirit. It can be unnerving at times; it can be uncanny and unbelievable, but for those brave enough to enter into the *Storybook Fairy-Tale Reality of the Kingdom of God*, it is exciting daily, never mundane, and full of surprises! Willing to enter?

ROMANS REVIEWED

You will be changed from the inside out.

Therefore, I strongly suggest to you, family, understand God's mercy. Daily present yourself and your agenda as an offering to the Lord, holy and pleasing to God—this is your true and proper worship.

Do not conform to the cultures of this world but be transformed by renewing your mind. Then you will think God's kingdom ways and live what God's will is—His will for you is good, pleasing, and perfect.

Romans 12:1, 2 (Laurie's translation)

Why *Romans*?

It is the basis of our salvation, the foundation of the depth of our perception of what Jesus did for us, and the freedom of our walk in Christ. It is our play-by-play book of how to transform our lives of sin into a resurrection of new life in Christ.

If we get saved and live a life without knowing *Romans*, then we cannot grow in the understanding of our inheritance, in the great expanse of our destiny, and the fullness of our power and influence here on earth.

It is a *Storybook Fairy-Tale Reality of the Kingdom of God*. We have not a clue what is before us in this spiritual life. Paul opens the door for us in *Romans*, and we get to take a peek at what God has for us. It is up to us to walk through and perceive what is right before our very eyes, not our physical eyes, but the eyes of our spirit.

Paul, the author of *Romans*, wanted to visit the Christians in Rome. He had heard of their convergence with Christ and wanted to disciple them into the "more of Christ;" unfortunately, he could not get to them, so he did not fuss over what he could not do. Instead, he did what he could do, picking up ink and putting it to papyrus paper.

CONTENTS

CHAPTER 1

Living the Truth

Read the complete chapter of *Romans 1*.

> *Paul, a servant of Christ Jesus, called to be an apostle and set apart for the gospel of God. (Romans 1:1)*

My Thought

Paul was a servant of Jesus Christ by a sudden conversion. He was so tenacious in his beliefs in Judaism that he did not notice the brief but distinct change that took place with the birth of Jesus. The Jewish leaders (mainly Pharisees and Sadducees) were staunch believers in the law. Caught up in the law, they missed the fulfillment of the law. Saul, belonging to the Pharisees sect, was quite aware of the new system spreading among the Jews. He was *not* going to let this recent move continue, so he went out, with permission from the High Priest, and persecuted this new breed of Jews (Jesus Christ believers). Unbeknownst to him, he was killing his God's people (because his heart was right but not his mind). So with a precise blow to Saul, Jesus knocked him off his high horse and turned this tenacious man into a servant of the most high God (*Acts 9*). He was called at that moment to be the apostle Paul and was separated from everything and set his eyes on one thing: the gospel of Christ. There is so much to say in this one verse. We must see this, precious family. In his loyal devotion to the law (religion), Paul was passionately persecuting his own people. He was tenacious in trying to persuade God how righteous he was. He was not going to let anyone change the law—his passions were in the wrong place. Instead of asking, God, have things changed? He went about in his "knowing" God's will. But God's ways had changed with the coming of Jesus—the change they had written about so many times in Old Testament scripture. The fulfillment of the law (Jesus) had come, meaning they no longer had to live out the letter of the law. This change was a change of law to grace. Paul was religious; his religion had blinded him from the truth because religion binds up. Knocked down, Paul became a servant. No longer tenacious after the law but now reserved to do God's will. That doesn't mean he didn't try to do his own thing; it meant that when he did, the Spirit would remind him who was in charge, and being a servant of Jesus, Paul would be subservient to what the Spirit of God said. Paul was not perfect, but he was teachable. Paul was separated to walk the truth of the gospel. A sermon in itself. We, too, need to be separated from all things and have our eyes set on Jesus and the cross!

Your Application

How can we practically do this? Meditate on this verse and then list some ways you, too, can become separated to Jesus and the cross.

> *The gospel He promised beforehand through the prophets in the Holy Scriptures.*
> *(Romans 1:2)*

My Thought

God promised throughout Old Testament scripture through the prophets of old that the gospel (the good news of Jesus Christ) was coming. The Old Testament prophecies are the living proof that the Word of God is true. Over three hundred prophetic words came true in Jesus's birth, life, death, resurrection, and ascension. No other book can give these statistics. God's Word is truly God's Word.

Your Application

Look up some of Jesus' Old Testament prophetic scriptures and match them with the New Testament scriptures.

> *Regarding His Son, who as to His human nature was a descendant of David.*
> *(Romans 1:3)*

My Thought

Jesus Christ was born of a woman, Mary, yet Jesus was living forever before the beginning and is never-ending. Deity chooses to become a man, designed to be in the lineage of David. David, our first true king in the flesh, modeled the greater king, King Jesus Christ. We see the limits of our flesh yet acknowledge the limitlessness of our king and leader, Jesus Christ. In our spirits, we can break the boundaries of the flesh. In faith, we can, by the Spirit, rise above the worldly limitations into godly expectations. We don't have to be bound to things here on earth when we understand that Jesus was born of a woman (limited in nature), yet He was also limitless in His life. He exemplifies what we can do. We, too, are born of women, but we too, can become limitless by the Holy Spirit in prayer, and in His desires for us, if we only believe.

Your Application

What stops you from reaching past your human limitations and visiting the realms of heaven? In *Romans*, Paul wants you to use the keys that unlock eternity and join others living in their full potential. Ponder on this and write a statement or essay.

> *And who through the Spirit of holiness was declared with power to be the Son*
> *of God by His resurrection from the dead: Jesus Christ our Lord. (Romans 1:4)*

My Thought

Jesus, born of woman, was proven to be the Son of God when He resurrected from the dead. He was given life from a woman, to surrender to death by men, and resurrected life by God. We are given the same opportunities as Christ. We are born of women, we see that life in this world by our own power is nothing more than vapor, and when we die to this life of flesh and resurrect to the life of Christ, we then live a life of substance and holiness (wholeness), being separated for kingdom purposes.

Your Application

How hard is it to hold vapor, to capture it and keep it? The beginning of real life is when you realize that life without Christ is fleeting. State the times you have been disappointed by the surface things of this world; when did your life begin to change from vapor to substance?

> *Through Him and for His name's sake, we receive grace and apostleship to call people from among all the Gentiles to the obedience that comes from faith. (Romans 1:5)*

My Thought

By Christ we receive our inheritance of grace and our destiny or calling. It's up to us to have the faith to accept it by believing and simply obeying. This is the Word that frees us to walk into our *Storybook Fairy-Tale Reality of the Kingdom of God*. We have been given grace. Therefore, there is now no condemnation. We are free from the law, free from religion, free from our own expectations.

> *Grace grants us the freedom to become ourselves without limitations or bondage. We become the ones we were meant to be in the plans of God. For Paul, it was to be an apostle; for each of us, there is a designated design. It is up to us to search what it is and to work it out.*

Your Application

This is where you stop and figure out what your designated design is. Some of you will already know, but for those who do not, how can you know? *Psalms 139* says that God has recorded all your life before you were born, so He knows your design! If you knew a person had the plans of your life, what would you do? Do it!

> *And you also are among those who are called to belong to Jesus Christ. (Romans 1:6)*

My Thought

Paul further encourages the Romans that they too are called by Jesus. We are all called by Jesus. It's up to us to accept that calling. So Jesus is not unjust in receiving some and rejecting others because *it's our choice*. He made the way; it's up to us to believe it. He is just in all that He does.

Your Application

Do you question God's ways? Write about it and give scripture that encourages you to believe that God is good, God is love, and God only teaches us what is best.

> *To all in Rome who are loved by God and called to be saints: Grace and peace to you from God our Father and from the Lord Jesus Christ. (Romans 1:7)*

My Thought

The first six verses were Paul's introduction to the Romans. Now he gives them a salutation. Paul says, "To all that be in Rome who…" are beloved of God and are called to be saints. Paul sends them grace and grants peace from God our Father and the Lord Jesus Christ. Paul demonstrates that they all belong to the same family. How important is this? We need to realize that we all belong to the same family who is the beloved of God and called to be saints. God is our father, and Jesus is the connecting force that brings us all together. Paul understood this and was able to love those he never met. If we don't get this portion of scripture, we will never have the ability to love with the love of the Father.

Your Application

Are you concerned with others outside your circle of influence? Do you weep for those who are hurting in other countries? Connecting to God's people is part of God's plan. Do something this week to connect to someone you don't know. (Hint: pray for them or write a letter or give your time or serve.)

> *First, I thank my God through Jesus Christ, for all of you, because your faith is being reported all over the world. (Romans 1:8)*

My Thought

Now Paul comes to the reason he is writing. He is thanking God for all of those in Rome who have accepted Christ Jesus. Paul is excited to share the fact that Romans are accepting Christ! When we hear of others' salvation, do we respond the way Paul did, or are we aloof to this fact? When reports come to us in a service that others in different countries have heard and accepted Jesus, do we want to take pen to paper and introduce ourselves and rejoice with them? We need to take a moment and check our hearts, for this was the very nature of our brother Paul. He was so excited that he granted them his time and expended energy to write a letter (New Testament book).

Your Application

Again, make a plan to connect with someone in Christ that you have not met and encourage them or find a missionary and commit to praying for and supporting them.

> *God, whom I serve with my whole heart in preaching the gospel of His Son, is my witness how constantly I remember you... (Romans 1:9)*

My Thought

Not only does Paul take the time to be excited for them and to write them, but now he is also praying for them. We need to remember that Paul does *not* know these people. He has no common connection to them. He has just heard about them and now wants them to be a part of him. The world, as we know it, gets up, pulls out of their garages by remote control, goes to work, comes back home, pulls back into their garages by remote control, never needing to see or talk with their neighbors. They go to church, worship, listen to the sermon, and go back home, never needing to converse with other congregants. This should not be. Paul says, rejoice when you hear of others' salvation. Write to them and welcome them into the family of God.

Your Application

Take a moment, ask God if you need to be more connected to His family, and ask Him how He would like you to do this. This week, I guarantee He will show you; that's how easy it is to learn from Him.

> *In my prayers at all times; and I pray that now at last by God's will the way may be opened for me to come to you. (Romans 1:10)*

My Thought

This is what Paul prays. I want to meet you. More conviction to our way of life; Paul hears, writes, and longs to meet them. Oh, that we would become more transparent to others. To leave our selfish side to come over to the desires of God's heart. Know your brothers and sisters. More clearly, God says, "Know my children for it is your family." We will live forever with each of God's children. We need to become connected here. We are so disconnected from our family of God that, in actuality, we are disconnected from our Father's heart.

Your Application

Let's stop right now and call on Him. Let's repent, "Oh God, our Father, we are so sorry for our aloofness to one another, how You long for us to love deeply, how You long for us to be connected as a family, to feel, to care, to rejoice and to weep with one another, to share what we have with each other. Lord God, we repent of our worldly ways and agree to walk in what You have for us. We agree to live our lives in the inheritance and destiny that You have for us. In Your name, Jesus, change us."

> *I long to see you so that I may impart to you some spiritual gift to make you strong. (Romans 1:11)*

My thought

As if we didn't get it, Paul longs to see those he has never met; *I long to see you that I might get something from you?* No! I long to see you that I might impart; Paul wants to impart some spiritual gift so they might be established. Oh, brother and sister, Paul longed to see them and wanted to impart a spiritual gift to them. Do you see Christ in him? Do you see the unselfishness, the desire to impart the gifts to them so they may be established, to give them a spiritual foundation? He had no selfish motive. Remember his passion at the first of the study? He wanted to persecute the disciples of Christ from his own self-righteousness; now, *his passions have been tampered by the Spirit, and Paul longs to do good towards them for God's purpose.* We no longer see Paul, but we see Christ in Paul (*Galatians 2:20*).

Your Application

Human nature is to get things for yourself, to look out for your own good, to manipulate, to negotiate, and to persuade people to see things your way. How do you rate yourself on these things? Are you more human nature, or has Christ turned you into His image? Meditate and honestly write out where you could allow Jesus more access to tamper with your character.

> *That is, that I may be encouraged together with you by the mutual faith both of you and me. (Romans 1:12)*

My Thought

As if Paul hasn't shown enough of Christ, he sets himself on the same level as they are. Paul knew Christ, he spoke to Jesus, he was a known missionary filled with the Spirit, but he compared his faith with theirs. The Romans were new converts and Paul wanted to reassure them and comfort them with the mutual faith they both had. He just leveled the playing field. He allows them to see that our faith is mutual. Our faith is shared. *There is no one better than the other in Christ, because His blood covers us all. We are all on the same playing field. If we get this, we are on the road to victory.* The one on the pulpit that seems to be elevated should be Christ, not the pastor. The pastor has the same mutual faith as we have. The ones we see on media that seem so holy is Christ; the man or woman representing God is on the same playing field as we are. That does not mean we do not appreciate them; it just means we are not to see them as elevated above anyone else. We are on common grounds, brothers, and sisters. We are all on the holy ground of Christ! That should comfort us all.

Your Application

Have you ever felt intimidated by another Christian, a leader, a person more knowledgeable than you? Why? Write it out and understand what causes you to feel this way. Christ is the only one who is to be elevated and put on a throne. All others are your brothers and sisters. We respect and honor others who have walked longer in Christ, but we all have the mutual faith of believing that Jesus Christ died for us all

> *I do not want you to be unaware, brothers, that I planned many times to come to you (but have been prevented from doing so until now) in order that I might have a harvest among you, just as I have had among the other Gentiles. (Romans 1:13)*

My Thought

Paul didn't want the Roman Christians to think that he hadn't made efforts to come to see them. Paul tried to come to Rome to meet his fellow family in Christ but was stopped each time. Paul wanted to be a part of the movement that was going on in Rome. He had helped further the kingdom of God in other Gentile regions; he now wanted to be a part of this as well. We want to do things for God, but God knows the right timing of when we should do the things for Him. Paul wanted to go in the prime of his calling, his apostleship, to the Romans, but God had other plans. Paul would go to Rome, but not in his prime, not in his strength, but in his prison days and in his last days.

Your Application

Oh dear Christian, for us to understand that God's timing and plans are perfect! Do you ever want to go ahead with your plans and forget God's? Will you consider why God's plans are better? Write out some attributes of God after reading *Job*, chapters 38–42.

> *I am obligated both to Greeks and non-Greeks, both to the wise and the foolish.*
> (Romans 1:14)

My Thought

Paul no longer has his own agenda; he is a debtor to all that would need a Savior. As a servant of Christ, he owed it to humanity to pay his debt, to preach the gospel of Jesus Christ to all who would listen. We, too, need to leave our agenda behind to pick up the debt we owe. Not our debt of sin, shame, or pain, that was all paid for when Jesus died on the cross. We owe a debt of love to our fellow man. Christ died for us while we were sinners. He gave us a gift of love when we were in our worst condition. As He beckoned Paul, He now wants us to pay back that debt of love to all who are lost.

Your Application

List ways to pay back Christ's love to others; make plans this week to do at least one on your list.

> *That is why I am so eager to preach the gospel also to you who are at Rome.*
> (Romans 1:15)

My Thought

Paul was ready. We must be prepared to preach, share, live out, and walk in the gospel to whomever God puts in our path. Are we ready? Are we ready to share the good news? If not, that's okay, because the study before us will prepare us to be ready.

Your Application

What are some areas in your life that you would like to change? Write them out and be prepared to see the change come as you meditate on His Word here in *Romans*.

I am not ashamed of the gospel, because it is the power of God, for the salvation of everyone who believes; first for the Jew, then for the Gentile. (Romans 1:16)

My Thought

Paul, who had persecuted the Christians for their faith, who had rebuked and made fun of these crazy people who followed Christ, was now unashamed of the gospel of Christ. He got it! He understood this very gospel is the power of God to save everyone who would believe. Everyone! In our cowardly-ness, we demote the power of the gospel in us. In our inability to proclaim the gospel of Christ boldly, we set ourselves up for failure. Paul's deep understanding of the power of the gospel made him unashamed. We get it backward; we don't understand the power behind the gospel, so we don't read it or study it. Therefore, we are ashamed, and we don't proclaim. We need to understand the power of knowing the gospel by studying it; consequently, we will not be ashamed, and we will proclaim boldly to anyone who will listen.

Your Application

To honestly know God's Word is to know God. To know God is to know who you are. Knowing who you are is to boldly be you and boldly proclaim with power the Good News to everyone. Make a point to set a time each day to know God through reading His powerful words!

For in the gospel a righteousness from God is revealed, a righteousness that is by faith from first to last, just as it is written: "The righteous will live by faith" (Habakkuk 2:4). (Romans 1:17)

My Thought

The gospel of Christ is the righteousness of God revealed, from faith to faith—"the just shall live by faith." Jesus Christ is the open Door into our *Storybook Fairy-Tale Reality* (*So Jesus again said to them, "Truly, truly, I say to you, I AM the DOOR of the sheep." John 10:7*). The gospel of Christ reveals the rightness of God. If we need to, we can go through the whole story of why Christ came. In God's goodness, He wanted to live with us, but He couldn't because we blew it (Adam and Eve) by being sinful (or better said, full of sin). Jesus loving His Father said, "I will go and take the place for their sin." The Father, desiring us so much, said, "Okay, Son." Jesus took our place on the cross to become our *sin*! Death took victory over Jesus, or so death thought. The Father, the Son and the Spirit broke all chains of sin, death, and Satan for eternity, thus the open Door to our *Storybook Fairy-Tale Reality of the Kingdom of God,* or abundant life. We walk into another world inside this world; our faith determines how far we go. *"Jesus said to him, 'I AM the way, the Truth and the life. No one comes to the Father except through Me' (the DOOR)." (John 14:6)*

Your Application

Meditate on and journal about the tragedy and glory of the cross. Personalize it. Read *John 10:9-10.* Explain what it means to see Jesus as the Door into another reality of living. Go into detail about this alternate life. What are the different ways we are to live? Unlike the world's standards what does this new life require of us? Use scripture.

> *The wrath of God is being revealed from heaven against the godlessness and wickedness of men who suppress the truth by their wickedness, (Romans 1:18)*

My Thought

The wrath of God is revealed. He hates anything that will trip up His children. All ungodliness, and all unrighteousness and all who hold the truth and twist it are in line to receive the wrath of God. Let's look in scripture to see why the wrath of God is actually the love of God turned against anything that would harm you, His child. *"Do you think that I like to see wicked people die?" says the Sovereign Lord. "Of course not! I want them to turn from their wicked ways and live." Ezekiel 18:23 (NLT)* That's God's heart. We may say like the Jews in the Old Testament said, '...The Lord isn't doing what's right!' "O people of Israel, it is you who are not doing what's right, not I. Therefore, I will judge each of you. O people of Israel, according to your actions," says the Sovereign Lord. "Repent, and turn from your sins. Don't let them destroy you! Put all your rebellion behind you and find yourselves a new heart and a new spirit. For why should you die, O people of Israel? I don't want you to die," says the Sovereign Lord. "Turn back and live!" Ezekiel 18:29-32 (NLT)*

We must not look away from the wrath of God. His wrath is not a scary thing for those who love and obey God, but a loving thing. If a parent demolished a poisonous snake who was close to their child would they be unloving? Our Father hates, deeply hates, all things that will harm us or turn our eyes from Him. He knows that He is Pure Love, and all other things are a mixture. Anything that is not of Him, but only a mixture of His truth, will lead His children astray; therefore, His wrath is against sin because it will destroy those He loves. Remember Your Father is not willing that any should perish (*2 Peter 3:8–10*).

Your Application

God's justified wrath is the side of God that the devil tries to pervert and make God seem unloving. God hates sin, disobedience, idols, anything taking our eyes off Him. Check out *Jeremiah 44:22, 23.* Write it out and hide it in your heart, *"all these terrible things happened to you because..."* Why? Because God is harsh or mean? No. It is impossible for God to be anything but *love*. Think of times in your life where God seemed uncaring or unloving or cruel. Work it out in your life that God's love does not change with your circumstances. God's love is pure, without mixture. Find scripture to back that up; now meditate and memorize and believe those scriptures. Share your sad event with someone and tell them how God's love didn't change even when you thought it had. Share your scriptures and say to this person if their circumstance makes it look like God is cruel or uncaring, to doubt what it appears to be, and to never doubt God's loving character.

> *Since what may be known about God is plain to them, because God has made it plain to them. (Romans 1:19)*

My Thought

All who have ever breathed are given the ability to know God, for God has allowed all men to know Him. Not all who know God actually "know" God. Every person knows, but not every person believes. God has given each person a sense of who He is, but as we know, not all people use their senses. God will not impose Himself on others, but He opens the Door (Jesus) for all humankind to come in; not all will, but it remains open for all.

Your Application

Deep! We got to get this. Does God give each person a chance to know and receive His salvation? Write out what you believe about this. Now ask God to show you if what you believe is true. Wait on Him.

> *For since the creation of the world God's invisible qualities—His eternal power and divine nature—have been clearly seen, being understood from what has been made, so that men are without excuse. (Romans 1:20)*

My Thought

This Door, although it is invisible, is also clearly seen by the things that are made, even to the extent of His power and the Godhead. There will be no excuses as to why one did not enter in. All know that God exists. How can that be? It is in the Word; therefore, it is truth. In the final judgment, there will be no excuses. Those who do not make it will not fall into eternal damnation; they will walk in with eyes wide open, with determined minds. Our Father is a just and righteous Father; He will not make anyone choose heaven—we have to do that on our own—but He will do whatever He can to show us the way. He gave us the greatest sacrifice of His life, *His Son!*

Your Application

Write out the names of people you know who resist Christ. Observe their ways; do you see times when they see the Light of eternity? Pray for them. Sadly enough, there will be those who will reject Christ and turn away from His open Door. Accept the truth that it is their choice, not God's.

> *For although they knew God, they neither glorified Him as God nor gave thanks to Him, but their thinking became futile and their foolish hearts were darkened. (Romans 1:21)*

My Thought

Even though they saw the Door, they didn't acknowledge Him as the Door. It was a way of escape, but they were not even thankful to have it. They (those who choose not to go through the Door) began to imagine other ways to be rescued, and it darkened their vision of the Door. The acknowledgment of Jesus Christ allows us access to so much more of Him and leads us into more *light*. The lack of acknowledging Jesus causes one to think of other ways to escape the sense of loss from within, darkening their path as they walk in foolishness of heart.

Your Application

Study Christ-rejecting people and look at how they create other ways to find peace and happiness. Do they appear to be at peace?

> *Although they claimed to be wise, they became fools. (Romans 1:22)*

My Thought

In their darkness, they believe things that are not true, they think themselves wise, yet they are fools. This is the sad state of the world. How many people profess to be wise, yet they walk in the darkness of fools? True wisdom only comes from God, for the fear of the Lord is the beginning of wisdom (*Proverbs 9:10*). Without God, one is not wise.

Your Application

Read *Proverbs 1:2–7, 20–35*. Write out what you understand these verses to mean.

> *And exchanged the glory of the immortal God for images made to look like mortal man and birds and animals and reptiles. (Romans 1:23)*

My Thought

Now, without God, man exchanged the Creator with deformed images of himself, like birds, four-footed beasts, and creeping things. Adam and Eve had God, and yet they forfeited it all for a creeping thing, their wisdom turned from true wisdom into a deformed man-made thing. *We all want to be someone, but without God, we become something which He did not want us to be.*

Your Application

Read *Genesis 3*. What is this chapter telling you? Why did God rush them out of the Garden of Eden? Write it out.

> *Therefore God gave them over in the sinful desires of their heart to sexual impurity for the degrading of their bodies with one another. (Romans 1:24)*

My Thought

God allowed them to walk in the darkness because the darkness is what they chose. They dishonored the only thing they had control of, themselves. God turned man over to his fantasies, sad to say it wasn't pretty, just as Adam and Eve were turned out of the Garden of Eden by their own choices; so, men and women who ignore the Door of Escape, Jesus Christ, will be turned over to their vain imaginations.

Your Application

Do you remember a time when you used your fantasies or imaginations to excuse a sin? How did that turn out? Write about it.

> *They exchanged the truth of God for a lie and worshiped and served created things rather than the Creator—Who is forever praised. Amen (Romans 1:25)*

My Thought

They saw the Door, but said it was not there. They created their own doors (paths) and worshiped and adorned them. People will act as though God is not the answer and will begin to form their own solutions through money, fame, humanity, drugs, sex, and lies.

Your Application

How was your door decorated before you found the open Door? What did you do to satisfy the longing in your soul?

> *Because of this, God gave them over to shameful lusts. Even their women exchanged natural relations for unnatural ones. (Romans 1:26)*

My Thought

God will allow them to worship their own ways because He is a just God and will not force Himself or the Door on anyone who does not want Him. He will allow the sickness of the world to penetrate their minds and their bodies, even to the place of believing what they are doing is right, even when what they do is against nature. As believers, God protects us in ways we don't even know or see. God protects us from the darkness of this world. We think we see some pretty nasty stuff, but even in that, we are protected by His holiness. *God is saying that as others decide they will not follow Him, God will allow them the fullness of the filthiness of this world, even to the extent of believing it to be good (Isaiah 5:20).*

Your Application

It all comes down to the deceiver of our soul. He is after everyone and will bring about his deception to make it look like truth. Read *2 Thessalonians 2:1-12*, it explains all about who our enemy is. It also explains Who is in control. Has there ever been a time you justified your sin and believed it to be okay? Write about it.

> *In the same way men also abandoned natural relations with women and were inflamed with lust for one another. Men committed indecent acts with other men and received in themselves the due penalty for their perversion. (Romans 1:27)*

My Thought

Men will begin to burn with lust for other men, as women for women. This unnatural act will be right in their eyes. But all things have consequences, and they will receive the just return of their sin within their own bodies and minds. God is not willing that any should fall into deprivation, but they will turn their bodies and minds into pits of anguish with their own choices. As will any sin bring us into depravity and anguish, Paul is pointing out this particular sin, but he will go on to call out all sin as debilitating.

Your Application

The sin of homosexuality is unnatural, yet today it is so prevalent that even some churches recognize it as a way of life. Study the history of homosexuality and see how it has transformed from unacceptable to acceptance in our society. What does that tell you about the subtleness of sin? Write about it.

> *Furthermore, since they did not think it worthwhile to retain the knowledge of God, He gave them over to a depraved mind to do what ought not to be done. (Romans 1:28)*

My Thought

Those who do not acknowledge God are now so far gone, they don't even remember the Door that was offered, so they desperately do things to ease the pain of hopelessness. Now sin becomes the only way of life; even if it is wrong, they see it as right behavior. Now those who have given themselves over to lawlessness have no constraints to keep them moral. All immorality seems right to them.

Your Application

This lawlessness has been since Adam and Eve, for once sin entered the scene, it has perverted the truth and tried to convince you the Door is too confining. You are free to make your own decisions. Give an illustration of how lawlessness creates havoc. (Example: The people of Israel in the Old Testament eventually turned into captives for 70 years for lack of obedience; or check out the book of *Judges*.)

> *They have become filled with every kind of wickedness, evil, greed and depravity. They are full of envy, murder, strife, deceit and malice. They are gossips, (Romans 1:29)*

My Thought

Most who find God non-existent become immoral, view sex outside of marriage to be okay, carry in them all wickedness, want what others have, cause pain to others, practice all kinds of envy, murder, debate, and deceitfulness, malign one's character, and gossip about others. *Sin is progressive.* It cannot stay in one place. It is like a fire that has to consume everything and everyone before it can quit.

Your Application

What are your thoughts on sin? What is your struggle with sin? Can it be tamed, or does it need to be destroyed by the blood of Jesus?

> *slanderers, God-haters, insolent, arrogant and boastful; they invent ways of doing evil; they disobey their parents; (Romans 1:30)*

My Thoughts

Backbiters, haters of God, spiteful, prideful, boasters, creating evil things, disobedient to parents; these are only a few of the lists that sin causes when we displace our worship of God for our own created things.

Your Application

Can you see the progression of sin? Think of a time in your life where you thought you could tame sin, but it got the best of you.

> *they are senseless, faithless, heartless, ruthless. (Romans 1:31)*

My Thought

Without understanding, covenant-breakers, without natural affections, relentless, unmerciful (bullies): These lists of sins now become human nature to those who reject the Door (Jesus). We can now understand why people can do terrible things and not even blink.

Your Application

Look back at the list Paul gave; examine your heart and see if any of these sins are permitted to live in you. If so, repent and change your ways by changing your mind about them. *We sin because we think the sin is "not that bad." All sin is bad; do not justify any sin as "not that bad."* How bad could it be to eat the forbidden fruit of the Tree of Life? We pay deeply for committing sins that we think are "not that bad."

> *Although they know God's righteous decrees that those who do such things deserve death, they not only continue to do these very things but also approve of those who practice them. (Romans 1:32)*

My Thought

Those without excuse know the judgment of God will be worthy of death, and yet they commit these things with pleasure. Not only do they do these things, but they approve of others who do them. This verse says they know the judgment of God. We cannot dispute God. He is all-knowing, so we have to trust that people who display such filthiness not only know they do evil but enjoy the sins they do.

Your Application

"Without struggle" is the keyword. God understands your struggle with sin; as long as you continue to give your battle to Him, He will help you. The problem is when the fight is gone, and you accept your sin as okay without conviction. Write about yourself or someone else who went from struggling with sin to giving in to the sin.

Romans One shows us how to live in the truth. Paul is happy to join new converts (the Romans) into the fold. Paul shows us there are none without excuse and some will refuse to see the Door (Jesus), even though they know it is there. They make the Door into a counterfeit and worship what they have made rather than the One who made them. *The law of this life is that everything falls apart, from order to disorder because of the fall, so their life's breath is degradation. So instead of life, they breathe death every day. Those who ignore the Door (Jesus) become like unto death.* There are two lives available to us. God has made it clear and without excuse. It is up to us which life we choose. The consequences of our choices are written in God's Word. Be very afraid to walk through the counterfeit door. Choose a life of truth!

My Prayer

Romans One has given us an understanding of You, God. You have given us Your truth. You want us to live in the truth. You are desirous that we know You; You love us deeply; You want us to be family, connected to one another. You have given us a Door (Jesus) to enter into another world, a *Storybook Fairy-Tale Reality of the Kingdom of God*. You say we can only live if we live in Your truth. To live in Your world, the air we breathe is truth and faith. Without it, it is impossible to live fully as You intended. It is impossible to please You. Faith takes us to different levels; to each of us who take the next level, there is more life to live. Help us to be filled with Your faith and truth daily, by asking, "Is there a sin in my life I am unaware of?" And "Am I believing a lie?" In Your amazing Name. Amen.

Write a summary of chapter 1.

Grace grants us the freedom to become us without limitations or bondage. We become the ones we were meant to be in the plans of God.
For Paul, it was to be an Apostle;
for each of us, there is a designated design.
It is up to us to know what it is and to work it out.

Our Worship

Graves Into Gardens ft. Brandon Lake / Live / Elevation Worship
https://www.youtube.com/watch?v=KwX1f2gYKZ4&list=RDMM&index=16

CHAPTER 2

Living Without Judgment

Read the complete chapter of *Romans 2*

> *You, therefore, have no excuse, you who pass judgment on someone else, for at whatever point you judge another, you are condemning yourself, because you who pass judgment do the same things. (Romans 2:1)*

My Thought

There are no excuses for those who judge; where one judges someone, one condemns himself, for those who judge are not without sin. We need to keep judgment to the Just Judge (*1 Peter 1:17, 2:23*). Those who are perfect and can read and hear the heart can judge correctly. If that is not our ability, which it is not, we need NOT judge other people. We ask, what is the difference between judging and discerning? Discernment is an understanding of a situation or person. Those with discernment might see things that are obscure to those around them. Discernment is a gift from God. Discernment is to be used carefully to restore a person; it is an act of love. We are the family of God, and we are to encourage and uplift. There is a time to rebuke, but *Galatians 6:19 (NLT)* says to be careful, *"Dear brothers and sisters, if another believer is overcome by some sin, you who are godly should gently and humbly help that person back onto the right path. And be careful not to fall into the same temptation yourself."* Judging the fruit on a tree (the behavior of a person) can seem right to judge, but is it? We can see the fruit, so we think we know the truth about the fruit, but what is there about the tree's roots that have produced that fruit? For example, the appearance of the fruit of kindness can be from the roots of manipulation. The fruit of promiscuity could come from a struggle of identity or a horrendous past. The tree's roots are unseen, so to judge the unseen is not for us to do. God knows what's in the heart and motive of an act. Judging becomes more personal and is usually hurtful. Judging says, "That person is bad. I am not that bad!" Judgments from our blurred sense of vision bring conflict and division. Remember, when we judge we are condemning ourselves, because we who pass judgment do the same things.

Your Application

Write about a time you judged someone, when all along, you were wrong about what you thought they were doing.

Now we know that God's judgment against those who do such things is based on truth. (Romans 2:2)

My Thought

We (Paul and present company) are sure that God's judgments are based on truth towards those who commit sins (*Romans 1:28–32*). The right judgments of sin are from God, who knows the heart and mind's intent and motive. We cannot judge! There is a time to discern what is right and wrong, but not to judge a person's motive. We can see an individual's fruit, but we cannot pass judgment on another human being. We must learn to leave all the judging to God, our Father. It's our job to love. Only the Perfect can determine where a soul will go. We must stand clear of thinking we are a judge of anyone.

Your Application

Have you ever been judged wrongly by someone? What happened? Give scripture, if you can, in your written essay. Check out the woman caught in adultery in *John 8:1–11*. What was wrong with this picture, according to *Leviticus 20:10*? What did Jesus, the Perfect One, do?

So when you, a mere human being, pass judgment on them and yet do the same things, do you think you will escape God's judgment? (Romans 2:3)

My Thought

Do you think you will escape the judgment of God when you do the very thing you are judging? Paul is not going to leave this alone. He wants to get down and dirty with the Romans, and with us. The Holy Spirit loves us so much; He wants us to see the error of our ways when we think we can judge. *None is righteous, no, not one (Romans 3:10).*

> *So maybe we don't sin precisely how the one we are judging does; the question is, we who judge, are we without sin?*

Your Application

Look up *Matthew 7:1–6; 15–20*, on judging, write a chart on judging the fruit of a false prophet versus judging a person (*He without sin cast the first stone. John 8:7*).

Or do you show contempt for the riches of His kindness, forbearance, and patience, not realizing that God's kindness is intended to lead you to repentance? (Romans 2:4)

My Thought

Do you despise the riches of God's goodness, His tolerance, and His patience, not understanding that the goodness of God leads to repentance? Do we want God to get others when they sin, but not us? Do we think our sin is okay, but the other sin is to be punished? God is so patient with us and others. We must not resent when God is disciplining us and seemingly allowing others to get away with their sin.

We must trust that God is just and good,
and He knows what He is doing.

Your Application

Has there been a time in your life that you felt God was disciplining you, and someone else looked like they were getting away with sin? Check out King David, King Saul, and Daniel. Did they have sin in their lives? How did God deal with each one of them? What did Jesus say to Peter when he asked, *"What about John?"* (John 21:21-22)

> *But because of your stubbornness and your unrepentant heart, you are storing up wrath against yourself for the day of God's wrath, when His righteous judgment will be revealed. (Romans 2:5)*

My Thought

Our hard and unrepentant heart sets us up to meet the wrath of God and to see the rightness of God's judgments.

When we get to heaven, at the judgment seat
we will see the perfect judgments of the Lord.

Let's not wait until then; let's believe what God's Word says is right; let's believe what we read and not what we think or feel.

Your Application

Practice on believing God's Word in times of doubt. Meditate on the truth of the Word, over the feelings of doubt. Look up scriptures about the truth of the Word of God. Memorize these scriptures for times of doubt. Knowing God's Word will keep your heart from becoming hard and unrepentant.

> *God will repay each person according to what they have done. (Romans 2:6)*

My Thought

At the judgment seat, God will reward each person according to their deeds on earth. Not just our deeds will be judged, but more importantly, the intent or purpose or reason we did what we did.

Thank God at the Judgment Seat our sins are forgiven
if we have Christ as our Savior, but God will judge us
for what we did with the time we had on earth.

Your Application

Become aware; pay attention to the motives of your kind deeds. What may seem like such a great thing to those looking on may be filthy to the Just Judge, who sees the intent and purpose of that deed. Write about when you did something nice for someone, but you were really manipulating for your own good. Honesty will open your eyes to see why you do what you do. Again, it is better to discover our wrong motives here on earth and be convicted and judged by a good God so we can change our ways, than to get to heaven and be judged and set for eternity with those actions.

> *To those who by persistence in doing good seek glory, honor and immortality,*
> *He will give eternal life. (Romans 2:7)*

My Thought

God will reward eternal life to those who choose to walk obediently for His glory, honor, and their immortality in God's kingdom. The reward for those who choose to walk in the rightness of God's ways will have eternal life. In other words, we live here on earth for the eternal and not the temporary.

Your Application

Read *Revelations 21–22.* What are some of the things you will most enjoy in heaven?

> *But for those who are self-seeking and who reject the truth and follow evil, there*
> *will be wrath and anger. (Romans 2:8)*

My Thought

The reward to those who are contentious, disobedient to the truth of God's Word, obeying the ways of unrighteousness, will be indignation and wrath. Rebellion, selfish motives, and pride will turn into a downward spiral cesspool. It will be a way of life that will render us powerless. We will try to free ourselves, but it may be too late when we realize we are trapped.

Your Application

Find scriptures on rebellion. Write out *1 Samuel 15:23, Proverbs 17:11, and Isaiah 30:1.*

> *There will be trouble and distress for every human being who does evil: first for*
> *the Jew, then for the Gentile; (Romans 2:9)*

My Thought

The punishment that will come to the disobedient will be (indignation and wrath v.8) tribulation and anguish, to every soul of man that does evil, of the Jew first and then the Gentile. Tribulation and anguish will come to the soul. The soul and the spirit live forever. The earthly body will die, but our soul and our spirit will live forever. For the righteous, they will live forever with their Lord. For the wicked, Christ-rejected sinner, they will live forever in anguish.

Your Application

Look up scriptures of hell and write a brief description of this real place.

> *but glory, honor and peace for everyone who does good: first for the Jew, then the Gentile. (Romans 2:10)*

My Thought

There is eternal life for those who walk in right relationships with Christ and glory and honor and peace to everyone who works for good, the Jew first and then to the Gentile. Glory, honor, and peace are the rewards for those whose deeds are judged acceptable. We do not work for our salvation. It was given to us freely by Jesus' sacrifice on the cross, but we do work for our sanctification (being made holy, complete, whole). Meaning we do good deeds from a heart of love for Jesus. The Holy Spirit creates in us clean hands and a pure heart. Our good deeds come from allowing the Holy Spirit to change us daily to be more like Jesus. Jews were first in line, but the Jews fell out of line by their unbelief, confusion, and rejection of the Messiah, then the Gentiles were given a chance to believe, and many did. When the opportunity comes for the Jews to understand who their Messiah is, they will get another chance to receive their reward.

Your Application

Why Jew first, then the Gentile? Why did the Jews miss the Messiah? What will help them recognize Jesus as the Messiah? Write out your answers and add scripture to back up your findings.

> *For God does not show favoritism. (Romans 2:11)*

My Thought

God does not have favorites. God does things as He sees fit. He is God; His actions are right, and we need to learn to acknowledge this without questioning His sovereignty. If we understood all that God did, we would not need faith. Remember, faith is the language of heaven; here on earth, we must learn to walk and talk in the language of heaven. One of the "truth" statements is, God does not have favorites! His love for you is perfect and true.

Your Application

Write out ten faith verses and commit them to memory.

> *All who sin apart from the law will also perish apart from the law, and all who sin under the law will be judged by the law. (Romans 2:12)*

My Thought

For those who sinned without the law (Gentiles), they will not be judged by the law but will still perish. The law will judge those who sinned within the law (Jews). This truth comes back to the scripture (*Romans 1:20*); there will be none without excuse. Those who live by the law will be judged by the law. Those who had no law will still perish if they turn their backs on the truth, for even the world's beauty declares God (*Psalms 19*).

Your Application

Look up some of the remotest places on earth. Have they been reached with the gospel? Begin to pray for their souls to be saved. Think about visiting them. (What's the most remote inhabited location on earth? A place called "Tristan da Cunha.") Tristan houses a school, hospital, post office, museum, cafe, pub, craft shop, village hall, and swimming pool. (Notice there are no churches.)

> *For it is not those who hear the law who are righteous in God's sight, but it is those who obey the law who will be declared righteous. (Romans 2:13)*

My Thought

Many will hear God's Word but will not be justified. Obeying the law will make us justified. James covers the same subject in his first chapter, verse *22, "But be doers of the Word and not hearers only, deceiving your own selves. 25: But whoso looks into the perfect law of liberty and continues to do it, he being not a forgetful hearer, but a doer of the work, this man shall be blessed in his deed."* Anyone can hear, but it takes a follower of Christ to do what he hears. To obey His word is to show deep love for Jesus. It isn't always easy to follow after His ways.

Your Application

Are you a hearer only? Do you do what the Word says? Jesus said, *"I knew you not; depart from Me..."* (*Matthew 7:21–23*). Who was he saying those words to? (Read about John Mulinde, http://www.charismanews.com/opinion/48597-all-along-i-thought-i-was-serving-god-john-mulinde).

> *Indeed, when Gentiles, who do not have the law, do by nature things required by the law, they are a law for themselves, even though they do not have the law. (Romans 2:14)*

My Thought

When the Gentiles live the law naturally without the law, it becomes a law unto themselves. The Jews had the law, the commandments were given to them from God via Moses. They were told how to live. When the Gentiles (non-Jewish people) came along and lived the law without knowing it, there is proof the law was written in the heart. Again, the premise is, God's law is written in our hearts, knowing not God but acting in a way that is right before Him. If our conscience knows right from wrong and we choose right, then God's DNA (Spirit) is inciting us to know Him more, live better and ultimately obey.

Your Application

Read *Hebrews 8:7–13*. What does that mean to you? Wrestle with these scriptures, do not just read them and let them go. Write out your final thoughts.

> *They show that the requirements of the law are written on their hearts, their consciences also bearing witness, and their thoughts sometimes accusing them and at other times even defending them.) (Romans 2:15)*

My Thought

The very nature of the Gentiles shows the law of God in their hearts, conscience, and thoughts. The law gives them a standard to live by; it either excuses them or accuses them. God sets heaven in our hearts. The law reveals in all men (even the atheist) there is a God, and the law points out right from wrong.

.

Your Application

God not only writes His law in the hearts of His Jewish people (*Jeremiah 31:33*), He also writes it in the hearts of all other people. His law has been written in your heart. How does that make you feel?

> *This will take place on the day when God judges people's secrets through Jesus Christ, as my gospel declares. (Romans 2:16)*

My Thought

"In the day…" According to Paul's gospel, there is coming a day when Jesus Christ will judge all secrets of men. There is a day coming when all secrets will be revealed. Sins covered by the blood of Christ are covered and forgiven, but unforgiven secrets hidden from the eyes of men now, all secrets, will be exposed and judged.

Your Application

If you think you are getting away with sin and there has been no consequence, oh precious friend, there is coming a day your secrets will be revealed; get rid of it today! Confess and repent to your loving Lord so you will not be caught unprepared and put to shame.

> *Now you, if you call yourself a Jew; if you rely on the law and boast in God; (Romans 2:17)*

My Thought

Consider, you who call yourself a Jew, who leans on the law, and boasts that you know God. Paul is setting up the prideful Jew; look at the wording: "*who calls himself a Jew.*" This prideful one leans on his knowledge that God has called his nation to be God's people. Not all who are Jews are God's people.

Your Application

Pride is an ugly thing, and God hates it. Do you have pride in your heart? Do you brag about the things you do as if you created your own gifts? Do you know that when you brag about yourself, that someone hears and feels put down because when you build yourself up, it is at others' expense? Pride blinds. Are you prideful? Does pride take any residence in you? If so, get rid of it. There is no place for pride in God's people. He did it all. We have nothing to brag about except Him!

> *if you know His will and approve of what is superior because you are instructed by the law; (Romans 2:18)*

My Thought

Consider, you who think you know God's will, and approve the things that are more excellent, you who are instructed out of the law. A hint of sarcasm is in Paul's writing. He is allowing the prideful Jew to recognize his ways. Paul incites us to consider. That is a serious word. Consider your ways, people. How many times do we stop to think about what we are doing? How many times do we consider why we do what we do?

Your Application

Stop and consider today!

> *if you are convinced that you are a guide for the blind, a light for those who are in the dark, (Romans 2:19)*

My Thought

Confident to be a guide to the blind, a light to those in darkness, as the Jews' chests begin to grow with the statements Paul says about them, he is honestly getting ready to set them down and teach them a hard thing.

Your Application

How hard is it to hear someone tell you something that you are doing is wrong or hurtful? Learn to receive rebuke and reproof. Have a teachable spirit and learn daily from what others may be saying to you. Do not shut out words that could make you a better person (*Proverbs 27:6*).

> *an instructor of the foolish, a teacher of little children, because you have in the law the embodiment of knowledge and truth (Romans 2:20)*

23

My Thought

A teacher of the foolish, a teacher of babes, which has the form of knowledge and of the truth of the law. The Jewish teachers were all caught up in the rules and regulations and ensured that everyone knew how good they looked outwardly, but what was going on in their hearts? Jesus called out the teachers of the law. He called them whitewashed sepulchers. *Matthew 23:27, 28 "Woe to you, scribes and Pharisees, hypocrites! For you are like whitewashed tombs which indeed appear beautiful outwardly, but inside are full of dead men's bones and all uncleanness. In the same way, on the outside, you appear to people as righteous, but on the inside, you are full of hypocrisy and wickedness."*

Your Application

Do you look good outwardly? It doesn't matter! What you will be judged for when you stand before your Just Judge will be what was inside of you. Your inward being is priceless and immortal. Where do you want to spend eternity? Live for the end result, not for the here and now!

you, then, who teach others, do you not teach yourself? You who preach against stealing, do you steal? (Romans 2:21)

My Thought

Do we practice what we teach? If we are preaching that a man should not steal, do we steal? Now Paul begins to point a finger with his words at the piousness of their ways. He asks them. "Are you practicing what you are preaching? Are you living the way you expect others to live?"

Your Application

Double standard is prevalent today. Do you know someone who lives a double standard life? What does that feel like to you? Check it out. Honestly, do you live a double standard life? *Paul says to you and me, "Live according to the law within your heart, not the outward shallowness of rules and regulations just to look good."*

You who say that people should not commit adultery, do you commit adultery? You who abhor idols, do you rob temples? (Romans 2:22)

My Thought

If we are saying a man should not commit adultery, do we commit adultery? We who loathe idols, do we worship others or material possessions? Paul begins to write to the Romans (Jews and Gentiles) with the Holy Spirit's convicting power to narrow in or maybe hinting on some of the secrets he said would be revealed. Paul is giving them a chance to confess and change. God is so good at revealing our sins to us before he sends a stronger messenger. Here in the form of a letter, God is opening up the Roman Christians' eyes, receiving this letter from Paul, that God knows what's going on.

Your Application

Paul is not judging them but declaring to them through the inspiration of the Spirit that their double standard ways have been noticed. God loves you too much to keep you the way you are. God will convict you and ask you to change, just as He did with the Roman Christians. Take heed to any hidden sin that you might have, yet you condemn it in others. Take note and change. Find an accountability partner who will help you.

> *You who boast in the law, do you dishonor God by breaking the law? (Romans 2:23)*

My Thought

We who hold strongly to lawful things making sure others follow the law; are we dishonoring God by secretly doing those things? Oh yes, we love the scripture *John 3:16*, God so loved the world that He gave… and yet do we carry bitterness in our hearts towards someone?

Your Application

You will not be perfect. God does not expect you to be. He does expect you to change by the power of the Holy Spirit into His image. Are there behavior traits in you that are not a part of His image? If so, bring them to God; He will know what to do.

> *As it is written: "God's name is blasphemed among the Gentiles because of you."*
> *(Romans 2:24)*

My Thought

God's law was not being followed, and the Jewish people were making a mockery out of God. Paul is saying, the Jews, in their disobedience in the Old Testament, were not being a good example among the Gentiles. As Jesus followers, we must be cautious to walk in a spirit of forgiveness without causing others to question our walk with God. If we fail, we must admit we are weak, but He is strong. His forgiveness covers our sins, but we cannot go around acting like we are perfect. In our weakness, He is strong. When we allow others to see our faults, they also see a big loving Father ready to forgive. We show the goodness of God instead of trying to act perfect and cover up our sins.

Your Application

Are you a good example among those you walk with throughout the day? Consider and write about it.

> *Circumcision has value if you observe the law, but if you break the law, you have become as though you had not been circumcised. (Romans 2:25)*

My Thought

Circumcision only profits by keeping the law, but if an Israelite breaks the law, the circumcision is not regarded as legit. The Israelite's circumcision is as though it is not if they break the law. The purpose of circumcision was to set the Jewish people apart. It was a ritual only the Jewish boys would do; therefore, a sign that they belonged to God. But it was an outward sign to an inward relationship with their King. In obedience, they were to cut their flesh to be different. If they didn't act differently, the cut meant nothing.

Your Application

Did you accept the plan of salvation from the Lord? Are you set apart for God's purpose? If your inward relationship shows no sign of walking a new walk, your salvation is now not legit if you walk in disobedience. Does that concern you? Write about it.

> *So then, if those who are not circumcised keep the law's requirements, will they not be regarded as though they were circumcised? (Romans 2:26)*

My Thought

Therefore, if the uncircumcision kept the rightness of the law, will his uncircumcision be counted as being circumcised? Now the opposite occurs. If those who are not cut are now living differently and belong to the King, following His laws, are they not as though they are circumcised? Then your relationship is legit!

Your Application

The sign of following Jesus is in your walk. Are you walking differently, thinking differently, living differently? Then you have the seal of the Lord on you!

> *The one who is not circumcised physically and yet obeys the law will condemn you who, even though you have the written code and circumcision, are a lawbreaker. (Romans 2:27)*

My Thought

To understand what Paul is saying, we need to look deeper into the times he lived. The Pharisees were always trying to make people live by the letter of the law by watching and keeping tabs on others. Yet they did not keep the law themselves. Paul is saying that some are uncircumcised (without the seal of the Lord) who follow the law better than those who are circumcised. Paul says, will not these people who are not sealed, condemn you?

Your Application

What does that mean to you? Write it out.

> *A person is not a Jew who is one only outwardly, nor is circumcision merely outward and physical. (Romans 2:28)*

My Thought

For he is not a Jew, which is one outwardly, neither is the circumcision validated if it is only outward in the flesh. Some in the church may not receive an inheritance because it was only an outward act. They acknowledge God with their mouths but didn't take it further into their minds and hearts; there was no inward commitment to Christ and His Word. There was not a change; there was not a new walk or real relationship with Jesus.

Your Application

You must not play church. You must enter into a real relationship with the King of the kingdom. Others will try to make you follow their rules, but God has an inward call in you, His Word, and you are to walk in obedience to that call only. You answer to God, not man. Read *Galatians 1*. What was Paul trying to teach you? Write it out.

> *No, a person is a Jew who is one inwardly; and circumcision is circumcision of the heart, by the Spirit, not by the written code. Such a person's praise is not from other people, but from God. (Romans 2:29)*

My Thought

But he is a Jew, which is one inwardly, and circumcision is that of the heart, in the spirit, and not in the letter, where praise is not from men, but from God. The real Jew will be the one who loves from the heart and in the spirit. The letter of the law died with Jesus. We are to receive praise from God and not men. God is responsible for our new relationship with Him because He sent His Son, Jesus, to fulfill the law that man could not. It's all about the heart now.

Your Application

Where are you with your relationship with God, our Father? Is it mechanical? Are you afar off from Him? Or is He living in your heart in an authentic and meaningful way? God loves you and wants to be close to you. Write out your relationship with Him. Is it all it could be? How can you draw closer to Him?

Romans Two instructs us not to judge, or we will be judged. God teaches us for our good. He insists that we not expect others to live the law and ignore it ourselves. He wants us to have a relationship with Him that is a light to others. Paul is insistent that spiritual circumcision is, most notably, a sign of the inward commitment to God. We cut our fleshly desires out, to live a life He has destined for us. He longs for us not to have an inner struggle with sin. He wants us to be honest and forthright in our relationship with Him. He doesn't want us to look good outside for others to see but be rotting away on the inside. God wants us to be a showcase for His glory. He wants us to live a lifestyle of grace, not judging.

My Prayer

Lord, we realize we have no excuse when we judge others, we need Your help not to behave that way, but to look at others as You do. Father God, it is Your kindness that leads to repentance, not us judging one another. Please clear our minds so we may be filled with the goodness of You! When we start to judge, convict us. Make us more aware of Your Presence so we too will walk in Your kindness towards others. We repent of judging; we know the enemy wants us to judge so we all the more want to walk in obedience to You to show that Satan has no stronghold on us. In the powerful Name of Jesus. Amen.

Write a summary of chapter 2.

When we get to heaven, at the judgment seat, we will see the perfect judgments of the Lord. Let's not wait until then; let's believe what God's Word says is true. Let's believe what we read, and not what we think or feel. Ask God daily to judge you and convict you!

Our Worship

Goodness Of God (LIVE) / Jenn Johnson
https://www.youtube.com/watch?v=n0FBb6hnwTo&list=RDMM&index=7

CHAPTER 3

Living A Changed Life

Read the complete chapter of *Romans 3*

God's Judgment Defended

> *What advantage, then, is there in being a Jew, or what value is there in circumcision? (Romans 3:1)*

My Thought

What advantage does the Jew have? Or what profit is it to be circumcised? If circumcision is of the heart and not of the flesh, why was it introduced to the Jew in the first place? Why does the Jew have an advantage? Paul asks us a question; maybe one of the *Romans* thought about this after reading the part of the letter he wrote about circumcision (chapter 2).

Your Application

Sometimes, questions are good to ask to prepare a person to think. Paul asked the question but didn't wait for an answer. His answer was on the way. He does this quite often in *Romans*. Try this with a person you would like to share the gospel with; ask a question that you already know the answer to—an intriguing question; then, like Paul, step right in with the answer.

> *Much in every way! First of all, the Jews have been entrusted with the very words of God. (Romans 3:2)*

My Thought

It does profit in every way! Mainly because to the Jew, God committed His oracles, His vision for all humanity. The Jews were selected from the beginning (Abraham) to be a nation that would receive the truths of God. God would start a family through the Jews. The cool thing is, God did start the family through the Jews but continued it on to the non-Jew, the Gentile, us! The two groups cover all mankind. Out of the two groups, those who accept Jesus become one, we become family.

Your Application
This week, find a Christian family member you have never met and introduce yourself. Like Paul, impart to them a gift and establish a relationship with them.

> *What if some were unfaithful? Will their unfaithfulness nullify God's faithfulness?*
> (Romans 3:3)

My Thought
So, what if some Jews did not believe? Should their unbelief change the faithfulness of God? Another question to stir up interest on this subject—Paul asks if some Jews didn't believe in all of this "God coming to make a family" stuff—does it make it not so?

Your Application
When dealing with unbelievers, it's important to know how to answer questions. Be prepared to know the answers to the questions that someone might ask. Better yet, ask the questions first, before they even ask and answer them with the truth of God's Word. Try that this week.

> *Not at all! Let God be true, and every human being a liar. As it is written: "So that you may be proved right when you speak and prevail when you judge."*
> (Romans 3:4)

My Thought
Paul answers the question, should some of the Jews' unbelief change the faithfulness of God, or the plans of God, with an astounding, "God forbid!" Let God be true and every man a liar; as it is written, that you may be justified in your sayings, and may overcome when you are judged. Paul says, "No! Absolutely not!" Use this verse in your arsenal of truth.

Let every man be a liar who contradicts God.

When others question what God says or what He does, we need to have the truth deep within us that God does not lie, nor does He contradict Himself; this is fundamental theology of staying grounded amid the storm of intellectualism. There will be "*smart*" people who will question us and try to persuade us that we don't know what we are saying. This verse says we will be justified in our sayings, and we will overcome when we are judged!

Your Application
It is good to practice sharing your faith with others. Ask a question like, do you think God is unjust when earthquakes happen, and innocent babies and children are killed? Then be ready to answer this question before they even answer. Have scriptures to back up your answer or give a testimony of an event that happened in your life that seemed terrible, but as you look back, you see the loving hand of God in it.

But if our unrighteousness demonstrates the righteousness of God, what shall we say? Is God unjust who inflicts wrath? (I speak as a man.) (Romans 3:5)

My Thought

If our sins speak well of the righteousness of God, what is to be said? Is God unrighteous who takes vengeance? (I'm just saying). A little girl was wearing a beautiful white dress; another little girl came in with a dress that was so dirty it made the white dress look even whiter. Is it the little girl's fault that her dress was so white, or did the dirty dress help make the beautiful white dress more apparent? *Our sins are so dirty; God is so brilliant.* Our sins next to Him makes us aware of how sinful we are. Is God unjust for inflicting punishment for our sinful nature? No. But, in His love for us, He gave us the Door (Jesus) to escape His wrath, if only we believe.

Your Application

God is called unjust and unfair all the time by those who do not know His nature. Look up scriptures that declare the goodness of God. Set them for memory and use them to speak to others who do not understand. Read Mark 9:2-8. Write about the comparisons between Jesus, the prophets, and the disciples. What did the Father say? What do you think that means? Job 9:20 speaks of our righteousness compared to God's. Write your thoughts.

Certainly not! For then how will God judge the world? (Romans 3:6)

My Thought

Paul answers, God forbid: how can God judge the world? Paul says God is not unrighteous for inflicting punishment on us, for God is the One who will judge the world. Oh, precious student, we have to get this.

> *It is not our friend, our family, or our teacher who will answer for what we did in this life of ours. They will not be there to give their opinion of how well we did. We will stand before a just God who will judge us individually for what we did. We must answer to Him then, so let's learn to answer to Him now.*

Let's make decisions that will bring us unimaginable investments in heaven and not worry about our immediate inheritance of praise from man here on earth.

Your Application

Check out why you do what you do. Is your faith based on your family, your friends, your mentors? Do you know what you believe? Can you give an answer to your Just Judge right now if He asked these questions? Know what you believe and why you believe, enough to be able to share it when needed. Write out the absolutes in your life.

> *For if the truth of God has increased through my life to His glory, why am I also still judged as a sinner? (Romans 3:7)*

My Thought

We must not think that God's glory covers our continued sin. Once we see that the dress is so dirty, we should not shrug our shoulders and say, "oh well." God has made a way for us to become clean, He's given us robes of righteousness so that we, too, shine brilliantly of His glory. Not to be mistaken that we now are righteous in our own merit, but we are an extension of His righteousness. No more wishy-washy: "I am unworthy" or, "I am so good…," we stand in the character of God. We are no longer living in shame and regret. We stand in the righteousness of God. We are not better than anyone. We are His. He gets us to a place of worthiness, and He gets ALL the glory, recognition, and praise.

We just get to be the models, walking in His robe of righteousness. We didn't make the robe; we didn't even put it on, He did.

We need to remember our rightful place so we can truly show the greatness of God without getting in the way and taking some of His credit.

Your Application

Do you walk in a place of sinfulness? Recognize it. Write about it and surrender it to God. Read *Ephesians 1–3* to gain a clear understanding of your rightful place in this *Storybook Fairy-Tale Reality of the Kingdom of God.*

> *And why not say, "Let us do evil that good may come?" —as we are slanderously reported and as some affirm that we say. Their condemnation is just. (Romans 3:8)*

My Thought

Obviously, some accusers of Paul said he said, "Let us do evil, for the glory of God." He is blatantly correcting this untruth. Paul confronts not only the theology of this way of life, but he also corrects the spreading of gossip about him. Some have reported, and some have agreed with the report that Paul was saying, "Do evil to show how good God is," so, therefore, it was something being spread about Paul's preaching justification by faith. Paul is an excellent example of how to deal with slander. Confront it with truth.

Your Application

Deal with slander and gossip head-on. Usually, people who are talking about you will stop if you just go to them. If not, then let God deal with them. Don't avoid these people or talk about them to others; it's what causes more craziness. Be an adult and deal with it head-on with truth and love.

> *What then? Are we better than they? Not at all. For we have previously charged both Jews and Greeks that they are all under sin. (Romans 3:9)*

My Thought

What then, are we better than they? No, we are not, for we have already said that Jew and Gentile are all under sin. There is no one better than the other. We are all under sin. The forbidden bite that was taken by Adam and Eve is a continuous bite that we each take. We are all smitten with the evils of sin. It's in our earthly DNA.

Your Application

Leveling the playing field helps us see ourselves and others as equals. There will never be another human being better than you; you will never be better than another human being. What can you do to help you walk in this truth? Do it.

All Have Sinned

> *It is written: There is none that is righteous, no, not one. (Romans 3:10)*

My Thought

Paul begins here in verses 10–18 to quote the Old Testament (*Psalms 14:1-3, 5:9, 140:3, and 10:7, and from Isaiah 59:7, 8*). He is using the truth to make his point. No one is born in their rightful place. We are all sinful and without hope, except that there is the Door (Jesus) we can all walk through. But without walking through the Door, we remain in our unrighteousness.

Your Application

Think of some of the sins you were trapped in before the King of Righteousness entered your heart. Is there someone you know you couldn't imagine being unrighteous? Look back at verse 10…there is none that is righteous. This righteous person is righteous because of the goodness of God only, not of their own merit.

> *There is none who understands; There is none who seeks after God. (Romans 3:11)*

My Thought

No one understands God. No one seeks after God! What? Does no one even seek after God? It is God pursuing us! Oh, dear saints, please see this. As Jesus pursued Paul, previously named Saul, it wasn't Paul's tenacity that pursued God. In His pure love, God came after Paul, as He does each of us. The God of gods, the King of kings, and the Lord of lords pursues you! He knows we don't understand, so He seeks us out to be in His family. Amazing.

Your Application

Write about the time you gave yourself to God. Think of how it was really God pursuing you.

> *They have all turned aside; They have together become unprofitable; There is none who does good, no, not one."* (Romans 3:12)

My Thought

Paul continues this theme of none being good. He says none are righteous. No one profits in themselves, none understand, they don't seek God, none are good. Not one? Nope, there is none. So, the argument does not work of the sweet little old lady down the street that doesn't know God, but she feeds the poor, is kind to animals, gives to charities, and always has a kind word and smile. How can she not be good? Remember the white dress and the dirty dress. No matter how hard we clean up that dirty dress. It is dirty compared to the brilliant white dress. This kind old lady may seem good compared to other dirty dresses, but she's not good compared to the pure whiteness of God. We must not compare ourselves to others and say, "See, I am not that bad!" At the Judgment Seat, we won't be compared to others but to the brilliant righteousness of Jesus. There is none that is good, no, not one, period.

Your Application

Hard theology is really simple if you believe that all of God's Word is true. Remember, no one can argue with your testimony; add the fact that God pursued you and share with others that even in your goodness it wasn't good enough to get you through the Door into your *Storybook Fairy-Tale Reality of the Kingdom of God*. It was all Him, Jesus, alone, that makes us right before God, our Father.

> *"Their throat is an open tomb; With their tongues they have practiced deceit; The poison of asps is under their lips."* (Romans 3:13)

My Thought

Their throat is an open grave, with their tongues they speak lies, their words are poisonous as asps. Imagine the smell of an open grave, the tongue tells lies, and their words are as poisonous as a snake. Paul is talking about whom? It appears to be all of us, Jew and Gentile alike. Paul is continuing the thought that none is good, no, not one. In our sinfulness, this is what we can expect to be.

Your Application

Have you ever lied, spoken gossip, or murdered someone with your words? Then you fit in this scripture as we all do. You must not be afraid to look at your bad (I call it "looking at our uglies"). You must be willing to see it and confess it and have God change it. A little saying, I learned from a wonderful Pastor, Jon Courson:

You can't change your heart, but you can change your mind
God can change your heart, but won't change your mind
If you change your mind, God will change your heart!

Change occurs in our lives as we allow God to invade our minds to think and know the truth. Then God will change our heart to follow after Him. God, our Father, through Jesus, sought us out to be His family. Without Jesus, we are not able to change our filthy clothes.

"Whose mouth is full of cursing and bitterness." (Romans 3:14)

My Thought

Paul goes on to explain all humanity without Christ speaks lies and bitterness. It isn't a pretty picture, but we all must agree that we have all been there. Cursing, whether in your mind or out loud, is still cursing because the One that will judge us can hear both. The bitterness of heart comes out in our attitude and the way we speak. Honestly, one can recognize a bitter person.

Your Application

Do you have bitterness inside? Do you curse others? Rectify this immediately. Ask God to judge you and convict you every day. Stay clear of these things.

"Their feet are swift to shed blood; (Romans 3:15)

My Thought

They are quick to harm or injure others. Wow, we might say, that's not me. Are we quick to add insult to injury when we are talking about someone we don't like? Are we quick to walk all over someone to get what we want? Again, we must face and acknowledge our uglies if we are to change them. If we deny we have them, we will walk around thinking we are okay.

Your Application

Take a hard look at these scriptures. Do you identify with them? Write a letter to Father God asking for His help to change you.

Destruction and misery are in their ways; (Romans 3:16)

My Thought

The way they behave brings destruction and misery. Instead of "they," let's put "the way we behave," brings destruction and despair. Let's take an even closer look at our lives. Do we bring destruction or misery to others? *Romans 3* sets us up to take a good, long look at ourselves.

Your Application

Write out a list of the areas that need to change in your life. Don't look at it as overwhelming. Ask Jesus which one He wants you to change first. Look up scriptures that can help you in that area. Listen to His Words and feel the love He has for you. Now begin to change for Him. All God wants is to walk with you daily in the "cool of the evening" to laugh, share, cry if necessary, and change your footing from this world into His kingdom. Read about Enoch walking with God.

And the way of peace they have not known." (Romans 3:17)

My Thought

There is no peace in us, and there is no peace around us without Jesus. Without a good dose of righteousness, there is no peace. Later on, in *Romans*, Paul will say that even nature knows that everything is not right. There is no peace without Him.

Your Application

At night before you close your eyes, do you experience the true peace of God? Do you worry and fret about things? Do you fantasize? Change your bedtime routine to reading His Word and then talk with Jesus about your day and pray yourself to sleep, then you will experience true peace.

"There is no fear of God before their eyes." (Romans 3:18)

My Thought

There is no fear of God in us. Remember, in *Proverbs 9:10*, it says the fear of the Lord is the beginning of wisdom. Therefore, where there is no fear of God, there is no wisdom. It is a fear of reverence and respect. It's like being in a library with a librarian who knows how to keep the place quiet. When you walk in, you know you have to obey her rules. The librarian is not mean, she just requires respect, or there will be consequences. We should all fear the One who controls our final destiny.

Your Application

Read *Matthew 10:28*. Look up scriptures that talk about the fear of the Lord. Understand that those who do not fear the Lord are actually pulling down destruction on themselves. Ask God to give you the fear of the Lord and ask God to give it to those who do not think they need it.

Now we know that whatever the law says, it says to those who are under the law, that every mouth may be stopped, and all the world may become guilty before God. (Romans 3:19)

My Thought

We know that the law is speaking to those under the law, for every mouth will be stopped before they make excuses and not only those under the law, but all the world may become guilty before God. Here Paul tells us the law condemns those under the law for no man can follow the law, but Paul is also saying that all the world (all of us) is guilty before God. We may think we have the best excuse for why we do what we do, but here God our Father says, there are no excuses, before Me all are guilty. The law condemns those under the law, the law condemns those outside as well, for all have sinned. The guilty sign is on us unless we ask God to vindicate us through the cross of Jesus Christ's death and resurrection and His blood!

Your Application

Has your guilt been taken away? You now can have victory in your life, and you are on your way to heaven. Stop for a few minutes and take that in, praise Him for that!

> *Therefore by the deeds of the law no flesh will be justified in His sight, for by the law is the knowledge of sin. (Romans 3:20)*

My Thought

No one will be justified by walking out the law, for it is impossible to live the law. For the law gives us knowledge of our sinfulness. We cannot in our own self follow all the law. Therefore, the law, which is perfect, shows us our imperfect, sinful self. This is the whole reason for the law. A man comes on the scene and without standards, thinks he is doing pretty well, until the rules come out, and he sees that he is way off course. He can then decide to work himself ragged by trying to follow all the rules, or he can ignore the rules altogether, or he can accept the truth that he is not able to follow the rules.

Your Application

Do you try to justify the love the Father has given you by working hard to get His approval? You cannot work for salvation. It is a free gift from God. You can work out your salvation by daily growing closer to Jesus and growing in Him; this is called sanctification. You have to acknowledge your sinful state and let the work done on the cross free you of sin. Look up sanctification and then read *Philippians 2:12 & 13*; what does it say to you? Write it out in your own words. Are you justifying your sin, or learning to work out your salvation with fear?

God's Righteousness Through Faith

> *But now the rightness of God without the law is seen, being witnessed by the law and the prophets; (Romans 3:21)*

My Thought

Now, Paul switches us over to the new covenant, the righteousness of God without all the law, no sacrificing of animals, no worries about what food we should eat, etc. The law and the prophets spoke of this new beginning back in the Old Testament. The new covenant is the part we can rejoice over. We could not live up to the standards of the law because we are not without sin. The law made sure we knew that. Now the new covenant says the righteousness of God is without the law. The law has done its part. Now we are given the new way, Jesus.

Your Application

How has your life changed after receiving Christ? Write about it. *For the law was given through Moses, but God's unfailing love and faithfulness came through Jesus Christ (John 1:17).* What does that mean to you?

> *even the righteousness of God, through faith in Jesus Christ, to all and on all who believe. For there is no difference; (Romans 3:22)*

My Thought

This righteousness of God is by faith in Jesus Christ to all and upon all who believe, for there is no difference. There is no difference as to who can receive this gift of righteousness of God through Jesus Christ. It is for all and to all. There is no exclusivity in Christ. He says all can come. God is not unfair or unjust as to who can enter into the kingdom. He does not choose some and ignore some. He is an open Door for all to come through. The sad thing is that not all will choose to go through. It is a choice each individual has to make.

Your Application

Make a point to introduce as many as possible to this beautiful life.

> *for all have sinned and fall short of the glory of God, (Romans 3:23)*

My Thought

For all of us have sinned. We cannot even stand in the glory of God's shadow. We all have sinned. We are all in the same boat, and it's sinking. It's funny how often we look at others as better or worse than us. When we understand this portion of scripture, we recognize that all of us are sinners; only those who accept the truth of salvation step over into another boat, and it's going places! We still need to remember that we are only there because of the blood of our Savior, not of our own accord. We must settle in our mind that none is better, and none is worse.

Your Application

Can you come to the truth that all have sinned? Mother Teresa has sinned. Daniel of the Bible sinned. Your parents have sinned. The one you hold up on a pedestal has sinned. Who do you hold up as higher or better than you? Bring them down so you can relate to them in the way the Lord wants us to, as a brother or a sister. We still respect those who have more wisdom and experience in the Lord. We can learn from them, but they are not to be set above, for they too have sinned. Read *Colossians 3:1-4.*

> *being justified freely by His grace through the redemption that is in Christ Jesus, (Romans 3:24)*

My Thought

So now it's understood His grace entirely vindicates us through the cross. Jesus exchanged our sin debt and gave us His free access to the Father. We cannot boast about anything. We did nothing to become the persons we are in Christ. He reconciled us while we were dirty, low-life people, and Jesus gave us this free washing for anyone who would come. In the cleansing of our sin, Jesus reconnects us to our Father

Your Application

It's hard for some to think of themselves as bad. *Romans* is going to continue to tell you that you are. We have to get this if we understand the fullness of the gospel (Good News). Write out some of the bad Jesus cleansed you from and then write a prayer of thanksgiving. Get your feelings involved in this writing; don't just automatically write something; be still for a while in His presence; let Him bring you to a deeper understanding. Ask for that.

> *whom God set forth as a propitiation by His blood, through faith, to demonstrate His righteousness, because in His forbearance God had passed over the sins that were previously committed, (Romans 3:25)*

My Thought

From the beginning, God set into action the plan of Jesus as appeasement for our dirtiness. Through faith in His blood, it was to affirm our Father's uprightness for the removal of past sins, through the forbearance (the action of refraining from exercising a legal right, especially enforcing the payment of a debt) of God. Think of the movies where there is an angry god, and he needs to be appeased for the sins of the people, so they throw a child or baby into the fire to let the anger ease up from the people. Our Father God is angry over sin, but unlike the movie, instead of throwing us into the fire (which we deserve), He sets up a plan to let His only Son take on His wrath. Symbolically, God, our Father, throws His willing Son into the fire (the cross). Our Father is so righteous, so right in all He does. He has nothing but love for us.

Your Application

Take a moment and let that sink in. Write a letter of thankfulness to God and His Son.

> *to demonstrate at the present time His righteousness, that He might be just and the justifier of the one who has faith in Jesus. (Romans 3:26)*

My Thought

The Father did this to declare, Paul says, His righteousness, that He proves He is right. The Father in His righteousness can justify all who believe in Jesus; this is an important scripture. God, our Father, put it there for us but also for those who question us. How do you know that God even has the power to do all this cleansing stuff? What if it's just make-believe? Who is He anyway? The Father said in verse 26 that He did this to declare His righteousness. He is the one writing the Book, so He is expressing right now to you and me who He is. "I am the One who is righteous, and I can give an explanation for your forgiveness of sin." Remember Jesus Christ was our appeasement, our propitiation, so now we stand clean before our Father. That is the only way we stand clean, not of ourselves or any other religion.

Your Application

Is there ever a time when you get to thinking you are a pretty good person in and of yourself? Be careful! Your goodness comes from God. Repent and settle this now.

Boasting Excluded

> *Where is boasting then? It is excluded. By what law? Of works? No, but by the law of faith. (Romans 3:27)*

My Thought

How can we boast? It is gone! How is it gone? Because of the law? Because of works? No, only by faith. We cannot boast in the law; we cannot boast in our good works. Our boasting can only be in the law of faith in the Son of God. We can only boast in what Jesus did for us. We can boast in the love of God. We cannot boast in ourselves, and when we do, we lift ourselves above the price Jesus paid.

Your Application

Think of something you made. What would you say if that very thing stood up and started saying how it came to be and how great it was, and started boasting about the greatness of itself? Sounds funny? Look around at mankind, because that is happening all around us, maybe in us? Analyze how you think of yourself. Do you take the credit for the things God has done in you and through you, or do you boast in the gifts and talents He has put in you? Revise your ways and acknowledge the True Creator of all these good things in you.

> *Therefore we conclude that a man is justified by faith apart from the deeds of the law. (Romans 3:28)*

My Thought

Now, we can conclude the matter that we are vindicated by faith without any works of the law. Without any good works on our part, we are now justified and blameless. Not because we are good, but only by believing (faith) Jesus took our sins away and put them on Himself.

Your Application

Do you work for your salvation? Are you always trying to be good so God will love you? Do you hate yourself when you blow it, thinking God will be angry or disappointed with you? This verse is for you. There is no need to work for God's Love because He loved you in your worse state, and He continues to love you. When you receive Him as your God and Savior, do you think now He will get you for not doing things right? No, He has set you into the freedom of getting to know Him without fear of punishment. He wants you to do good because you love Him, and He wants you to obey because you understand it is for your good, and it's the way you show you trust Him and love Him.

> *Don't work for your salvation. It's already been paid.*
> *Just splash in it. Your Father loves it when*
> *you are having fun in Him.*

Or is He the God of the Jews only? Is He not also the God of the Gentiles? Yes, of the Gentiles also, (Romans 3:29)

My Thought

Is our Father the God of the Jews only? Is He the God of the Gentiles as well? Yes, He had us all in mind when He put the plan of salvation into effect. Paul is now going to break it down into the whole matter. God is the God and Father of all. He is not only for the Jew but also for the rest of society! I love this. God's plan of salvation from the beginning of time included you and me. He didn't add us in when the Jewish people denied Him. We were and have always been on His mind as well. Just like today, He has the Jews on His mind. We are one big happy family, just waiting for Jesus to return so we can finally all be together.

Your Application

God called all; you have brothers and sisters that you have not met, but one day you will. If you have had a happy family, you can understand how this will be. If you haven't, you now have something great to look forward to understanding! Write an essay about what it will be like for you.

> *since there is one God who will justify the circumcised by faith and the uncircumcised through faith. (Romans 3:30)*

My Thought

So there is One God. By faith, the circumcised will be justified, and the uncircumcised will be justified through faith. As a result of faith, the Jews will be justified. The Jewish nation was established to house faith. So, they are vindicated from their sin as they believe the original plan that God is their King. In the course of faith, all others will be acquitted. All others were brought through by believing in the Door of Redemption, Jesus. We are all joined together because of faith; we need each other.

Your Application

Know what you believe and believe what you know. Then convince others what you know you believe, that's called the Good News (gospel)! There is only One God. This is the scripture you can use when others say there are other gods. *Romans 3:30* says there is one God. You must learn to use scripture as your basis of all truth.

Do we then make void the law through faith? Certainly not! On the contrary, we establish the law. (Romans 3:31)

My Thought

Is the law needed now that we have faith? God says, Yes, we establish the law. Yes, the law is necessary because it creates the necessity for faith. We cannot accomplish the law requirements, so we need to have confidence in Jesus that He completely satisfied the law. So why do we need the law? The law tells us about our Father, about Jewish history, what is good for us, and how to behave appropriately. We are given the freedom to read all about our brothers and sisters of the Old Testament. If we didn't have the law, we would be clueless about our origin. Yes, we need the law today. Do we need all the rituals of the law? No, they were fulfilled in Christ, and now as we stand in Christ, as Christ is in us, the law is fulfilled in us, too. What a tremendous plan God provided for us who believe!

Your Application

Choose a brother and sister of the Old Testament and read about them. Write your thoughts on them and why they are essential. What did you learn from them?

Romans Three shows us victory in life is based on simple and fundamental truths. We believe that God is good, He has set a plan of saving us from our sins, and He is carefully watching over us. Life doesn't just happen to us; life is for us. Hopefully, you believe this. If not, why not talk with your Father about this and ask for a deeper understanding of this truth.

My Prayer

Lord Jesus, we realize that no one is righteous, no not one! No one is wise; no one is even seeking You. We have no excuse; we have all sinned. Yet, You came after us to bring us into a sonship with the Father! Amazing! How much You must love us to plan from the foundation of time to seek after us and to sacrifice Your life, shedding Your blood, for our sin so we could be set free as we place our faith in You. You make us right in Your sight. We truly are living a changed life, thank You! We love you! In Your most wonderful Name. Amen.

Write a summary of chapter 3.

We just get to be the models, walking in His robe of righteousness. We did not make the robe; we didn't even put it on, He did. Do not work for your salvation. The price has been paid. Just splash in it. Your Father loves it when you are having fun in Him.

Our Worship

Jireh / Elevation Worship & Maverick City
https://www.youtube.com/watch?v=mC-zw0zCCtg

CHAPTER 4
Living in Faith Part 1

Read the complete chapter of *Romans 4*

Abraham Justified by Faith

> *What then shall we say that Abraham our father has found according to the flesh? (Romans 4:1)*

My Thought

Our father Abraham found that in his flesh, there was no good thing. He celebrates the fact that all he has comes from God. Through his own works, he knows that he created division (Ishmael), but when he let God do what God had promised, in God's timing, God gave Abraham, Isaac.

Your Application

How often do you see your ability to perform God's will your way? How often have you produced Ishmaels? Understand that God will bring about His will in His timing. Wait for the things of God and let your flesh learn to be patient for the perfect timing of God. Read *Genesis 12-25*, as a novel of Abraham's life. Write down what you learned through him. There is a song called "Take Courage" by Bethel Music, Kristene DiMarco, in which part of the lyrics is "He's in the waiting…" So good to be reminded of that. Why not listen to it now and be encouraged?

> *For if Abraham was justified by works, he has something to boast about, but not before God. (Romans 4:2)*

My Thought

Abraham was a good man and a rich man. He could have boasted in these things, but even what he had was given to him by God. We need to realize that all we have been given comes from God. Our talents, our personality, and our abilities to create wealth are from God. *But remember the LORD your God, for it is He who gives you the ability to produce wealth, and so confirms His covenant, which He swore to your ancestors, as it is today (Deuteronomy 8:18).* We can boast about these

43

things, but we shouldn't, because there are consequences (*Daniel 4*). In all that we have been given, we should always give thanks to God for all of it.

Your Application

Read the story of King Nebuchadnezzar in *Daniel 4*; write out what happened to him.

> *For what does the Scripture say? "Abraham believed God, and it was accounted to him for righteousness" (Genesis 15:6). (Romans 4:3)*

My Thought

Looking into Scripture is so important. Paul is looking back in the Old Testament to give us the basis of faith. Abraham believed God first. Abraham's faith came before his works. Abraham didn't work for his righteousness; his belief in God credited him for right standing before God.

Your Application

Know that faith will always come before works. Your faith in God is the most crucial aspect of your walk with God. You need to be "working out your salvation" (*Philippians 1:6*), but not before your simple child-like faith. Examine your walk with Christ: are you working for your right standing with God, or is your faith simply living it by believing God?

> *Now to him who works, the wages are not counted as grace but as debt. (Romans 4:4)*

My Thought

Working for our righteousness is useless, for it becomes works. Works without faith is placing your righteousness before the blood of Christ. If you work for your right standing with God, you will owe Him forever because it is impossible to pay your debt. We have to walk in our salvation in the proper order. We have to believe God sent His Son to die for our sins. The work is finished, we receive His grace, now we accept the cross' complete work. We can then work out our salvation by daily giving our lives over to Him to grow in our faith (sanctification).

Your Application

What order are you living out your salvation? Write a letter to Jesus, thanking Him for His Grace.

David Celebrates the Same Truth

> *But to him who does not work but believes on Him who justifies the ungodly, his faith is accounted for righteousness, (Romans 4:5)*

My Thought

By faith in God, we are validated through Jesus. Now Paul is including the Romans and us in the story. Paul is saying if we do not work but believe on Him, our faith is credited to us as right standing before God, just like Abraham. People, you need to understand this concept. Faith came first, then Abraham was given God's righteousness. We need to believe first, and then we are given God's righteousness. We are not to work for our righteousness, no matter what you have heard; Paul is making it very clear that our rightness before God is a Gift given to us through the price of Jesus Christ on the cross.

Your Application

Understand this concept, dear friend; struggle with it until it is in your head, but more importantly, in your heart. It means we accept that He loves us. He has done the work for us, and now we enjoy the process of walking with Jesus, growing in His goodness without trying to get Him to love us because He already does.

just as David also describes the blessedness of the man to whom God imputes righteousness apart from works: (Romans 4:6)

My Thought

Paul goes back to the Old Testament to prove his point. He uses King David's words from the Psalms. Use the Word to make a point. Our opinions are just that, an opinion, but God's Word is unchangeable truth. We can build a case on God's Word.

Your Application

How often do you use God's Word to bring the truth of what you are saying? Literally, open the Word and read straight from it, practice using scripture this week in your conversation with others.

Blessed are those whose lawless deeds are forgiven, and whose sins are covered (Psalms 32:1); (Romans 4:7)

My Thought

King David says, happy is the man and woman whose sins are covered by the blood of Jesus. Also happy is the one who, after breaking the law, is now forgiven of that wrongdoing. Sin is so ugly, and we are so weak in dealing with it, but we have a way out through the precious blood of Jesus. We are covered and forgiven.

Your Application

How often do you remember the effects of your sin on your Savior? How often do you ponder on the price of your forgiveness? Do it today.

> *Blessed is the man to whom the LORD shall not impute sin (Psalms 32:2)*
> *(Romans 4:8)*

My Thought

King David continues, happy are we whose sin has not been charged against our lives! We deserved a penalty for the wrongful acts we have committed, but we are free, no longer owing a debt. The blood of Jesus Christ cancels out our debt.

Your Application

Remembering this daily gives us a constant connection to our Savior. Does someone owe you today? Cancel that debt and feel what it is like to forgive a debt that was owed. Thank Jesus today!

Abraham Justified Before Circumcision

> *Does this blessedness then come upon the circumcised only, or upon the uncircumcised also? For we say that faith was accounted to Abraham for righteousness. (Romans 4:9)*

My Thought

Is this promise of sins being forgiven only for the circumcised, or do the uncircumcised get the same benefits? Paul once again goes back to the Old Testament to clarify his answer. Faith made Abraham righteous, not the seal or sign of faith.

Your Application

What makes you righteous? Do you read hours of the Word? Do you give generously? Do these acts make you righteous? Are you continually serving the poor and needy? Does that add to your righteousness? Think about what makes you righteous. Look back at the scripture; what is Paul saying made Abraham righteous?

> *How then was it accounted? While he was circumcised, or uncircumcised? Not while circumcised, but while uncircumcised. (Romans 4:10)*

My Thought

When was Abraham given his righteousness, before or after he was circumcised? He was made righteous before the circumcision. He did nothing to bring about his righteousness. It was his faith in God that made him righteous.

Your Application

Again, look into what you think makes you righteous. Are you working so hard to receive your right standing before God? Are you worn out being a Christian? God never intended you to work for your salvation. He wants you to receive the gift of grace freely from Him (read *Galatians*). Write your thoughts.

> *And he received the sign of circumcision, a seal of the righteousness of the faith which he had while still uncircumcised, that he might be the father of all those who believe, though they are uncircumcised, that righteousness might be imputed to them also, (Romans 4:11)*

My Thought

Circumcision is a seal, just like a ring is a seal between a husband and a wife. Circumcision is a picture of dying to our flesh. Circumcision is a picture of purity, nothing hidden from God. The sign of Abraham's seal of righteousness (circumcision) came after he believed God. God just allowed the seal to be placed on him because he already believed God to be the true and only God. Circumcision had no importance in itself, just as a wedding ring means nothing without two people committing to one another. The love of a man and woman grows first, and then the ring has its meaning or sign of love. The seal of circumcision set the Jews apart to be God's people.

Your Application

What comes first to you, your works, or your faith? Do you act out your works to prove your faith? Do you say you have a ring, but no one wears it, there's no relationship? The ring means nothing. Works do not work without faith first.

> *…and the father of circumcision to those who not only are of the circumcision, but who also walk in the steps of the faith which our father Abraham had while still uncircumcised. (Romans 4:12)*

My Thought

Circumcision is not the topic here. It's not circumcised, or uncircumcised—the issue is faith. And Abraham is the father of all who believe. God is amazing in how He set this whole thing up. He knew we would be people that get tripped up with working hard to gain God's love and affection, so He took that out of the equation. God made it very simple for His sheep (us). He said, just have faith in Me. Circumcision is the sign God used to separate His people of faith. It is also an example for us today to separate our flesh from our spirit. Circumcision wasn't just a cut, but it was a ceremony of a covenant with God.

Your Application

Are you separated from your flesh? Or does your flesh expose wrong motives of your good deeds? Is your spirit alive and well, breathing freely without the flesh, or is the flesh still surrounding your spirit and looking horrible on you? Learn to be like your father Abraham and cut off the flesh of your heart and let the spirit be free to live the life God intended for you, an abundant and free life.

The Promise Granted Through Faith

> *For the promise that he would be the heir of the world was not to Abraham or to his seed through the law, but through the righteousness of faith. (Romans 4:13)*

My Thought

The promise God our Father passes down to us through Abraham is faith, not the law. Abraham believed, and God credited his faith as righteousness. God did not reward Abraham as righteous because he strictly followed the law; that was impossible. God just asked Abraham to believe. Faith is our goal. We have to begin to experience faith as a child. God says it, we believe it, and it is settled in our hearts as faith.

Your Application

Do you want to earn your righteousness? Do you want to make your own robes of righteousness? That is impossible. The law could not and cannot be followed, for if you break one letter of the law, you have broken the complete law (*James 2:10*). Take time today to set into action a part of scripture that is hard for you to believe. Increase your ability to let faith grow in you by spending time with God, like your father Abraham did. As Abraham spent time with God, his faith came naturally.

> *For if those who are of the law are heirs, faith is made void and the promise made of no effect, (Romans 4:14)*

My Thought

The law does not make us heirs. The law made us aware of our need for a Savior. The law shows us our bad. The law opened our eyes to see we were orphans in search of family. Faith made us an heir; faith in God made the promises come true.

Your Application

How many times have you sat still to let faith grow? Take the time right now to allow God to fill you with faith.

> *because the law brings about wrath; for where there is no law there is no transgression. (Romans 4:15)*

My Thought

The other thing that the law does is make us aware of the wrath upon those who are not righteous. God's wrath is set on the sin of the unrighteous. God hates sin, and the law shows us our sinfulness. If we did not have the law, we would not have a standard of righteousness, and we would not know that we are sinners. We would be unaware of the bad that lives inside of us.

Your Application

How happy you must be to learn that the law is your friend, it does expose our weaknesses, our vulnerabilities and our wickedness, but it also directs us to the source of our redemption! *Wounds from a friend can be trusted, but an enemy multiplies kisses. (Proverbs 27:6)* Are you trusting the law as a friend to wound you into truth? Sit and ponder.

> *Therefore it is of faith that it might be according to grace, so that the promise might be sure to all the seed, not only to those who are of the law, but also to those who are of the faith of Abraham, who is the father of us all... (Romans 4:16)*

My Thought

God invites all into this wonderful family. Not only those of the law but all who are of the faith of Abraham. That includes us! We live in this family of God with our Jewish brothers and sisters. We will forever live together in harmony in our lives to come. We also need to value each other in our *Storybook Fairy-Tale Reality of the Kingdom of God* here on earth. We need to begin to see the importance of praying for each other and especially loving each other.

Your Application

How connected are you to your fellow brothers and sisters in Christ, whether they be those you know or those you have never met? We connect to all our family through prayer. Begin to pray daily for your kingdom family.

> *...(as it is written, "I have made you a father of many nations") in the presence of Him whom he believed—God, who gives life to the dead and calls those things which do not exist as though they did; (Romans 4:17)*

My Thought

Faith believes in the things that do not exist. Abraham believed God for the things He said, and yet Abraham did not see these promises. In fact, the promises were incredible to believe. Abraham, old and having no children, with a barren wife Sarah, who was past the childbearing stage, would be the father of all nations. How is that possible? Abraham must have seen something in this God of his to know that what He spoke could make the very thing that did not exist become existent!

Your Application

How is your faith, friend? Do you believe in the promises God gives you? Are you of Abraham's inheritance, and do you carry his faith? Do you walk in the "things that do not exist as though they do" faith? If so, rejoice, for you will see those things God promised you come into existence. If you do not walk in your Father Abraham's faith, why not? Make changes to see your faith increase. Read *Hebrews 12*.

who, contrary to hope, in hope believed, so that he became the father of many nations, according to what was spoken, "So shall your descendants be." (Romans 4:18)

My Thought

Hope is the expectation of coming good! Abraham, contrary to believing what he saw, expected something good in the promised Word of God. The outcome was that he became the very thing God promised him. What did not exist in Abraham came to existence because Abraham believed the Word spoken over him by God.

Your Application

Do you have a Word spoken over you by God? Yes, you do; read His Word. Do you believe the Word spoken over you? Become like your father, Abraham, live out your life in faith. Find a verse or two that speaks a word over you. Try *Psalms* 139.

> *And not being weak in faith, he did not consider his own body, already dead (since he was about a hundred years old), and the deadness of Sarah's womb. (Romans 4:19)*

My Thought

Here are the reasons why God's promise could not come true. Abraham was old, and Sarah was dead in her womb. That's a pretty safe defense for not receiving His promise. Once again, our Father Abraham must have seen something in his God's eyes or heard something in his God's voice to be so confident that what God said was more substantial than what his eyes and mind could figure out.

Faith stands higher than what we can work out in our minds.

Your Application

Faith is yours if you will only take hold of it. How does faith grow? By knowing the One who speaks the promises to you. Faith grows by living more in the *Storybook Fairy-Tale Reality of the Kingdom of God*. This kingdom does not exist for many. If you listen to those who do not believe, they will give you the reasons why. What would have happened if Abraham listened to those who said he couldn't be a father of nations? Your faith will grow if you believe the impossible truths God is speaking to you. What is stopping you? Experience an encounter with God now. Look into His eyes and hear His voice, then you will believe in the things that do not exist as though they do!

> *He did not waver at the promise of God through unbelief, but was strengthened in faith, giving glory to God, (Romans 4:20)*

My Thought

He did not waver because he did not listen to the voices of unbelief. He gave God glory; he knew what God said was true; his faith strengthened him. He believed and God credited Abraham as righteous. The more we use our faith, the stronger our faith becomes. It is in stepping out in the impossible promises of God that we become strengthened in our Christian walk.

Your Application

What was the last faith walk you took? Have you walked in faith lately or are you living your Christian life on the momentum of the faith-walk you lived in the past? Why not do something today that requires faith?

> *and being fully convinced that what He had promised He was also able to perform.* (Romans 4:21)

My Thought

Abraham was convinced in his mind that what God had promised him was going to come to pass because Abraham believed what God promised, God could make happen. Abraham was thoroughly convinced. Why? Again, he knew something about God that maybe many of us are missing. We hear about God from the pulpit, we might even read about God from the great men of faith, but are we walking with God as Abraham did, as some pastors are or as the men of faith did? Are we putting these people on pedestals? Is their faith better than ours? Nope! What do we need to be convinced as Abraham was? Abraham had an encounter with God. He met God, and from that point in his life, he was confident that God could do anything He said He would do.

Your Application

Have you had an Abrahamic encounter with your God? Read Genesis 18. How did Abraham know it was God? What was the first thing Abraham was asked to do when he recognized God? If your faith is lacking, ask for an encounter with God.

> *And therefore "it was accounted to him for righteousness."* (Romans 4:22)

My Thought

Abraham was convinced and believed, and God credited it into Abraham's account as righteousness. God is looking for people that will believe in what He says. God does not want to jump through hoops for us to believe. God wants to count us righteous by our belief in Him. He is looking for good men and women to just believe in their General, who through blind faith, know what He says He can perform, and who walk in the Word of our God. God is looking for our faith to convince others of His kingship. Abraham believed, and those looking saw God's promise come into existence when barren Sarah birthed Isaac. God's righteousness was placed on Abraham because he believed what was impossible to be possible due to an encounter he had with the One who does the unthinkable.

Your Application

Your righteousness comes from your faith in the One who wants to show you how incredible life can be if you only believe. Hopefully, you understand the contradiction of faith. You believe in what you do not see. Things that do not exist can exist if you believe in the One who says they exist. Oh, faith is so much fun. Faith astounds the brightest of earthlings, and our Father has only begun to show His unimaginable signs and wonders. Believe in God's promises before you have time to think. Read *Habakkuk 2:4, 2 Corinthians 5:7, Romans 10:17, and Romans 1:7.*

Now it was not written for his sake alone that it was imputed to him, (Romans 4:23)

My Thought

Abraham's story of faith is great, but it wasn't for him alone. God uses Abraham as an example for all his inheritance. Abraham is the father of all nations, so we as his children can read about our heir and receive the reward of his faith.

Your Application

Know that what you do will be passed down to your heirs. Are you passing down good spiritual genes to your future family? Remember to live a life worth repeating and make good decisions for the ones yet to come.

but also for us. It shall be imputed to us who believe in Him who raised up Jesus our Lord from the dead, (Romans 4:24)

My Thought

Abraham's faith affects us. His faith not only imputes righteousness into Abraham's account, but our faith imputes righteousness into our accounts as well. As we see our Father Abraham walk by faith and follow his example, we receive! We can say, "Ah, that's nice for Abraham," but it's when we see the effect on our lives that we begin to understand we need to appropriate it into our lives. Honestly, we are selfish beings and need to see the "what's in it for me" before getting it. God knows that; it is why He included this scripture. What is the faith we need? The faith God is asking for is to believe in Him who raised Jesus from the dead. It is not just about Jesus but also believing in God the Father who Jesus represented while on earth. People want to believe part of the story, but our God asks us to believe it all.

Your Application

Now that you see the benefits of faith for your life, why not begin to live in faith daily? How? Begin with the encounter. See God's face through the Word. Hear God's voice through the Word and the Holy Spirit. Then as you see His face, faith will begin to grow. What people say is "impossible," you will see as possible. Write about your encounter.

who was delivered up because of our offenses, and was raised because of our justification. (Romans 4:25)

My Thought

Jesus was delivered up to the cross because of our sins. Jesus was raised from the dead to bring undue justice to us. We are now justified because of His blood, just as if we never sinned. If we look at the accounting sheets of our life, we see the debt of our sins and know the debt can never be repaid. With the faith of Abraham, we can believe that which does not exist as though it does, and we see *not guilty* stamped on our ledger! By faith in the Son of God, our debt is paid, and we are free to live in our *Storybook Fairy-Tale Reality* with joy and anticipation every day to see what new things God our Father will bring us as we just hang out with Him.

Your Application

Faith is the real deal. Faith grants you access to live in the *Storybook Fairy-Tale Reality of the Kingdom of God*. We walk through the open Door (Jesus), but we must have faith to stay in this kingdom. The greater your faith, the higher your status of believing in the "things that do not exist as though they do." Grow in faith and let your life truly begin.

Romans Four shows us to have faith over good works. We are to have both, but faith comes first. Good works are a product of our faith as we mature in our salvation, we want to do good works, but our righteousness is credited to us through our faith in God who forgives our sins, as it was with Abraham, our spiritual father of faith. *Abraham believed in the God who brings the dead back to life and who creates new things out of nothing* ((Romans 4:17). Abraham was fully convinced that God would do what He promised, even the impossible. Because of that faith, God credited Abraham as righteous. It benefits us too as we believe in Jesus' sacrifice with His shedding of blood; we are credited righteous as well.

My Prayer

God, we are learning faith is the evidence of things not seen. Father God, in chapter four, we are granted the privilege of looking into Abraham's life. We see his incredible faith, although we also know that he did waver in his faith in *Genesis*, as did Sarah. They both decided that what You had asked was going to take a bit of help from them. In their assistance, they made an Ishmael. Their faith became greater when they realized You didn't need their help. How often do we get in the mix with You, God? We place our hands in with Yours, to help You. We, too, make Ishmaels. God, you were so patient towards Abraham and Sarah. You kept Your promise to give them, an Isaac. God, you are so good to us; we must learn from our Father Abraham not to help You, but if we do, we will remember You are gracious and patient with us. You will keep Your Word. Faith stands alone. We become better for believing and waiting even if it's twenty-five years. God bless us as we wait in faith. In Your Son's Name. Amen.

Write a summary of chapter 4.

Faith stands higher than what we can work out in our minds. Believe in God's promises before you have time to think of how you will help Him.

Our Worship

Most Beautiful / So In Love (feat. Chandler Moore) / Maverick City Music
https://www.youtube.com/watch?v=oCAY_qeDo-w&list=RDMM&index=2

CHAPTER 5

Living in Hope

Read the complete chapter of *Romans 5*

Faith Triumphs in Trouble

> *Therefore being justified by faith, we now have peace with God because of our Lord Jesus Christ, (Romans 5:1)*

My Thought

We are vindicated! We stand before God just as if we never sinned. We have access to the Father at any time. We do not have to worry about the wrath that was on us. It is completely gone! Why? Our Lord Jesus Christ took on His body the wrath that was meant for us. He took the penalty of our sin so we could be at peace with our Father.

Your Application

In this verse, Paul calls Jesus Christ, "Lord." Look up, Lord, and write out the meaning. Now ask yourself, is Jesus Christ "Lord" of my life? Write out what you discovered. If He is not Lord, why not act now and give Him access to all of you and trust Him to control your life.

> *through whom also we have access by faith into this grace in which we stand, and rejoice in hope of the glory of God. (Romans 5:2)*

My Thought

By Jesus Christ, we also have access into this undeserved favor (grace) because we believe this whole story; we also rejoice in the expectation of the coming good (hope) of the splendor (glory) of God. As we walk by faith through the Door (Jesus), we can enter into this *Storybook Fairy-Tale Reality* where love is unlimited, and we have an undeserved peace with God, our Father. In this world, we are joyfully enjoying life with our Father and Jesus. Even during sickness, hurt, and tragedy, we can still have joy in knowing He will never leave us or forsake us, and He will bring us through. We wait expectantly for the coming of our real life and live forever in the splendor of God.

Your Application

How many times do you daydream about the Coming of Jesus Christ? Make it a point to think/daydream of the place Jesus has gone to prepare for you. Read *John 14:1–4* and daydream right now.

> *And not only that, but we also glory in tribulations, knowing that tribulation produces perseverance; (Romans 5:3)*

My Thought

Don't just be happy in all these promises of God; we also need to be content in God during tribulation, knowing that tribulation brings about patience in us. If we look at people's lives, most people have learned the most during difficult times. God, our Father, teaches us through Paul, to not resent the difficult times in our lives. We must understand this if we are to live in the *Storybook Fairy-Tale Reality of the Kingdom of God*. Did Cinderella have it good? Did Peter Pan? Did Snow White have an easy life? Did the Fantastic Four? What about Belle? Do you think living with a Beast is easy? All these fairy tales have the "difficult times," but the characters persevere. They become better people. Our Father wants us to learn to persevere through tribulation, for it will work patience in us. What kind of patience does our Father want to work in us? Are we waiting for something good to happen? Yes, but what if the good doesn't happen soon enough—do we put a limit on how long God can allow our difficult times? Or does our Father want us to be like the Three Hebrew Boys, who said, *"Our God can deliver us,* but if He doesn't, we still won't give in, or throw a temper tantrum" (*Daniel 3:16–18*)

Your Application

Are you patient with God, or do you set time limits on Him? He has given you the greatest gift He could give. Do you really deserve more? Your witness to people around you is to believe when all others quit. Remember the Three Hebrew Boys? Read their story again (*Daniel 3*) and ask God to impart that courage and faith into you, so no matter what, you won't give up even when God seems to be taking His time.

> *and perseverance, character; and character, hope (Romans 5:4)*

My Thought

Not only does tribulation bring about patience, but patience also brings experience, and experience brings hope. Again, our Father is teaching us, His children, how to navigate through life. He says, "You will have difficult times, but through them, if you do not give up, you will come out a patient, experienced, hopeful child of God."

Your Application

If you were to hire someone to work in your business, would you want someone who had experience? Would you like someone patient, and who was hopeful? Your Father gives you an opportunity to have all this if you go through difficult times, trusting Him. How do you usually handle difficult times? Write about it.

Now hope does not disappoint (or put us to shame), because the love of God has been poured out in our hearts by the Holy Spirit who was given to us. (Romans 5:5)

My Thought

Not only do difficult times bring patience, experience, and hope, but with all that, we are not ashamed, because the love of God is spread in our hearts by the Holy Spirit. We have been under the cover of shame ever since Adam and Eve sinned. As we continue to walk in sin, we walk in shame. Now, God, our Father says, with these difficult times, I will show you my glory and no longer will you be ashamed, for you are now Mine. I can see a farmer spreading his seeds throughout his land, expecting a generous crop. That's the picture God wants us to see. He spreads His seeds of love in our hearts, and He gives us the Holy Spirit to cultivate His love.

Your Application

Do you still have shame in your life? Take a moment to meditate on this verse. Allow the Lord to wash away all your shame. As a child of God, all shame should be as far from you as the east is from the west! Rejoice and use this verse next time condemnation or shame come to haunt you. Difficult times produce patience, which builds experience that God is faithful in what He says, which creates hope, an expectation of coming good, which causes you not to be ashamed!

Christ in Our Place

For when we were still without strength, in due time Christ died for the ungodly. (Romans 5:6)

My Thought

For when we had no strength, at the right time, Christ died for us. When we were helpless to do anything about our sin, Christ came and died at the right time. We have to get this, dear saint. Jesus Christ came at the perfect time according to His all-knowing knowledge and wisdom. His timing is excellent, and when we get impatient with Him and give up or get mad at Him, we show our lack of understanding of how *big* God is. Simply put, we do not know, but He does. What else is there to discuss, ever? *He is a big God, and we are little people.* We must understand that our difficult times are there for a reason. Just as Jesus came in His perfect time to die on the cross for us, He sets up our lives with good and hard times. Accept it and move on in Him with patience, experience, and hope of never being ashamed! Receive everything He has for you, the good with the tribulations. That's a true disciple.

Your Application

Again, Paul camps here because you need to understand this truth to move successfully into your *Storybook Fairy-Tale Reality of the Kingdom of God.* Do you know that God is in control of all your life, good and bad? Write out what you believe about this; use scripture.

For scarcely for a righteous man will one die; yet perhaps for a good man someone would even dare to die. (Romans 5:7)

My Thought

The point Paul is making is that it is rare that anyone would die for someone. Possibly one would die if the person is good, and yet, Jesus is born to die for us, the wicked, the sinful.

Your Application

Would you give your life for anyone? Seriously think about it and answer that question?

But God demonstrates His own love toward us, in that while we were still sinners, Christ died for us. (Romans 5:8)

My Thought

God expressed His love toward us that while we were so deep in sin, Christ died for us. Some might die for a good man, but God expressed His love towards us while we were wretched in our sin. We hear it so often we sometimes just say, "I know that." Get out of the old mindset and hit refresh. Hear it for the first time. We were unable to live out the perfect law, so our destiny was death. The Prince of Peace rescued us because of His deep love for His Father, and because our Father loved us so much, and wanted us reconciled back to Him. Jesus stepped in and died for us while we were not good, but sinners.

Your Application

Can you understand this kind of love? If not, ask the Holy Spirit to deepen your ability to take this all in.

Much more then, having now been justified by His blood, we shall be saved from wrath through Him. (Romans 5:9)

My Thought

There's more?! Being vindicated by Jesus' blood, God's wrath is no longer an issue. God's wrath is as great as God's love. If you can imagine His love and how vast it is, then know God contains the same amount of wrath towards sin. Think of it this way, you have a pet lamb, and you love him very much. There is a wolf that wants to destroy the lamb. You see the wolf coming after the lamb. Do you just sit there, or do whatever is necessary for the lamb to escape the wolf? There is something within you that loathes the wolf that is trying to kill the one you love. Now you see the lamb desiring to be with the wolf (sin) and not you. You know it will destroy the lamb, but the lamb turns to the wolf. As the wolf eats up the lamb, your wrath lashes out to kill the wolf, and your wrath is justified. So it is with God: His wrath is justified because He has made a way of escape for all people, but some will not take that way, and God's wrath will consume sin and those attached to it.

Your Application

God's wrath will be on all who choose sin (the wolf). The wrath is towards sin, but God's wrath will destroy both if the person joins with sin. There is a way of escape for all, but for those who do not take that path, there will be the price to pay for the penalty of sin—death. Read this verse again and understand that you are free from the wrath of God because of Jesus. Share with someone this week, this wonderful truth. Read Ezekiel 8-9:11 to understand more of the wrath of God. Write out your thoughts.

> *For if when we were enemies we were reconciled to God through the death of His Son, much more, having been reconciled, we shall be saved by His life. (Romans 5:10)*

My Thought

When we were enemies, we were reunited to God by the death of Jesus, His Son. How much more will Jesus' life save us? If His death caused us to be reunited with our Father, how much more will we be saved through His resurrected life? The death of Jesus reunited us to God, our Father. The resurrection of Jesus brings us to another dimension of life, abundant life. We become complete and whole because of His life.

Your Application

Are you missing something in your life? Is He your Shepherd? *The Lord is my Shepherd I will not want.* Are you wanting? Then you need to recheck your status with the Lord because if you are wanting, He isn't your Shepherd. Read *Psalms 23*; search your heart.

> *And not only that, but we also rejoice in God through our Lord Jesus Christ, through whom we have now received the reconciliation. (Romans 5:11)*

My Thought

We not only have life but abundant, joyful life in God because of Jesus Christ. By Him we received our atonement (satisfaction or reparation of a wrong done or an injury). Our lives with God are not a life of trying to repay God for giving us His Son. Our life with God is abundant and joyful. He is so happy that we accept the sacrifice of Jesus. He allowed this to happen so He could have a relationship with us. He loves hanging out with us. He loves it when we put other things aside and set Him as top priority.

Your Application

Do you understand that God wants more than anything to be with you? He has made a way for you to be close to Him. How close are you to Him? Evaluate this question and write out if you need to change your life to set Him as a priority. You are guaranteed to have a joyful, abundant life if you do.

Death Through Adam, Life Through Christ

> *Therefore, just as through one man's sin entered the world, and death through sin, and thus death spread to all men, because all sinned—* (Romans 5:12)

My Thought

By one man (Adam), sin entered the world, and sin meant death. Death was mankind's destiny, for all have sinned. Simply put, Adam, who was the best specimen of humanity, didn't pass the test of temptation. He failed; therefore, we failed. Death is inevitable for all of us because all of us have sinned. We need to understand we are on a downward spiral because we tend to sin. We want our way. We will get what we want in whatever way we can. We are selfish individuals.

Your Application

Do you recognize the selfishness in you? Do you acknowledge when you do things that are not ethical just to get your way? Don't be shocked; that is part of our DNA. We are sinful people. Write out ways that you try to get your way.

> *(For until the law sin was in the world, but sin is not imputed when there is no law. (Romans 5:13)*

My Thought

The law recognized sin; where there is no law, sin is not recognized. The purpose of the law was to let us see our own bad, for us to acknowledge our sinfulness. If there were no laws to break, then we would not be lawbreakers. The purpose of the law was to point out our inadequacies, our flaws, and our sins.

Your Application

It's okay to know you're bad. Knowing it is the beginning of surrendering because you realize you cannot change without Jesus. You require a stronger power, Jesus. Your world shouldn't revolve around you. There is someone bigger, with the complete picture of life. What are some of the sins in your life? Lay them at the feet of Jesus and talk with Him about them. He will not condemn you! He will show you how to let go of them.

> *Nevertheless death reigned from Adam to Moses, even over those who had not sinned according to the likeness of the transgression of Adam, who is a type of Him who was to come. (Romans 5:14)*

My Thought

As mentioned earlier, death entered with Adam's sin. Death continues to have dominion into Moses' era, even to those who had not sinned in the same likeness of Adam (rebellion and disobedience). Adam was a shadow of Jesus, who would be our Rescuer. Adam had one rule, "Do not eat the fruit."

One rule! He could not be the one to rescue us because he could not follow one rule! Don't be too hard on Adam; he was our Olympic choice; we could not have done any better. Why does it mention sin that reigns from Adam to Moses? Moses represents the law, so sin reigned until the law. Then the law was given to show us our inability to live sinlessly. The law showed our sinfulness, and there was only One way to have forgiveness of sin, a Perfect Person who could keep all the law, Jesus. Although Adam and Eve were given the consequence of sin by being led out of the garden, sin did continue to invade humankind. When Moses came along, God gave him a set of rules and regulations to live by and instant consequences for breaking them; death being the ultimate consequence. God also made a way for forgiveness of sins by continual sacrifices of animals which was the picture of what Christ would do on the cross. When sin entered the world, death was the destiny for all; even if we didn't sin precisely as Adam did, we have all sinned (*Roman 3:23*). Adam was the shadow of the Perfect Adam that was to come, Jesus. Adam failed, allowing death to enter all mankind; Jesus did not. Through His one-time sacrifice He bought life for all, but only those who will believe will receive it.

Your Application

From Adam to Moses, there were no written laws by God, yet people were responsible for their conduct. How would you live if you knew you wouldn't be accountable for your actions? Now think about your written response and ask yourself, would I follow after Christ if I were not destined to hell?

> *But the free gift is not like the offense. For if by the one man's offense many died, much more the grace of God and the gift by the grace of the one Man, Jesus Christ, abounded to many. (Romans 5:15)*

My Thought

Adam brought about death, so Jesus brings us the free gift. Through the sin of Adam, we had death. More significant than that, we have the grace of God through the greater than Adam, Jesus Christ, giving us the gift of grace to many. The difference between the two men, Adam and Jesus, is Adam was us, and we were given a chance to live in harmony with God, but we failed. Then we received the perfect Adam, Jesus, who lived on this earth in communion with God without sin. Now we have, through the kindness of God, the gift of grace (not receiving what we deserve). We deserve to go to hell, but we are getting what we don't deserve because Christ took upon himself the death we deserved. Grace is given to many, but not all will receive because there will be those who will not believe.

Your Application

What helped you to believe? So many do not believe this story. You can convince them by knowing what made you believe. Write out what convinced you that Jesus Christ is real. Share that with someone this week.

> *And the gift is not like that which came through the one who sinned. For the judgment which came from one offense resulted in condemnation, but the free gift which came from many offenses resulted in justification. (Romans 5:16)*

My Thought

Sin entered by Adam and all sinned, just as the salvation's gift entered through Jesus, and all were given a chance to receive it. For the judgment came to us through Adam to condemnation, but the free gift covered all sins leaving us standing as if we had never sinned. Let's not give Adam a bad rap for failing because he was the best of the best. We would not have been any different. The same "all" that sinned under Adam have the same opportunity to receive a gift of justification (just as if we never sinned) of our sin. If we choose to stay in the first Adam account, we condemn our self. If we decide to believe and receive the gift of grace, we live as if we had never sinned.

Your Application

Living under grace is underestimated. Grace is a free gift given to you so that you might live without the chains of restrictions (sin), therefore being free to be who you were meant to be. What would you do if you had no restriction on your life?

> *For if by the one man's offense death reigned through the one, much more those who receive abundance of grace and of the gift of righteousness will reign in life through the One, Jesus Christ.) (Romans 5:17)*

My Thought

For if through one man's offense death reigned by one, how much more to those who believe will receive an abundance of grace and the gift of living without sin through the life of another one, Jesus Christ. If a mere man could bring about such a mortal life for us, how much more could a God/Man bring about an abundance of grace and rightful living for each of us.

Your Application

What is your ultimate concern today? Can the One who washed away your sins by His blood also take care of what concerns you today?

> *Therefore, as through one man's offense judgment came to all men, resulting in condemnation, even so through one Man's righteous act the free gift came to all men, resulting in justification of life. (Romans 5:18)*

My Thought

Summing it up, Paul stays on this subject because it is the foundation of our lives as Christ's followers. We need to understand this because it is our choice to follow one man or the Other. To follow one man will condemn us; to follow the Other is to vindicate us. There will be no one without excuse, so making this choice is life determining!

Your Application

So much theology, and yet it is covered here in *Romans 5*. Take time to read and reread this chapter until you thoroughly understand the depths of the riches that are yours.

> *For as by one man's disobedience many were made sinners, so also by one Man's obedience many will be made righteous. (Romans 5:19)*

My Thought

Why many and not all? For all were made sinners from the disobedience and rebellion of Adam. It is not singling out that some didn't become sinners; it says that not a few but countless or innumerable became sinners. The consequence of sin affected many, but by the obedience of Jesus, many (all), the same amount that was made sinners, now have the ability to become vindicated of that penalty. All of us are sinners; all get a chance to change the verdict. Sadly, not all will choose Christ.

Your Application

Don't let the scriptures confuse you. All words in the Bible are ordained. There is not one contradiction. *1 Timothy 5:18* tells us that the scriptures are God-breathed, meaning God spoke into men through the Holy Spirit every word written. If something is confusing in scripture, doubt your confusion, not the scripture. Go figure it out, but look to the confusion, do not look to find a mistake in the Bible; there is none. Here is some help to explain this verse: *The Judicial View: According to this position, all persons were "made sinners" and "made righteous" in the same sense—judicially. That is, both Christ and Adam were our legal representatives. And while in Adam all of his race were before God made sinners officially, nonetheless, in Christ, all are officially made righteous, though not actually and personally. And just as every person, when they come to the age of accountability (see comments on 2 Samuel 12:23 and Romans 5:14), must personally sin to be personally guilty, even so everyone must personally accept Christ to be personally saved. Christ removed the official and judicial guilt that was imputed to the race because of Adam's sin. This does not mean that everyone is actually saved, but only that they are no longer legally condemned (http://defendinginerrancy.com/bible-solutions/Romans_5.19.php).*

> *Moreover the law entered that the offense might abound. But where sin abounded, grace abounded much more, (Romans 5:20)*

My Thought

The reason for the law was to show us our offenses. Where sin flourished, the gift of grace grew more. The law made us aware of our sinfulness. If there are no laws, there are no breaking of laws. Therefore, when God put the law together, He was making us aware of our bad. The remarkable thing is that God overcomes sin with more grace. That means there is nothing that we can do that will disqualify us from God. Whatever sin we might commit, God's grace is greater and more powerful. In our love and appreciation for God's gift, we learn to sin less. We recognize that grace is not cheap, but Jesus paid a great price for it.

Your Application

You must recognize your tendency to sin, accept it, and acknowledge that God's grace covers all your sins. You must also acknowledge living daily in the power of the Spirit will give you the ability to walk in obedience and sin less. That is your goal.

> *so that as sin reigned in death, even so grace might reign through righteousness to eternal life through Jesus Christ our Lord. (Romans 5:21)*

My Thought

Sin's final destination is death. Even more incredible is grace reigning in your life, which leads to eternal life by Jesus Christ, our Lord. There are two destinations in life, the second death (*Revelations 2:11, Revelations 20:6, 14, and Revelations 21:8*), and eternal life. That's it. This last verse in *Romans 5:21* tells us if sin reigns in our lives, we will end up in eternal death (damnation, never to be with our Father). It also says that if Jesus reigns in our lives, we will have eternal life. This is a serious decision we each must make.

Your Application

Sit and think about your relationship with Jesus. Are you a follower, but not a believer? Do you follow because you want to have eternal life, but don't do all that is in the Word? Are you obedient to the point of death, or to the point of just making it into heaven? Do you want to know Christ and make Him Lord of all your life, or do you still want to call the shots and have Him bless your endeavors? Do you believe what the Bible says is true? Consider your answers and evaluate your relationship. In times of persecution, you need to know what your response will be.

Romans Five explains because we are made right with the Father, we have peace with Him. The one sin of the first Adam caused death to all. The second Adam, Jesus, in His gift of death and resurrection, caused abundant life to all. Living a life of hope is only possible through faith and acceptance. The law was given so we could see how sinful we were. Where sin did abound, His grace did much more increase so we could be in right standing. We now have eternal life through Jesus Christ!

My Prayer

Thank You that we can live in hope every day because of the second Adam, Jesus Christ. You are our hope! When we acknowledge this truth, we will be on the path to a new and exciting destiny. Faith in You, Jesus, leads us on a "hope" journey of ups and downs. As we walk in obedience, we will gain the promised perseverance, character, and hope. We have no room for shame because Your love covers our sin, guilt, and shame. Our expectation of coming good (hope) is the driving force that makes us able to walk uprightly and live abundantly through the power of the Holy Spirit. When we were powerless in sin, You, our loving Father, sent Jesus to give His life for us while we were yet sinners. Our hearts brim over with so much hope and love in response to what You have done for us. You spared us from a life of deserved wrath to reconciliation with our All-Powerful Father-God. Thank You! In Jesus loving Name. Amen.

Write a summary of chapter 5.

> *The Word of God well understood and religiously obeyed is the shortest route to spiritual perfection. And we must not select a few favorite passages to the exclusion of others. Nothing less than a whole Bible can make a whole Christian.*
> *A. W. Tozer*

Our Worship
Have My Heart (feat. Chandler Moore & Chris Brown) / Maverick City Music
https://www.youtube.com/watch?v=U3Skc4MQlqU

CHAPTER 6

Living in Sin or Obedience

Read the complete chapter of *Romans 6*

Dead to Sin, Alive in Christ

> *What shall we say then? Shall we continue in sin that grace may abound?*
> *(Romans 6:1)*

My Thought

What will we say? Will we continue to sin so grace can increase? There is more grace when we sin, so should we sin so we can show grace? If bleach gets the dirt out, should we go out and get dirty to show the bleach's power? Sometimes we don't think clearly. We want to show how grace works, so we sin to show that we are covered?

Your Application

Is there ever a time you think, "I can sin because God will forgive me anyway?" Write what you think that does to God's heart when you have that attitude towards grace, God's priceless gift to us.

> *Certainly not! How shall we who died to sin live any longer in it? (Romans 6:2)*

My Thought

Paul answers the above question with God forbid. How can we who are dead to sin, continue to live in it? As we gather up salvation into our hearts, we realize that we have choices to make. We can jump into His grace and His ways and die entirely to our old practices and agendas, or we can use His grace to do our own thing and call upon the gifts of God when we get in trouble. The first is the real relationship God prepared for us. It is what He desires. The second is man's way of using God's gift of grace without making a full commitment to Him. We are manipulators, and we strategically use God for our benefit. It should not be.

Your Application

Do you find times in your life where you use God? Write about it.

> *Or do you not know that as many of us as were baptized into Christ Jesus were baptized into His death?* (Romans 6:3)

My Thought

Baptism represents our mutual death with Jesus. We are now dead to our self, our will, and our way. We are to wake up every day as if we no longer live, but Christ lives in us. What does He want to do in us and through us today? What is His agenda today? Are we supposed to do nothing? No. We are to daily surrender our lives to Him and then go on our way. He will direct our days if we just allow Him to, that's living in the *Storybook Fairy-Tale Reality of the Kingdom of God* or abundant life!

Your Application

How often do you set your day aside to allow Jesus to rule and reign? What would that look like if you did? Try it. Read *1 John 2:15–17.*

> *Therefore we were buried with Him through baptism into death, that just as Christ was raised from the dead by the glory of the Father, even so we also should walk in newness of life.* (Romans 6:4)

My Thought

We no longer live as if we are lost people. The "old" us dies in baptism, and we are made new.

We have a new life, with new thinking, kingdom thinking. We do not see things as the world sees them. We walk out of the old life into the Storybook Fairy-Tale Reality of the Kingdom of God. We are now kingdom people with a purpose and a mission. Each of us, doing our part that completes the Father's business! It's a special mission; an extraordinary life is accomplished with the death of our old self. If we do not die, we never really see all that is before us.

Your Application

How often do you underestimate your calling? Every child of God is called into a mission. Do you know yours? Search it out. Read *Galatians 2:20.*

For if we have been united together in the likeness of His death, certainly we also shall be in the likeness of His resurrection, (Romans 6:5)

My Thought

As we die to self, we will also have the ability to walk in the newness of life. As we understand Christ's death and know that His death killed our sin, we too need to align our old man with death so we can be free from the slavery of sin. We can walk in the newness of life. It's like falling in love; everything seems new and fresh and beautiful. That is what Jesus wants for us, His newness of life every day. We can have that if we place our sin under His death, and we walk in the newness of His resurrection.

Your Application

What stops you from this death to life experience? What stops you from committing? Write it out and think about what it means for Jesus to give you newness of life.

knowing this, that our old man was crucified with Him, that the body of sin might be done away with, that we should no longer be slaves of sin. (Romans 6:6)

My Thought

Know this, our old man dies with Christ, and sin is destroyed; we do not have to serve sin anymore! With our newness of life, we have a new perspective! Our old man knows one thing, how to sin; when we crucify the old man and old ways, we no longer serve sin.

Your Application

What sins do you serve? None? Really? Are you held captive by anything? Is there something that you don't want to do in your life, but you find yourself doing it? Sin is a slave master to anyone who lives in their old man. How does it feel to be a slave? Write about it.

For he who has died has been freed from sin. (Romans 6:7)

My Thought

He that is dead no longer sins. If a man dies to sin, he has no one to answer to. He does not have to sin anymore. He is dead.

Your Application

Have you ever experienced being dead? Not a real-life death, but dead to something you no longer want to have a hold on you. Dead to cigarettes? Dead to an old boy/girlfriend? Dead to the anger and bitterness towards an abusive parent? These sins/hurts can call for you, but you no longer have your heart attached to them. Are you dead to sin? Is your heart still attached to the old way of life, or are you free from sin? Write about being free from the old life of sin, or write what still has a hold of you, keeping you a slave. Read *Genesis 4:6-7*

Now if we died with Christ, we believe that we shall also live with Him,
(Romans 6:8)

My Thought

This "dead" concept is essential in our walk with Jesus in our *Storybook Fairy-Tale Reality*. We have to get this. We are dead to sin, we now live with our Prince of Peace. We are no longer paupers, debtors, or sinners. We are now royalty. We are priests and kings in His world (*Revelation 1:5, 6*). We walk in His power and authority to change atmospheres, or at least we should be.

Your Application

How often do you walk around believing that you are royalty and priest in God's kingdom? You are missing out on the real living, the abundant living, and the powerful living of the demonstration in His kingdom. If you understood this, how would your life be different? Write about it.

knowing that Christ, having been raised from the dead, dies no more. Death no longer has dominion over Him. (Romans 6:9)

My Thought

To understand this, we have to remember the account of Adam and Eve. They had dominion or control over the earth, but authority was given over to Satan when their sin entered the world. He was given the title deed (to control the corrupt world system) over the earth. Death had a sting, and the grave had victory because there was no Savior. There was no one to rescue us, so we were doomed. When Jesus came to die, His death conquered sin, death, the grave, and the enemy of our souls. Jesus didn't need to go to the cross for Himself. He did it for us. Satan has no hold on our great and powerful Savior. Jesus died to free us from sin, death, and Satan's grasp. One day the Lion of the tribe of Judah will open the seal to the deed of the earth and will take back all dominion of the earth (*Revelation 5:1-14*). His rightful plan all along. Until then we will see corruption, greed and manipulation on this earth, but we do not have to be controlled by it when we give our lives over to Christ.

Your Application

You no longer need to fear eternal death for your Savior has conquered it for you. How does that make you feel? How can you apply that to your life today? Read *Job 1:6–11, Colossians 2:15, 1 Peter 3:19, John 12:27-33, Ephesians 2:2, 1 Corinthians 4:4, 1 John 5:9, Hebrews 2:14, 15, Colossians 2:13-15, Revelations 5:1-14, Revelations 20:10.* What understanding of Satan do you find in these scriptures? Write it out.

For the death that He died, He died to sin once for all; but the life that He lives, He lives to God. (Romans 6:10)

My Thought

What does that mean? Jesus' death demolished sin, never to be a burden to us, but His life is to the highest form, it is to live with God forever. Jesus reconciles us to the highest form of life! We live in a new world, with a new life, living abundantly here on earth until we live our perfect life in His world, He has prepared for us.

Your Application

Think of the best time you have had in life. Think about the most beautiful place you have ever experienced. Think about the most incredible emotion you have ever felt. Now put them all together; heaven will be greater. Take a moment to imagine heaven. We get to live there, eternally. Write it out.

> *Likewise you also, reckon yourselves to be dead indeed to sin, but alive to God in Christ Jesus our Lord. (Romans 6:11)*

My Thought

Just as with Jesus, we too are dead completely to sin, but alive unto God through Jesus Christ, our Lord, so what Jesus received from dying, we receive it also! We are dead to sin and alive in Him. He worked it out for us. He suffered and died, took on sinfulness at its worst to freely give us the gift of life. We are no longer alive to sin if we die to ourselves. How can that be?

Your Application

Work this verse out. Chew on it, meditate and ask the Holy Spirit to give you illumination. Write out what you get and then share it with someone this week.

> *Therefore do not let sin reign in your mortal body, that you should obey it in its lusts. (Romans 6:12)*

My Thought

Given permission to no longer let sin reign, we can now live a life where we do not give into lusts and sin. How, do you ask? By daily dying to our agenda. If we have no agenda, no will, no desire to see our ways lived out anymore, we can now live for the glory of God.

Your Application

If sin reigns in your mortal body, in your old man, then it proves that you have not died daily to self. Write out what is hard to give up: Your dreams, your way, your desires, what is keeping you from dying to the old man, and living to the newness of life? Read *Luke 9:23.*

> *And do not present your members as instruments of unrighteousness to sin, but present yourselves to God as being alive from the dead, and your members as instruments of righteousness to God. (Romans 6:13)*

My Thought

We can use our minds and hearts for good or evil, but not both. We are either living our lives fully for God, or we are still living life our way, and we use our hearts and minds for tools of selfishness. Does that mean we are perfect? Never. We will not be perfect until heaven, but it does mean that we give our hearts and our minds for His use. When we allow God to have our heart and mind (*Colossians 3:1, 2*), we will continue to live in this world, but we will see things from the *Storybook Fairy-Tale Reality of the Kingdom of God*, and the things of this world won't get to us.

Your Application

What world do you live in, this present world or His kingdom? Think about it.

> *For sin shall not have dominion over you, for you are not under law but under grace. (Romans 6:14)*

My Thoughts

The law came so we could see we are lawbreakers, sinners. Now we no longer are under the standard of the law. We are now under grace. Grace covers our sins, and the law, which once pointed out our sin, is no longer there to make us ashamed. A woman lives under her family's name until she is married, and then she is given her husband's name. Our family was the law, but when we married Jesus, He gave us His name, grace. We are no longer assigned to the law but committed to our new Husband. We now live by His rules: to love Him with all our hearts, souls, minds, and strength and love others the same way we love Him.

Your Application

Is it confusing to you that God dismissed the law with grace? Think of what God's commandments are now. What would it look like to treat your God or fellow man by the commandments of Jesus? Write about how good God is to take away all the confusing rules and regulations we were obligated to follow, and now God set only two commandments for us to live out. How hard is it to love? Why? Is it proof that death has not completely taken place?

Slaves to Righteousness

> *What then? Shall we sin because we are not under law but under grace? Certainly not! (Romans 6:15)*

My Thought

Paul states that we are not to run around as if we are lawless because we are no longer under law. Grace raises us to a higher standard. It does not lower us to lawlessness and defilement. We are now under a new covenant of love. We are royalty, living a life of devotion to our Father first, and then to others in this world. Love rules and reigns in our hearts.

Your Application

Describe what love looks like in your daily walk. Write an essay or draw a picture of love.

> *Do you not know that to whom you present yourselves slaves to obey, you are that one's slaves whom you obey, whether of sin leading to death, or of obedience leading to righteousness? (Romans 6:16)*

My Thought

Don't you know that whomever you give yourself over to obey, that person becomes your master? Your master is either sin that leads to death or obedience that leads to right standing before God. In this life, it has been narrowed down to two masters, sin to death or obedience to God. It's that simple. It is not complicated or complex; it is one or the other. We are either sowing to righteousness or sowing to death. It is one or the other all the time. We do not want to see it that simple because we want option three: Do what we want and go to heaven. According to scripture, there are only two options, and we must choose one. If we do not choose Christ, then the choice is sin and death. What if we are choosing obedience and still failing? It is a process, it is a heart position, and God knows that you want to obey, but you are struggling in a sin; He loves you and will get you through. It's the one who chooses to sin or chooses not to make a choice; those are the ones who will choose eternal death. Stay clear.

Your Application

> *"There are only two kinds of people in the end: those who say to God, 'Thy will be done,' and those to whom God says, in the end, 'thy will be done.'"*
> *C S Lewis (the Great Divorce)*

What have you chosen? Why?

> *But God be thanked that though you were slaves of sin, yet you obeyed from the heart that form of doctrine to which you were delivered. (Romans 6:17)*

My Thought

Thank God, you obeyed the new covenant and are not slaves to sin anymore. Paul is thanking God that the Romans got it. They received the word of truth that was given to them, and they now walk in the forgiveness of sin and are called to Him who died for them. The Romans heard, and they accepted the gospel.

Your Application

How did the Romans receive? Because they heard it! No one will receive unless they hear, and no one will hear unless we are sent. Make sure you share your testimony as often as you can. Do it today sometime. It is the good news! Read *Romans 10:14-15*

And having been set free from sin, you became slaves of righteousness.
(Romans 6:18)

My Thought

Paul recognizes the saved Romans are free from their former way of life, and he is accepting them as his brothers and sisters. He is getting geared up to share with them the life of righteousness. He is about to paint a picture of what living as a servant of holiness looks like.

Your Application

What does being a servant of righteousness look like to you? Think about it. Write it out if you want to make it more real.

I speak in human terms because of the weakness of your flesh. For just as you presented your members as slaves of uncleanness, and of lawlessness leading to more lawlessness, so now present your members as slaves of righteousness for holiness. (Romans 6:19)

My Thought

"I am speaking frankly to you because of the sickness of your flesh, for as you gave your minds and hearts over to servants of uncleanness and iniquity unto progressively worse iniquity, even so now give your minds and hearts over to servants of holiness." Paul is stating clearly that the old way of life was making them sick in their bodies and minds. They were giving themselves over to uncleanness and sinfulness. Now he impresses on them to live in the fullness of what is right and therefore brings their bodies into wholeness, set apart for God.

Your Application

What percentage of your life do you live for God? Take a look at your daily activities. How much of those activities in your day reflect God? Chart it out and comment on how you faired. There is no condemnation in this assessment, only recognition to change if need be. Ask the Holy Spirit to help you in this conquest. It is supremely fun to be open to what the Spirit shows because He also empowers us to transform our ways.

For when you were slaves of sin, you were free in regard to righteousness.
(Romans 6:20)

My Thought

We cannot serve two masters. We will either love one and hate the other or obey one and reject the other. We cannot serve both sin and righteousness. We have to make a choice.

Your Application

What choice does your life reflect? Ponder this.

> *What fruit did you have then in the things of which you are now ashamed? For the end of those things is death.* (Romans 6:21)

My Thought

The life of the flesh, a selfish life, what good came of it? The result of living for our self is shame and death. God, our Father, cares so deeply for us. He wants us to live a rich, abundant life. He desires for us to bear fruit that only comes by being planted in the soil of His love. In our own selfish soil, we produce shameful behavior, and we produce death.

Your Application

What does death look like to you? What shameful behavior have you produced? Think about that for a moment. Write a brief essay on the second death, the death that leads to eternal destruction. Add scripture.

> *But now having been set free from sin, and having become slaves of God, you have your fruit to holiness, and the end, everlasting life.* (Romans 6:22)

My Thought

But now that you are made free from sin, and you are a servant to God, you have wholeness, and your end is everlasting life. The fruit of sin is being ashamed and then death, an eternal death. The result of cutting off the life of sin and living as a servant to God is a rich life of wholeness, completeness, fulfillment, and contentment, and at the end of life, you live forever with your loving Father and the family of God!

Your Application

Why do you think many will choose to be the servants of sin and miss this tremendous opportunity to live with Christ? Write a few paragraphs about this subject.

> *For the wages of sin is death, but the gift of God is eternal life in Christ Jesus our Lord.* (Romans 6:23)

My Thought

For the salary of living a sinful life is death, but the gift from God is eternal life through Jesus Christ, our Lord. Paul sums it up by stating the wages and gifts of either choice. *One choice is eternal damnation, forever alive, but not living. Option two is eternal life because of the precious price Jesus Christ paid for us.* Every human being who has ever been born will have to settle his account before a beautiful, merciful God.

Your Application

At the end of life, will you receive the gift of God, eternal life? Or will you receive the wrath of God's hatred towards sin that you opted for when you chose to be your own master? Thank God this second question does not have to apply to you, but it will apply to those who choose not to believe.

Romans Six shares with us that the choice is ours, live a life of obedience to eternal life or live a life of sin to eternal death. Paul sets out almost as a lawyer to convince a jury with his closing arguments. He sets up what serving sin will do and what it looks like to be obedient to God. He is showing the Romans and us the life choices we have. Paul wants us to see a new life option is available to us through grace. *"We are buried with Christ through baptism into death in order that, just as Christ was raised from the dead through the glory of the Father, we too may live a new life"* (*Romans 6:4*). He is showing us that if we died with Christ, we are set free from sin. Being raised with Christ, death no longer has mastery over us. We no longer have to let sin reign or rule over us. We are free to live a life of obedience.

My Prayer

Help us, Lord, to make the right decisions for our lives. Help us to die to sin continually, so we feel uncomfortable living in it. Don't let sin control the way we live. Help us not to give in to sinful desires. We don't want to be a slave to sin, but rather free in You. Please help us to remember that sin loses its power over us because we are baptized with You into death to rise again with You in right relationship with our Father God. In Your gracious Name. Amen.

Write a summary of chapter 6.

We no longer live as if we are lost people. The 'old' us dies in baptism, and we are made new. We have a new life, with new thinking, kingdom thinking. We do not see things as the world sees them. We walk out of the old life into the Storybook Fairy-Tale Reality of the Kingdom of God. We are now kingdom people with a purpose and a mission. Each of us doing our part that completes the Father's business! It's a special mission, an extraordinary life that needs the death of our old self to be accomplished. If we do not die, we never really see all that is before us.

Our Worship

This is the Kingdom / Elevation Worship / Pat Barrett
https://www.youtube.com/watch?v=wEFHy-NSW8I狀

CHAPTER 7

Living in the Battle

Read the complete chapter of *Romans 7*

Released From the Law, Bound to Christ

> *Don't you know brethren, (for I am speaking to them that know the law—the Jews) that the law has dominion or control over a man as long as he is alive? (Romans 7:1)*

My Thought

To the Jews, they lived by the law and understood the only way out of the penalty of sin was through death. *Leviticus* speaks of all the sacrifices of animals for the Jews' sins to be removed.

Your Application

What kind of covenant do you know of that you can only get out of through death? For better or worse, in sickness and in health, 'til death do us part. How strong is that covenant today in our society?

> *For the woman who has a husband is bound by the law to her husband as long as he lives. But if the husband dies, she is released from the law of her husband. (Romans 7:2)*

My Thought

The purpose of a marriage covenant was to be a firm commitment for two people to stay together until "death do they part." Today, most marriages have turned into a cheapened vow to be together until they do not like how things work out. This marriage contract was supposed to be a strong covenant that lasted until the death of one.

Your Application

How did marriage become so casual? Look up statistics on marriage today and then look up statistics on marriages in the 50s, 60s, and even the 70s. Why the change? What can you do to strengthen your outlook on marriage? Write about it.

> *So then if, while her husband lives, she marries another man, she will be called an adulteress; but if her husband dies, she is free from that law, so that she is no adulteress, though she has married another man. (Romans 7:3)*

My Thought

Paul goes on to explain the rules of marriage. If the woman's husband is dead, she is free to commit to another, but if the husband is still alive and she commits to another, she has committed adultery and is in penalty of the law. Christ died to fulfill the law so therefore it no longer has a hold on us. We can now be committed to Christ and not the law.

Your Application

Understand that Paul is talking to the believers in Rome, but we also need to get his message. He is trying to dissolve the importance of rules and regulations, and he is trying to build a case to replace the law with a deep, meaningful relationship with Jesus. Does Paul want you to be a lawless individual that does whatever you want? Does Paul want you to live a life of rebellion? No, Paul is trying to get you to understand that through a meaningful relationship with Jesus, you will be who you are predestined to be. Do you have that relationship with Jesus, or are you into the religious rituals? Write about it. Does it sound like the truth or an opinion?

> *Therefore, my brethren, you also have become dead to the law through the body of Christ, that you may be married to another—to Him who was raised from the dead, that we should bear fruit to God. (Romans 7:4)*

My Thought

Going back to chapter 6, Paul states that if we are dead to the things of this world, then we are dead, in a sense, to the old husband, the law. Now we can be married to our new husband, Christ. The law, our old husband, is right and just, but also strict and unforgiving. If we are dead to the law, then we no longer have to live by the law. If we are resurrected with Christ, we are now under His rule, grace, and truth. We will produce fruit from one of these marriages. Whose children will you have? Will you produce the fruit of the Spirit or produce the fruit of the law that leads to failure?

Your Application

Whom would you rather have a covenant with? A strict and unforgiving husband—but live how you want, or a grace-giving and truthful Husband to surrender your will and ways to Him? It seems so simple, although so many times you want to make your own decisions. This is how it is: make your own decisions and live under the law, which calls for eternal death. Or surrender your all and live God's ways, which leads to eternal life. Who is dead to you, the old man under the law or Jesus and His gift of grace? Write about your choice.

> *For when we were in the flesh, the sinful passions which were aroused by the law were at work in our members to bear fruit to death. (Romans 7:5)*

My Thought

For when we were in the flesh, the consequences of sins regulated by the law did work in us to bring forth the fruit of death. Our flesh is held under the law's judgments, so when we sin, we are judged by the law, and we cannot live up to the law's regulations. Therefore, the fruit of our fleshly life is death; remember the wages of sin is death.

Your Application

Do you ever try to be good on your own? How has that worked for you? Discuss this with someone.

> *But now we have been delivered from the law, having died to what we were held by, so that we should serve in the newness of the Spirit and not in the oldness of the letter. (Romans 7:6)*

My Thought

The switch is taking place. We have two masters, and we must decide whom we will serve. Look at the words: we will serve in the newness of the Spirit or serve the old covenant. Just listening to the wording, God gives us a clue whom we should serve, along with the fact that one leads to death, and One leads to abundant life, and that, life everlasting.

Your Application

Why do you think living for God is so hard? Write it out in essay form.

Struggling with Sin

> *What shall we say then? Is the law sin? Certainly not! On the contrary, I would not have known sin except through the law. For I would not have known covetousness unless the law had said, "You shall not covet." (Romans 7:7)*

My Thought

What will we say then? Is the law sin? Paul says no. No, I would not know sin, unless the law pointed it out. I did not realize wanting what someone else had was wrong, except the law told me not to do it. Here is the situation of sin in our bodies; we know what sin is because we have a code of ethics in the law. Just because the law shows us our sinful state does not mean that the law is sin. The law is only the flashlight that illuminates the sin in us. Should we be mad at the law? How dare the law show us our sinfulness, right? The law is our friend because the law gave us the smarts to know that something in us is not quite right. If we do not recognize this, we will not change or seek after that which is good.

Your Application

When did you first notice you needed a Savior? Share the story with someone this week.

> *But sin, taking opportunity by the commandment, produced in me all manner of evil desire. For apart from the law sin was dead. (Romans 7:8)*

My Thought

The sin in us, illuminated by the commandments, worked in us all manner of sinful desires. Without the law, we would not know sin, therefore sin was dead. The commandments, the law, made us aware of our lustful desires for our selfish gain to satisfy the longings in our flesh. "We will not covet or desire what is someone else's," says the commandments. If we didn't know that commandment, we would not be guilty of desiring what is not ours. So, the law shows up and tells us we are guilty of these things.

Your Application

What commandment have you broken? What commandment is difficult for you to live out? If you were the loving God, how would you look at a man who breaks your commandments and gives the excuses you give? Discuss this topic.

> *I was alive once without the law, but when the commandment came, sin revived and I died. (Romans 7:9)*

My Thought

As children, we are without the law for we do not understand the commandments of the Lord, but when the commandments come to our awareness, and we know our sin, then sin comes to life to tangle us and trip us up and eventually strangle us to death. There is an age of accountability. For each person, it is different. For each person, it is the time when we become aware we are naked and become ashamed. Remember Adam and Eve?

Your Application

Write about when you became aware that sin had dominion or control in your life.

> *And the commandment, which was to bring life, I found to bring death. (Romans 7:10)*

My Thought

The law that was to lead to life was leading me to death. We could not live up to the standard of the law that leads to life, so now we were condemned to die. It's like playing on a team with the most outstanding athlete, and we are to play with Him. The rules are laid out, but we are not capable of playing by the rules because we were undisciplined and imperfect to follow the rules. We wanted to play the game, but we wanted to play by our own rules. There is only One who can play the game and win. By watching Him play by the rules and not breaking one, we become aware of our own inability to win. The game is only for the Perfect, and since we are not, we see that we are disqualified from playing.

Your Application

You can sometimes convince yourself that everything is okay in your world. You can say you can do it on your own, but to be truthful, can you? Can you play the game of life by yourself? What are some of the clues that show you need help? Ask Jesus right now for help.

> *For sin, taking occasion by the commandment, deceived me, and by it killed me.* (Romans 7:11)

My Thought

Sin is deceiving! Sin looks fun for a season, but then the judgment of the sin leads to death. Sin deceives me into sinning and then points the finger at me for sinning. Sin is not our friend. Sin is our enemy. Sin is out to condemn us, shame us, and eventually slay us. It's the evil dragon in our *Storybook Fairy-Tale Reality of the Kingdom of God*. Sin is a fiery, destructive dragon ready to incinerate us. Stay clear.

Your Application

Remember a time when sin deceived you? What did it feel like when you realized it? Write about it.

> *Therefore the law is holy, and the commandment holy and just and good.* (Romans 7:12)

My Thought

Sin is deceitful, but the law is holy, and the commandments are righteous and just and good. The law may seem to be the tattletale, but the law is there for our good. The law is holy (perfect), just (honest and truthful), and sound. We need to be happy for the law and be pleased that the law illuminated in us our sinfulness.

Your Application

Read *Psalms 119*. Write out some of the verses that talk about the law. Did this change your outlook on the law?

Law Cannot Save From Sin

> *Has then what is good become death to me? Certainly not! But sin, that it might appear sin, was producing death in me through what is good, so that sin through the commandment might become exceedingly sinful. (Romans 7:13)*

My Thought

Was the law, which is good, made to be death for me? Paul says, no! The law, which is good, was given to reveal sin in me and sin works death in me, that sin, illuminated by the commandments, might show itself exceedingly sinful. The law did not lead us to a death state. The law showed us how terrible sin is and showed us that we are full of it. If we don't get this, we won't know how badly we need rescuing. If we don't see the dragons in the kingdom, we will not understand our Hero's sacrifice. He came to defeat the dragon—sin, so we might not be smitten by such a deadly fate.

Your Application

Do you understand the severity of sin? Do you justify your sin or elevate sin to different levels? A dragon is a dragon is a dragon, be it seemingly small or large. It is out to do the same thing, deceive and destroy by fire. Sin is not your friend! Leave all sins behind and ask God to give you His holiness.

> *For we know that the law is spiritual, but I am carnal, sold under sin. (Romans 7:14)*

My Thought

For we know that the law is spiritual, meaning it comes from God: but I am carnal, meaning I measure things from my understanding, from a physical approach; I was sold under sin. We need to understand that interpreting the law from our physical senses will not help us understand the law from the spiritual realm. The law, written by God, is clearly for the spiritual man, not the carnal man. The carnal man cannot keep the law for he is sinful, but the spiritual man can do it through Christ, who had already proved His ability to have power over sin when He came to earth, was fully obedient and kept the whole law.

Your Application

How often do you try to keep the rules and regulations on your own terms? Do you fail? The law illuminates humankind's sinfulness. Through dependence on Christ, you can live a righteous life!

> *For what I am doing, I do not understand. For what I will to do, that I do not practice; but what I hate, that I do. (Romans 7:15)*

My Thought

Why are we doing what we do? We don't understand. For what we want to do, we don't do, but what we hate, we do. The old adage of life, what we see good and desire to do, we end up not doing it. What we see as evil and desire not to do it, we behave in that manner. We get frustrated with ourselves and promise not to do it again, but we end up in a continual battle, doing what we do not want to do. My teenage struggle was ice cream; my father had it every night. As a teenager, I knew it wasn't good for me, so on my way home I said, "I am not going to have ice cream," but I just kept *thinking* how good it was and how much I wanted it and before I knew it, I was biting into a spoonful of chocolate ice cream! Afterward, I was mad at myself because I did what I did not want to do and what I wanted to do; I did not do.

Your Application

My desire for ice cream dominated my thinking instead of allowing my mind to be transformed by the Holy Spirit (*Romans 12:1, 2*). What is an example of a self-battle that you deal with in your life? Write it out.

> *If, then, I do what I will not to do, I agree with the law that it is good. (Romans 7:16)*

My Thought

If we do what we do not want to do, we agree with the law that it is good. The law points out that we are not capable of keeping it and that the law is right. The law is good, and we are full of sin. When we are full of sin, we become slaves to sin. We no longer have mastery over what we say and do, but sin is our master.

Your Application

Do you agree that the law of God is good? And yet impossible to keep?

> *But now, it is no longer I who do it, but sin that dwells in me. (Romans 7:17)*

My Thought

To sum it up, it is not us who do these things, but it is the sin that lives in us. As people, we come into agreement that we are good. "I'm okay, and you're okay." This scripture contradicts that philosophy. It says that we are not even in control of what we do. We do not do these things, but the master, sin, does it within us. Sin has the lordship of our lives, and we submit to walk in its sinful ways.

Your Application

Do you agree with this scripture that it is not you who do these things, but it is the sin you have allowed to live in you? Meditate on what that means. Who is Lord or lord of your life?

> *For I know that in me (that is, in my flesh) nothing good dwells; for to will is present with me, but how to perform what is good I do not find. (Romans 7:18)*

My Thought

For we know that in our flesh lives no good thing, for the will to do good is present in us, but how to perform the good we wish to do, we do not know how. Again, we are naturally selfish and sinful people (look at Adam and Eve). There is no good thing that lives in our flesh. We need to get this in order to understand this principle of sin and the law. We have in us a desire to do good, we see how it looks, but we are not capable of righteous living without the spiritual side of us awakening to the One who made a way for us. Jesus is the Door we must walk through. As we walk through the Door, we surrender our bad, we die to our sinfulness, and live in the ability of His Spirit to do the things we once could not do, but now we can do!

Your Application

This concept is confusing, yet the Spirit wants you to get this; it is a huge step to overcoming sin's dominance. Of course, it's going to be the tough one. You can understand the good in the thing you want to do, but you cannot perform that good. The flesh in you does not understand the things of the Spirit. The spirit in you understands the Spirit of God. Meditate on this until it begins to make sense.

> *For the good that I will to do, I do not do; but the evil I will not to do, that I practice.* (Romans 7:19)

My Thought

Again, Paul reiterates verse 16 in another way: For the good that we would, we do not do; but the evil that we do not want to do, that we do. If we see good but do not do it, and if we see evil and think not to do it, but we do it, we have a problem, right? We say we are not going to lie, but when the time comes, we lie. We say we will help our brother or sister, but then we don't do it. We are struggling with an inner battle of good and evil. Who is our master? We no longer have the power to do what we want because what we want is to control our destiny; but to have control, we must surrender our control to the Spirit, therefore not having control. *"My old identity has been co-crucified with Christ and no longer lives. And now the essence of this new life is no longer mine, for the Anointed One lives His life through me—we live in union as one! My new life is empowered by the faith of the Son of God who loves me so much that He gave Himself for me, dispensing His life into mine!"* (Galatians 2:20 TPT) We are wired to serve someone. We will either serve ourselves, and sin will rule over us, or we will surrender our agenda to God and allow Him to rule and reign in our lives. There is no halfway, even if it looks like it.

Your Application

Are you completely surrendered? Write about it.

> *Now if I do what I will not to do, it is no longer I who do it, but sin that dwells in me.* (Romans 7:20)

My Thought

Another time, Paul continues into this debate as in verse 17. If we do what we do not what to do, it is no more we who do it, but sin that lives in us. Paul is staying with this subject with the Romans because it is a human condition, we all need to address. If we are stuck doing what we do not want to do, who is in control or who is our master? Us, or sin living in us? If we can understand this, we will be able to walk in the fullness of what God has planned for us here on earth.

Your Application

What is the condition of your heart and mind? Are you harboring sin inside? Or are you leaning on the One who made a way for you? *"Who is this coming up from the wilderness leaning on her beloved?"* (Songs of Solomon 8:5 *NIV*)

> *I find then a law, that evil is present with me, the one who wills to do good.* (Romans 7:21)

My Thought

We find then this law is at work, that when we would do good, evil is present in us. If you think everything is redundant, it is. It is like a child who has to be told repeatedly about not touching the electrical outlet. He doesn't understand why he can't play with it; it is just a small plate on the wall with holes. It looks harmless. The child is curious and wants to check it out. We all know what would happen if the child put something metal in the small holes. It is dangerous and could lead to death. Paul is teaching us as he would a child. He continues to say the same thing because he wants to keep us from getting enslaved to sin. Paul cared about the Romans. God cares about us. Sin seems harmless, and we are curious. Others have gone before us; they have gotten burned or electrocuted by sin, and they are warning us just to stay away.

Your Application

Are you curious? Where has it led you? Destruction?

> *For I delight in the law of God according to the inward man.* (Romans 7:22)

My Thought

For we delight in the law of God, that is our inward man: Our spirit gets God. Our spirit communes with God, and our spirit delights in the laws of God. Our spirit understands the *Storybook Fairy-Tale Reality of the Kingdom of God.* We see the greatness of the law leading us to follow in Jesus' footsteps. Jesus is guiding us through the Holy Spirit to an upward battle leading us to dependency on Him. The longer we walk with Jesus, the more we see the invisible world (things not seen) than we see the temporal (the here and now). We learn to rule and reign in heaven with the inward man (our spirit).

Your Application

Write about a time that you were so full of the light of God and understood His will and way.

> *But I see another law in my members, warring against the law of my mind, and bringing me into captivity to the law of sin which is in my members.* (Romans 7:23)

My Thought

But we see another law in us, warring against the law of our mind, and bringing us into captivity to the law of sin, which is in us.

> *The battle is clearly between two entities living in each one of us. Our inward man, who communes with the Spirit of God, loves the plan of grace. Our outward man who deeply wants attention is prideful, does not listen, and wants things his way. We continue to fight between the two until we settle once and for all who will have dominion. That's the battle.*

We have the Spirit of God calling us to holiness, and we have the enemy of our soul deceiving us to walk in the selfishness of our desires.

Your Application

Write about a time you saw the battle within yourself between good and evil.

> *O wretched man that I am! Who will deliver me from this body of death?* (Romans 7:24)

My Thought

O wretched that we are! Who will deliver us from ourselves? Paul was so tired of fighting the fight between his spirit and his flesh. Obviously, the flesh was winning, and he called himself wretched. This struggle is where hopelessness comes in and tries to persuade us that there will not be better days. It's a lie. There will be good days and bad days, but there is always hope in Jesus. He makes a way where there seems to be no way. *(Isaiah 43:19)*

Your Application

Have you ever felt so low that you just wanted to quit? Hold on; there is good news coming just around the corner.

I thank God—through Jesus Christ our Lord! So then, with the mind I myself serve the law of God, but with the flesh the law of sin. (Romans 7:25)

My Thought

Paul asks, who will deliver us from us? His answer, I thank God through Jesus Christ, our Lord. So then with the mind, we serve the law of God, but with the flesh the law of sin. Two laws fight inside of us. Who will win? Who can deliver us from all these crazy battles in our bodies? God! Through the death and resurrection of Jesus Christ, our Lord, yes, Jesus Christ has to be our Lord in order for us to be delivered. Is He your Lord?

Your Application

If Jesus is your Lord, then you are in a good place. If He is not your Lord, you can make Him your Lord today. Just simply tell Him you want Him to live in you. *1 John 1:9* says, *"If we confess our sins, He is faithful and just to forgive us our sins and to cleanse us from all unrighteousness."* Confess your sins to God. Walk through the Door into a new world with your Father God. Get to know Jesus by reading His Word. Talk with Him regularly and expect to hear from Him. Ask Him questions and look for the answers. This is the beginning of an extraordinary, abundant life living in the *Storybook Fairy-Tale Reality of the Kingdom of God*. It is only the beginning; in chapter 8, we will see some very interesting paths to take to deepen our walk even more.

In *Romans Seven*, we see the battle between our flesh and our spirit. We see that our flesh pulls us in the direction of selfishness, "what's in it for me," pride, and disobedience. When we are in the flesh, we deceive ourselves into thinking we can make right decisions, but really sin is our master. Paul is sharing with us his inner battle between flesh and spirit, helping us relate to him. *"The good I want to do; I find myself doing the opposite. The wrong decisions I don't want to do, I do"* (Romans 7:18). In his humble, honest state, he shows us that all struggle and all need to decide whom they will serve. The law shows us we are not capable of living the law. Jesus came and demonstrated He could live the law perfectly, and He invites us to die to our old self and be joined with Him and win the battle of our souls. Who can? We can!

My Prayer

Lord, You know there is a battle going on inside each of us; the struggle is not over until we choose whom we will serve. Will we choose Your law of love, which is grace and abundant life leading to our eternal home or, will we choose the law of sin? We have the victory in You, but we oftentimes want to do things our way. Help us, Lord, to see that Your ways are what's best. Help us to realize how much You love us in that You made a way for us. Help us to listen to Your voice, Your Word, and Your Spirit residing in us to make the choice today to serve you. In Your loving Name. Amen.

Write a summary of chapter 7.

> *The battle is clearly between two entities living in each one of us. Our inward man, who communes with the Spirit of God, loves the plan of grace. Our outward man who deeply wants to be seen, is prideful and does not listen, wants things his way. We continue to fight between the two until we settle once and for all whom will have dominion. That is the battle.*

Our Worship
You're Going to be Ok / Jenn & Brian Johnson
https://www.youtube.com/watch?v=R0PCblOjOxg

CHAPTER 8

Living in the Spirit

Read the complete chapter of *Romans 8*

Life Through the Spirit—Free from Indwelling Sin

> *There is therefore now no condemnation to those who are in Christ Jesus, who do not walk according to the flesh, but according to the Spirit. (Romans 8:1)*

My Thought

After *Romans 7*, after declaring to accept Jesus as Lord, there is now no one to condemn us! Oh, what a statement, what a verse! If we walk after the Spirit and not after the flesh, we are free to walk in this world without ever again being condemned. Never!

Your Application

Do you ever feel judged? Do you ever feel others condemning you? Do others make an opinion of you without knowing you or the intent of your heart? It does not matter, because God said if you walk in the Spirit, you are no longer under condemnation, judgment or shame.

The God of the universe frees you from those feelings; why are you letting mere man, who is on the same playing level as you, bring up feelings of condemnation that are no longer yours? You live differently now, you live in the *Storybook Fairy-Tale Reality of the Kingdom of God*, and there isn't condemnation here! Your sins are abolished! How do you feel? Write it out!

> *For the law of the Spirit of the life in Christ Jesus has made me free from the law of sin and death. (Romans 8:2)*

My Thought

So, the two laws we studied in the last chapter are back, but we understand that the same Spirit that lived in Jesus while on earth lives in us. We have the same Spirit to overcome the law of sin and death, that gave Jesus the power to overcome. That's how we are delivered.

Your Application

Is it all making sense now? Write about how awesome it is to have the same exact Spirit living in you that was living in Jesus. What is the difference between our flesh and our spirit? What is the difference between the law of the Spirit and the law of sin and death? Write it out.

> *For what the law could not do in that it was weak through the flesh, God did by sending His own Son in the likeness of sinful flesh, on account of sin: He condemned sin in the flesh,* (Romans 8:3)

My Thought

The law could only show us our inability to follow the rules. The law had no power to change us. God sent His own Son in an earthly body to experience the likeness of what we experience. God sent His Son to take our place. God condemned and punished our sins through His Son. The law could not save us. It could only reveal in us our sin. The law opened our eyes to our inability to be good. God allowed Jesus to experience what sin was all about, how evil it is, and how it can capture and enslave a soul. As Jesus experienced all this, He was without sin. Although He was in the world and experienced being in His flesh, Jesus did not sin. He did not fall into the temptations of the flesh, but through the Spirit living in Him, He was able to say 'no' to all temptations. His Father gave Jesus His agenda daily, and Jesus obeyed. God condemned sin because Jesus overcame sin, so sin has no rule over us. In chapter 8, we will learn about the law of the Spirit, the Spirit of Jesus. This Spirit that was in Jesus to help Him overcome sin while He was on earth is the same Spirit that will help us overcome our bad and change us.

Your Application

Read the account of Jesus in the wilderness, *Matthew 4* and *Luke 4*. What three temptations did Jesus overcome? What did Jesus do to overcome temptation? What does that teach you about how you can overcome temptation? Find and memorize some scriptures you can use against temptation, just like Jesus did!

> *that the righteous requirement of the law might be fulfilled in us who do not walk according to the flesh but according to the Spirit.* (Romans 8:4)

My Thought

Jesus condemned sin so that the law's righteous requirement would be fulfilled in us as we walk in the Spirit. The purpose of the law is to show us our sin. Jesus came to conquer sin for us; now, the purpose of the law is fulfilled. We recognize our sin, and we also accept Jesus' sacrifice for sin, so we no longer have to be slaves to sin, if we walk in the Spirit.

Your Application

If you walk in the Spirit, the fulfillment of the law is made perfect in you. If you continue to walk in the flesh, the power of the Spirit is void. The reason for your wavering happens because you struggle between who will rule your life, you, or the Spirit of Jesus. Sit down and think through your day. Did you let your flesh call the shots today, or did you allow the Spirit of the living Lord permeate your day?

> *For those who live according to the flesh set their minds on the things of the flesh, but those who live according to the Spirit, the things of the Spirit. (Romans 8:5)*

My Thought

This is where the split, the chasm begins, right here. We either live after our flesh's paths, which are our selfish desires and dreams. We want to control our life while in the flesh. Or we live in the Spirit, meaning we die to self and live after the desires and dreams of the Spirit. We are no longer in control. This is where working out our salvation (*Philippians 2:12*) becomes real or fake. If we want our own way but also want to follow Christ, we struggle with His will versus our will. We cannot serve two masters, so we end up loving one and hating the other, thus the struggle in many Christians. To walk after the Spirit is to walk out our Christian life as Jesus did. He did not come to have His way. He was in constant contact with His Father through the fellowship of the Spirit. We have the same advantage as Jesus because when Jesus left this earth, He sent the same Spirit that was inside of Him, to us. We can now walk in the power and love of the Holy Spirit. Why do we struggle so? Our own will is a strong force. In our understanding of the two forces battling for control of our soul, we either win or lose the battle.

Your Application

Write about the two forces inside of you. How does it feel? Who seems to have more control? Why?

> *For to be carnally minded is death, but to be spiritually minded is life and peace. (Romans 8:6)*

My Thought

To think worldly is death but being spiritually minded is life and peace. If it is that easy to choose: death, or life and peace, why do we struggle? Along with our struggle, lives an evil entity with great deceptive powers, convincing us as we do our own thing our eyes will be opened. The devil is trying to convince every believer that God is trying to control them and keep them from fun. The devil works his distorted magic and makes destruction look appealing. The Father knows what is on the other side of deception and calls out loud and clear for us not to follow, but we want what we do not have, and for a season, sin is fun. If we continue to think worldly, gratifying the senses, only seeing what our physical needs are and how to meet them, then we choose death. If we think spiritually and understand that God only wants what is best (*Isaiah 48:17*), we acknowledge that our soul requires a Savior! We connect our soul to His Spirit, and we have real life and peace.

Your Application

In words, it seems so simple. In reality, it is dying daily to the strong selfish force in you that wants its own way. In reality, it is the hardest decision to do, and you have to make that decision every moment of every day for the rest of your life. The great thing is you do not have to do it alone; the Spirit comes in to help, and it gets easier each time you say no to the flesh and yes to the Spirit. How can you strengthen your "yes" to the Spirit when you have been saying "yes" to your selfish ways? Ponder and write about it. Read *Luke 9:23–25*; what steps will you take to save your soul, how often did Jesus say to take up their cross? Write out the actions you will take and memorize Jesus' words in *Luke 9*.

> *Because the carnal mind is enmity against God; for it is not subject to the law of God, nor indeed can be. (Romans 8:7)*

My Thought

Think of archenemies trying to live inside of us, each one trying to have control over us. We have the ultimate decision; the one we listen to wins. Each one is stating the advantages of why we should follow after them. One is honest and requests us to die to ourselves, follow Him, and live after the Spirit; it won't be easy, but He will give us what we need when we need it. The other is lying, but it appeals to our flesh, our own senses, and it looks much easier. Everything the flesh taunts us with is against what God's law stands for. The enemy inside us cannot stand the ways of God and cannot even follow them. It's a tug of war for our soul.

Your Application

You will end up following one and rejecting the other. Understand that living after your flesh is a desired way of life. Look around. To follow after the ways of the Spirit is a disciplined life. It is giving up your own will to listen and follow the practices contrary to the way you would think to live. List scriptures that talk about flesh and the scriptures that talk about the Spirit. Check out the ending of each path. *Many of those whose bodies lie dead and buried will rise up, some to everlasting life and some to shame and everlasting disgrace. (Daniel 12:2 NLT)*

> *So then, those who are in the flesh cannot please God. (Romans 8:8)*

My Thought

So, after verse 7, we see that those who choose the fleshly ways cannot please God. Brother Paul will break it down so clearly that we cannot refute the words he is ordained to say. If we walk in our ways, we cannot please God. Wow. Think about that. He has a single path for us to walk in, the way of the Spirit. Any other way is displeasing to God; any other way is destructive to us… even if the way seems harmless. We all have to make the choice, those who do not, even though they seem like good people, will be accountable for their decisions.

Your Application

Do you waiver between your flesh and your spirit? Why not commit some of these scriptures to memory and use them next time you find yourself wanting to walk after the flesh.

> *But you are not in the flesh but in the Spirit, if indeed the Spirit of God dwells in you. Now if anyone does not have the Spirit of Christ, he is not His. (Romans 8:9)*

My Thought

Roman Christians, you are not in the flesh, but in the Spirit, if the Spirit of God lives in you. Now, if any man does not have the Spirit of Christ, he does not belong to Jesus. When the Spirit of God lives in us, we no longer live in the flesh, but now we live in the newness of the Spirit. If we live in the flesh, the Spirit of God is not in us, and we do not belong to God. How does that work when we struggle between living in the flesh and living in the Spirit? Our initial way of life is self-centered, so when Christ comes to live in us, we struggle to let Him control us by the Spirit. So usually, it's a process. For some, it takes a lifetime, while others get it quite quickly. *It's a matter of the heart.* King David was after God's heart. King Saul was after his own ways.

Your Application

Study the two kings and see if you can get some perspective on flesh versus spirit. You know that David sinned with Bathsheba, but King David was said to have a heart after God, and yet Saul's little disobediences throughout his reign cost him his kingship. Why? Write about it.

> *And if Christ is in you, the body is dead because of sin, but the Spirit is life because of righteousness. (Romans 8:10)*

My Thought

If Christ is in you, the body is dead along with sin, but the Spirit is alive as well as righteousness. If we are full of Christ, then His Spirit lives in us and produces holiness (wholeness, set apart, right living). If we are full of Christ's Spirit, then we cannot be full of ourselves, right? The body is referring to the flesh/sin part of us. Think of it this way, a full glass of water cannot take any more water, or it will overflow, but if the glass is half full of the Spirit, then the flesh can come in as well. We have to learn to empty ourselves daily as the scripture says, die daily (*Galatians 2:20*), and be filled with the Spirit. Fill my cup Lord, I lift it up Lord, come and quench this thirsty heart of mine. Bread of Heaven feed me till I want no more, fill my cup, fill up until I'm whole (https://www.umcdiscipleship.org/resources/history-of-hymns-fill-my-cup-lord).

Your Application

What stops you from emptying your cup/life daily? Write about it.

But if the Spirit of Him who raised Jesus from the dead dwells in you, He who raised Christ from the dead will also give life to your mortal bodies through His Spirit who dwells in you. (Romans 8:11)

My Thought

But if the Spirit of God that raised Jesus from the dead dwells in you, He that raised Christ from the dead will also come to life in your mortal bodies by His Spirit that dwells in you. God, our Father, raised Jesus, our Savior, from the dead. God will set in our spirit the same Spirit that was in Christ. We get so caught up with our own inner struggle that we lose focus of the bigger picture of going into all the world and making disciples. We convince ourselves that unless we get it right, we cannot go. God is saying in this passage, "I have brought My Son to live in you through His Spirit. Go, do what I have commanded. Don't worry about getting it right; I will make it right as you do My kingdom Business." What is His kingdom Business? To Love God with all our heart, soul, and strength and love others as we love ourselves. If we do this, we are making disciples.

Your Application

Do you get caught up in "you," so you don't do what you were destined to do? You will not be perfect, but you can be full of Jesus' Spirit. Delve into what the intention of your life's destiny is, don't get caught up in the trivial things of life. Go forth in the Spirit to subdue your enemy's distractions and live your life to the fullness of the *Storybook Fairy-Tale Reality*. It truly is magical in the purest sense of the word.

> *Therefore, brethren, we are debtors—not to the flesh, to live according to the flesh. (Romans 8:12)*

My Thought

Therefore, since our mortal bodies come to life in the Spirit, brothers and sisters, we are not debtors to the flesh, and we do not have to live after the flesh. Scripture says it; therefore, it is truth!

We do not have to live a life after our ways, wills, and wants; we are not ruled by our silly, childish flesh anymore! Or are we? Why are we still stagnant and not changing? Could it be, we are acting as if we still owe a debt?

If we owned a huge bank loan for buying land in Florida that we later learned was full of quicksand, and an Investor came along and paid our debt and took the lousy piece of land off our shoulders, why would we continue to pay for the land? It sounds ridiculous, yet in the kingdom, the angels scratch their heads when they see how we behave. We no longer owe a debt to our flesh. We are free to live in the Spirit.

Your Application

Do you want to live in the Spirit? Do you want to die daily to your flesh? What keeps you from fulfilling your destiny in this *Storybook Fairy-Tale Reality of the Kingdom of God*? Write it out.

> *For if you live according to the flesh you will die; but if by the Spirit you put to death the deeds of the body, you will live. (Romans 8:13)*

My Thought

There is an action that needs to take place through the Spirit; CRUSH the deeds of the body/flesh. Think of crushing a spider. When it is finished, there is no longer any resemblance of a spider; it's just a small dead blob; our flesh needs to look like that. We live in an age where we are so self-important. We need attention; we don't know how to crush our sinful selves. Oh, but God knows how to do it and is waiting, so He can bring you real-life through His Spirit. There is no comparison to living our lives our way to living our lives the way He sets forth for us in His Spirit.

Your Application

Are you ready to CRUSH your flesh and its sinful ways to live in the Spirit? Have you already done it? Write out where you are in comparison to this scripture.

> *For as many as are led by the Spirit of God, these are sons of God. (Romans 8:14)*

My Thought

All that are led by the Spirit of God; they are the sons of God. We are God's sons and daughters if we let His Spirit lead us! According to this truth, we can meditate on this scripture for hours and set a standard of our life's behavior.

Your Application

Do you behave like a son or daughter of God the Most High, Creator of all things? Stop and ponder. Let this scripture infiltrate into your soul. You are His! *To all who believed Him and accepted Him, He gave the right to become children of God. They are reborn—not with a physical birth resulting from a human passion plan, but a birth that comes from God (John 1:12, 13).*

> *For you did not receive the spirit of bondage again to fear, but you received the spirit of adoption by whom we cry out, "Abba, Father." (Romans 8:15)*

My Thought

Once an evil stepfather ruled us, intending to use us for his own good and then planned on destroying us, but once Christ came to rescue us from the evil stepfather, He brought us to a new place and adopted us into the Good Father's Family. We no longer have to ever fear again the stepfather and his bondage of sin he set on us, unless we go back and live with him.

Your Application

Do you still live in bondage or fear? That bondage will come over you again and again. This scripture reassures you that you are adopted into a new family, and the Father will not let the old stepfather get you. For this to happen, you have to stay close to the Father. How can you remind yourself your evil stepdad (Satan) is dead to you; you no long have to fear? You are now alive in Christ. Write out steps with scripture reinforcement to remind yourself you are free from your evil stepfather (the enemy).

The Spirit Himself bears witness with our spirit that we are children of God, (Romans 8:16)

My Thought

The only way we can understand God is through our spirit. Our spirit knows the truth of the matter. We have to live in the Spirit for our spirit to accept that we are now children of God. Our flesh will tell us different stories to entice us to stray. God doesn't want us to be confused, so He tells us to die daily to our flesh. He says, "Don't listen to your flesh, for your flesh is connected to your evil stepfather, who will convince you I am lying, just like he did to Adam and Eve. I love you and do not want you to listen, for your own safety. Do you understand?"

Your Application

How often does your flesh lead you astray? How can you lower that number? Read and commit to memory: *Nevertheless, God's solid foundation stands firm, sealed with this inscription: "The Lord knows those who are His," and, "Everyone who confesses the name of the Lord must turn away from wickedness"* (2 Timothy 2:19 ESV). This scripture is a great reminder of who you are and what you should do. Read *2 Corinthians 1:21-22*, what does Paul mean by these words. Meditate on all these scriptures until you fully know the truth, you are your Father's child!

and if children, then heirs—heirs of God and joint heirs with Christ, if indeed we suffer with Him, that we may also be glorified together. (Romans 8:17)

My Thought

Since we are children of God, then we will inherit the things of God, and we will be joint heirs with Christ; as we suffer with Him (dying to our flesh and being persecuted by those who do not believe), we will also be glorified together. We are in this life together. We are family, connected by Jesus' blood, adopted by the Father and empowered by the Spirit. We do not have to live this life alone because we have the Spirit of Jesus, and we have each other as sisters and brothers. Neither do we have to fret over finances in what God has set up for us, because we are heirs of His kingdom, which is limitless in its resources. That doesn't mean we don't have to work; we just don't need to fret over finances when it comes to God's projects. We need to do due diligence in our finances and not be ignorant about them. We need to learn what God's heart is about wealth for us. Where He guides, He will provide! I guarantee it! But not if we sit on the couch and wait for it, we must be proactive, knowledgeable about our wealth path.

Your Application

Do you know you are part of a great big family? You are not alone. Do you know God is your good Father? Do you know that God will supply your needs according to His riches in glory (*Philippians 4:19*)? That's a lot of riches He has stored up for those who walk in His Spirit. Learn about God's thoughts and intents of wealth. Look up scripture and understand we are to influence our community by our giving and investing. Our attitude towards finances says a lot about our relationship to our Father. (If you want to learn more about your wealth path with God, go to WealthWithGod.com)

> *"No one can take better care of us than Father God!"*
> *Jim Baker*

Present Suffering and Future Glory

> *For I consider that the sufferings of this present time are not worthy to be compared with the glory which shall be revealed in us. (Romans 8:18)*

My Thought

We believe the sufferings we go through are not worthy of being compared with God's glory that will be presented in us. Paul is moving us into the *Storybook Fairy-Tale Reality* in saying that our present suffering, no matter how bad it might seem, is nothing compared to the other side of death, heaven. What God will reveal in us is far greater than our sufferings and pain. Paul is painting a picture for us to move forward in our pain and suffering because there is something greater coming! Our suffering will pale in comparison to the plans God has for us in glory.

Your Application

Suffering is a real and painful event, but it is just that, an event; it is a happening that will pass. Have you camped out in your suffering, making it a lifestyle? God does not plan for you to live forever in your suffering; He has other purposes for you. Endure the suffering for as long as He allows but learn to walk out with Him when it's time. There is more for you not only in the time after death but also here and now. He has promised you abundant life (*John 10:10*), so go after it! Write about your suffering. What is it that God wants you to do amid your pain? Are you going through a Gethsemane suffering planned for a greater purpose, or have you caused this pain by making poor choices? A wise pastor once said, *"You have a crummy life because you make crummy decisions"* (*Glen Berteau*). Find scriptures on suffering and meditate on them, remember a time is coming that will wipe away all thoughts of your suffering. Read *1 Corinthians 4*.

> *For the earnest expectation of the creation eagerly waits for the revealing of the sons of God. (Romans 8:19)*

My Thought

Creation waits in eager expectation for the children of God to be revealed. Creation was perfect once. Creation longs for the time to live in perfect harmony again. God placed all that exists on this earth in six days, and there was harmony of the highest calling. Creation longs for those days. There is coming a day in which we, His children, will be revealed in our full glory, and it is such a day that even creation waits for it. We live as if today and tomorrow is our life. Creation knows there is so much more. We have to move from the mindset of this life and enter the *Storybook Fairy-Tale Reality of the Kingdom of God*. If we haven't experienced it, it is so much greater than we know. Living here on earth in the mystery of His kingdom is living out God's promised abundant life. Move into such an experience by lessening the importance of all that surrounds you and improving your ability to see the invisible life that is right before your very eyes.

Your Application

Today, open up the eyes of your spirit to see what He has for you.

> *For the creation was subjected to futility, not willingly, but because of Him who subjected it in hope; (Romans 8:20)*

My Thought

Creation was frustrated and held back, not by its own choice, but by the will of the One who exposed it, in hope… Oh, what a good picture we have here: "not by its own choice" is a picture of God, allowing something frustrating in creation to take place to bring about change. God allows us to be frustrated when we become complacent or too comfortable in our life. We settle for something, and God says, "Oh, there is so much more, don't camp there," and He places a thorn in our life to move us forward. Ha! What a good God we have. He has so much love for us. He sends things into our life to frustrate us so we can move forward in Him.

Your Application

Do not settle! Look for "the more" of the Lord. Improve your Christian life by looking at your frustrations in another light. Don't get frustrated. Get moving to the next level of intimacy with God.

> *because the creation itself also will be delivered from the bondage of corruption into the glorious liberty of the children of God. (Romans 8:21)*

My Thought

In hope, creation will be liberated from the bondage of decay. God will also bring creation into the freedom and glory of the children of God. Creation was exposed to frustration in hope that it would be liberated from its bondage of decay (caused by sin entering the world). Creation knew perfection, but now creation sees its own decay, in the fact that life does not live forever anymore. Creation longs for that day when it is no longer under the effect of sin. Thus, the words "in hope" appear in our passage. Hope is "the expectation of coming good." Creation hopes for a better day. Creation knows a day is coming when the children of God will be free from the bondage of decay and go into freedom and glory, and with that, creation will no longer be subject to the lower elements of life.

Your Application
Are you looking forward to that day as much as creation is? Creation knows that day is real, do you? Look into scriptures today that talk about the Garden of Eden and Heaven. What do they have in common? Write it out.

> *For we know that the whole creation groans and labors with birth pangs together until now. (Romans 8:22)*

My Thought
Paul says that we know that the whole creation has been groaning as in the pains of childbirth right up to the present time. If we knew of a greater day to come, would we be comfortable living in the lesser? Creation has experienced life at its best and groans for those days to come back. There is a birthing process taking place, and creation feels the labor pains of what is coming. Creation longs for, hopes for, and feels the labor pains of the coming of what was in the Garden. The earth is about to transform into what it was meant to be all along. Are we as readily groaning for the coming of our Lord?

Your Application
He is coming back to restore what was—to its proper place. Do you know how to groan like creation, to call into place the transformation of your new life in Him? Creation is your example today; learn from its longing to be restored. Read *Psalms 96:11–13* to see why creation groans for the coming of the Lord.

> *Not only that, but we also who have the first fruits of the Spirit, even we ourselves groan within ourselves, eagerly waiting for the adoption, the redemption of our body. (Romans 8:23)*

My Thought
Not only creation but we, who have the first fruits of the Spirit, we groan inwardly as we wait eagerly for our adoption into the family, the completeness of our bodies. Not only does creation desire this, but we desire this. Our spirit knows as much as creation that this isn't all there is. There is so much more—and we, our spirits in us—groan to complete our adoption and the trade-in for our new bodies. Are we adopted? Yes! Is our adoption complete? Yes and No. Think of it this way: we are Ethiopian orphans, and we have been told that we are adopted! We have met our loving parents, and we are now theirs. They have given us their name, and we call them Mom and Dad, learning all about them and having a growing relationship with them. We are truly adopted, but there is more. They are taking us home. They know where we are going, but we have never been there. Our adoption will be complete when they take us from this place and bring us into the home they have prepared for us

(And if I go and prepare a place for you, I will come back and take you to be with me that you also may be where I am. John 14:3). Not only are we going to another place, our real home, but we also have been given new abilities and freedoms that we could not enjoy when we were adopted yet still living in Ethiopia. Similarly, we long to see our new home, and we groan in unexpressed words to have the liberty to be complete. Our spirit within us gives us this inner groaning and yearning to be home and have our new, amazing bodies. We love Jesus, and it's wonderful to be in His presence, but through the Spirit, our spirit groans, for there is so much more!

Your Application

Take time to meditate and groan for "the more" of the Lord.

> *For we were saved in this hope, but hope that is seen is not hope; for why does one still hope for what he sees? (Romans 8:24)*

My Thought

Who hopes for what they already have? Paul states in verse 20 and 21, "in hope" creation will be liberated and brought into freedom. Creation has not seen the return of its fullness but waits in expectation of it to come to pass. If we think this is it in our Christian life, then we settle. We camp and live life as if this is all there is. There is no expectation of coming good because we think we have it all. Think about how we will live our lives if we think that way. We will just live day in and day out as if we have received it all—"mundane." Why do you think some Christians' lives are boring (yawn, yawn)?

Your Application

Do you expect something every day, or do you think you have all that there is? Look for more. What do you want? What are the dreams God has placed inside of you? Don't settle, ever.

> *But if we hope for what we do not see, we eagerly wait for it with perseverance. (Romans 8:25)*

My Thought

If we hope for what we do not yet have, we wait for it patiently. Our spirits groan inside, saying, "There's so much more!" Are we listening? There is more; we have not exhausted God's resources. He wants so much more for us. He wants us to know His love in a more significant way. He has plans beyond our understanding. If we know there are things expected to come, will we not wait for them? We cannot live life as usual when God calls us to a higher level of living. We must wait for the expected coming good of what our Father has in store for us.

Your Application

Are you tired of waiting? If you are, then do you really expect something greater is coming? Does it seem God has let you down in an area in your life, and you are now shutting down? Look again at the verse. Renew your hope in Him. Wait patiently for it; wait expectantly for it; it is coming! *Psalms 43:5* is a verse for you, *Why, my soul, are you downcast? Why so disturbed within me? Put your hope in God, for I will yet praise him, my Savior and my God.* Meditate on it until your expectancy is set back in its proper place, my dear hopeful one. Check out how your father Abraham and brothers Isaac and Jacob handled promises not yet fulfilled in *Hebrews 10:8–15*. Record your findings and thoughts.

> *Likewise the Spirit also helps in our weaknesses. For we do not know what we should pray for as we ought, but the Spirit Himself makes intercession for us with groanings which cannot be uttered. (Romans 8:26)*

My Thought

In the same way, the Spirit helps us in our weakness. We do not know what we are to pray for, but the Spirit Himself intercedes for us with groans that words cannot express. Paul is talking about creation and our spirit, longing for what is to come—as if we know there is something more. In the same way, Paul is now telling us the Spirit within us intercedes for us with groans without words because we cannot fully express it yet. We groan along with the Spirit's intercession in us for the hope that is to come. We have to understand there is so much more than us. There is a more excellent language, a greater hope, and a greatness that our bodies cannot contain. He that lives in us is far greater than any words, so our spirit connected to His Spirit groans to be let out of our weakness long enough to express the fullness of who He is and all that He deserves. Our spirit, connected to His Spirit, groans for the more extraordinary things to come.

Your Application

Try practicing connecting your spirit to His Spirit by quieting your soul (mind and body) and meditating on His Word. Slow down your thoughts and open your mind to Him. Play worship music or—better yet—just sing your own song to Him. Concentrate on one of Jesus' attributes, then let His Spirit take your spirit to a higher understanding. It is a hard discipline to attain, but you begin to understand "the more" of the Lord when you have achieved it.

> *Now He who searches the hearts knows what the mind of the Spirit is, because He makes intercession for the saints according to the will of God. (Romans 8:27)*

My Thought

He who searches our hearts knows the mind of the Spirit because Jesus intercedes for God's people in accordance with the will of God. We have a need, we set our request before the Lord, and He who searches our hearts knows exactly what we are thinking. He knows our small and insignificant thoughts that make up our prayers, and He who knows our heart also knows the mind of the Spirit who intercedes for us (and maybe even chuckles at the different directions the prayers are going).

We pray our hearts, and the Spirit prays God's will. How, oh how, do we connect the two? We pray, "Lord, take away the problems of this person who is going through such terrible pain and suffering." The Spirit prays, "Sustain this precious saint to endure their pain and suffering so that their prayer, to know You more, comes to fulfillment." Ha! We are quite funny and little in our "noble" request while the Spirit is direct and perfect in His prayers for the saints. We must connect to the will of God by praying in accordance with Jesus' intercession for God's people and agreement with the intention of God.

Your Application

Oh, precious one, if you grasp this today, your prayer life will never be the same, and I guarantee your life will change as well. Practice praying for others with your spiritual eyes open, let your spirit connect with the Spirit, and pray the prayers that release God's will.

More Than Conquerors

> *And we know that all things work together for good to those who love God, to those who are the called according to His purpose. (Romans 8:28)*

My Thought

In life, we know God works good for those who love Him and whom God calls according to His purpose. God works for your good in all things. "All things" mean death, murder, rape, poverty, war, abandonment, betrayal, fires, tornadoes, floods… all means all. Therefore, instead of thinking up things that God doesn't work for your good, flip that switch and begin thinking your God will work for your good with anything that comes your way. God can put the good in any circumstance because God is good. Even in the bad, He creates a silver lining of good. We need to feel this verse in the core of our being. Understand that if God in verse 20 of this chapter said that creation is frustrated, "not by its own choice," then God will allow things to come our way, not by our own choice, but the more excellent thought is, God will work it for your good. How? *I do not know how, but I DO KNOW He will*. The bad that comes our way by our own doing is the consequence of bad choices. God can still work them out for good if we humble ourselves and repent and change our ways. The bad that comes from consequences outside of our power to control, God will work out for our good under two conditions: if we are among those who love Him and for those whom God calls according to His purpose.

Your Application

So, do you love Him? Read scriptures on how others will know we love Him. Are you called according to His purpose? What exactly is His purpose for you? Read *Psalms 119:175, Ephesians 1:11–12, 1 Corinthians 11:1, Philippians 4:4*, and *Revelations 4:11*. Find other scripture that pinpoints your purpose here on earth. Write them out and meditate on them until your spirit bears witness with His Spirit and confirms your purpose.

For whom He foreknew, He also predestined to be conformed to the image of His Son that He might be the firstborn among many brethren. (Romans 8:29)

My Thought

For those God already knew, He also set their destiny to be conformed to the image of his Son, that Jesus might be the firstborn among many brothers and sisters. Whom did God foreknow? He is God, right? This verse gets so much attention. Some say, "Hey, God predestined people, so He isn't just and fair," or "He has favorites, and He sets some high and some low." Whom did God foreknow? He is God. He knew everyone before they were. So, whom God foreknew, He also predestined them to be conformed to His Son's image. How just and fair can our God be? He predestined all (...*not willing that any should perish, but everyone to come to repentance. 2 Peter 3:9*) to conform to the image of His Son. The sad point in this scripture is, not all will respond. What was our purpose? To be a family! God predestined us to be brothers and sisters in the image of our Father's firstborn, Jesus! Father God is gracious to want all of us to be a part of His plan.

Your Application

You are a part of a large family! Today, introduce yourself to another brother or sister you have not met. Share this scripture with them.

Moreover whom He predestined, these He also called; whom He called, these He also justified; and whom He justified, these He also glorified. (Romans 8:30)

My Thought

And (What, there's more?) those He set a destiny for, He also called. Those He called, He also justified. Those He justified, He also glorified. What the scripture is saying is all are called, but not all will be justified and glorified. The incredible point of verse 29 is God predestined everyone to be in the image of His Son, but not all will respond. For those of us who respond to our destiny, we are called by the Father to join Him. We live just as if we had not sinned, with Jesus' robe of righteousness placed on us (we are holy, set apart for His purpose), and we are definitely valued.

Your Application

You are predestined to live in the family of God. You are called to be a brother or sister of Jesus. You are justified from the sinful state you lived in, and you are glorified to a greater value. How does that make you feel? In times of doubt, build your faith by letting this scripture enforce the truth in you.

God's Everlasting Love

What then shall we say to these things? If God is for us, who can be against us? (Romans 8:31)

My Thought

What do we say in response to these things (verses 28–31)? If God is for us, who can be against us? Paul is speaking to the Romans after sharing doctrine and emphasizing who we are in God. After all this, he now says, "What can I say!" He has built a case for the Roman Christians, and now He says if God is for us (Paul, his fellow companions, the Romans, and all who believe), who can be against us? We must let this scripture ruminate throughout our minds, our hearts, and our spirits.

Your Application

Set this as the primary weapon verse when an enemy comes against you. Throw that verse out, and like David killed Goliath, watch your enemy fall. Today, go chop off the devil's head to silence him, run after all other smaller enemies and stand in your victory! Bow low to the One who makes this all possible.

> *He who did not spare His own Son, but delivered Him up for us all, how shall He not with Him also freely give us all things? (Romans 8:32)*

My Thought

God the Father did not spare His only Son, but gave Him as a sacrifice for every one of us—how will He not also, along with giving us Jesus, graciously give us all things? "All things" mean all things, according to His will for what is best for us. Do not go naming and claiming material things here. This is serious stuff. God is generous, and He is ready to give us all things to live a life of victory. If He is for us, who can be against us? Father God gave His Son for us to have a victorious life! He will now graciously give us all things to continue that victorious life. We need to long for the deeper things of the Lord. He is so ready to graciously provide them to us. Are material things bad? Does God not want us to have things? *"Seek first the kingdom of God and His righteousness and all other things will be added" (Matthew 6:33)*. God wants you to go after the things of God, and He will give you the things you need and unimaginably more! You take care of His business (Look after the widow and the fatherless, *Psalms 68:5, 6*. Bring hope to the hopeless, set God's people free and come against the enemy, *Isaiah 61:1, 2.*), and He will take care of yours.

Your Application

Your Father did not spare His own Son, but gave; how will He not also graciously give you all things? He loves you so much. Are you speaking and understanding His language of love? It is not material things He cares about; it is YOU! Change the way you see God and ask Him to give you the tools you need in your life to live victoriously and abundantly. Read *Psalms 44:1–8* and put it to memory.

> *Who shall bring a charge against God's elect? It is God who justifies. (Romans 8:33)*

My Thought

Who will bring any charge against those whom God has chosen? It is God who justifies. Who can judge us? Who can slander us? Who can charge us with anything? If God is for us, no one can! It is

God who validates us, and if He loved us so much to give us His Son, then no charge will stand as we walk in the Spirit.

Your Application

Do you allow charges to come against you, worse yet, do you bring charges against yourself? Do you stack up accusations against yourself and set yourself as the culprit? Stop it now. No one, not even you, can bring any charges against you because God has chosen you, and He has validated you. Write out those who bring charges against you. If there is wrong done, take care of it. If there are accusing words, and they are not justified, cross them out with the words, "I'm justified by God!" Paul fully understands this verse and probably had to remind himself of it often. Remember, he killed his own brothers and sisters of Christ in his tenacity towards the law to ensure no new cult came in to redefine it. He made sure the letter of the law was fulfilled by his own hands, not realizing it was God's Son who had come in the flesh to redefine the letter of the law. Jesus was the fulfillment of the law, so it was no longer rendered as alive. The new law was a law of love and grace written on the hearts of those who believed. Paul had to live every day with this fact and had to call himself justified by God, his Father.

> *Who is he who condemns? It is Christ who died, and furthermore is also risen, who is even at the right hand of God, who also makes intercession for us. (Romans 8:34)*

My Thought

Who then is the one who condemns? No one. Christ Jesus, who died—is at the right hand of God and is interceding for us. Who can ever condemn you again? No one! Let this word be in you. Who condemns? The Enemy. In this chapter (*Romans 8*), Paul started out saying, "*There is, therefore, now, no condemnation.*" He carries the thought through to the end, restating that no one can condemn you when you know that Jesus Christ died for you, it is all over. Where is Jesus Christ? He is at the right hand of the Father interceding for us, He is living in each of our hearts contending for us, and He is waiting to give us the tools to fight each battle that comes our way. We cannot help but win when we do it His way!

Your Application

Battles can be hard, but it is not the battle that counts; it's how you choose to fight the battle. Are you fighting on your own? Or are you letting the tools of the Word and the completion of Christ's death and resurrection bring you victory? Set aside weapon verses to use during conflict and battles. Memorize them so you can use them effectively in times of trouble. Here are a few: *2 Corinthians 10:4, Ephesians 1:3, Ephesians 6:11, 12, Colossians 1:16, Colossians 2:15, 1 Timothy 1:18*. Look up more and use them! "It is written," said Jesus during His battle.

> *Who shall separate us from the love of Christ? Shall tribulation, or distress, or persecution, or famine, or nakedness, or peril, or sword? (Romans 8:35)*

My Thought

What are the things that can separate us from the love of Christ? Will trouble, hardship, persecution, being hungry, having no clothes, danger, or the sword separate us from the love of Christ? The last five verses in chapter eight deal with who can separate us from the love of Christ. It all comes down to the truth of the matter, not one person, not one entity, not one problem, or hardship or famine or nakedness or danger or sword can separate us. There is only one who can separate us...it will all come down to our response to His call.

Your Application

Today, respond to His call to come closer and hunger for more of Him and less of what you want and less of the world. Realize how much God loves everyone in this world, everyone! The only one stopping people from Him is each person's right to choose whom they will serve. Encourage someone today to take a closer look at the love of God.

> *As it is written: "For Your sake we are killed all day long; We are accounted as sheep for the slaughter." (Romans 8:36)*

My Thought

As it is written: *"For Your sake we face death all day long; we are considered as sheep to be slaughtered"* (Psalms 44:22). This scripture sounds like *Romans 8:28.* He works for our good, all things bad or noble. The verse says, "for Your sake...," for whose sake? For God's sake. It says "for God's sake" we face death all day long. If we continue to read *Psalms 44:25, 26, "We are brought down to the dust; our bodies cling to the ground. Rise up and help us; redeem us because of your unfailing love."* David declares that God's love is unfailing even in the most difficult times, and he will not be separated from it.

Your Application

In the most challenging times, God loves you! Set that in your mind and your heart. Deepen your resolve to go through difficult times with confidence that God's love is near you, beside you, and in you.

> *Yet in all these things we are more than conquerors through Him who loved us. (Romans 8:37)*

My Thought

In all hardships, troubles, persecution, famine, distress of finances, fear, or anything terrible we go through, we are more than conquerors through God who loves us. If we resolve in our hearts and minds that nothing can separate us from the love of God, then we are on the road to being conquerors. We can overcome anything if God is for us and if God loves us. It is up to us to determine the scriptures to be true to our individual lives. We have to believe these scriptures about God's love. We have to believe that nothing can separate us from God's love. Our victory is determined by what we believe. If we believe He loves us, no matter what comes our way, we will walk in the covering of our Father God's love and will not waiver. If we begin to doubt the love of God and listen to our enemy, we will start to act like orphans again and try to deal with the invisible enemy with our own physical senses. It is impossible to fight a spiritual battle with our physical resources. We are out of our league, and we will lose, but if we fight with the resources God has given us, if we rest in His love for us, we will win every time and be *more* than conquerors, and we will act like adopted children of God in the *Storybook Fairy-Tale Reality of His Kingdom.*

Your Application

What are your biggest battles? Write them down. Take a good look at how you fight. Are you fighting in your own strength and understanding? Or are you allowing the love of God to fight for you with all the resources He has for you to win? Change your strategy if you need to and ask God to give you the faith to believe you are continuously loved, and you are more than a conqueror!

> *For I am persuaded that neither death nor life, nor angels nor principalities nor powers, nor things present nor things to come, (Romans 8:38)*

My Thought

"For I am convinced that neither death nor life, neither angels nor demons, neither the present nor the future, nor any powers…" Our past is covered, our present is covered, and our future is covered. The blood of Jesus is proof of God's love for us. He covers us entirely and continuously.

Not Death	Not Life
Not Angels	Not Demons
Not Past or Present	Not Future

Nor any powers can separate you from God's love!

Your Application

What is trying to separate you from the love of God? Check it out; Paul is giving us an extensive list of what cannot separate us. Have you found your enemy in this list? If not, there is more on Paul's list. Better yet, make a list of your own and declare as Paul did: "Nothing can separate me from the love of God…" and put your list under your proclamation. Put it somewhere you can see it every day. Live the truth!

> *nor height nor depth, nor any other created thing, shall be able to separate us from the love of God which is in Christ Jesus our Lord. (Romans 8:39)*

My Thought

Paul sums it up with, *"nor anything else in all creation..."* Paul is leaving nothing uncovered. He lets the Roman Christians and all who will read his book of *Romans* know that there is no way that we can ever be separated from God's love.

Your Application

"What's the big deal," you might say. Well, it has everything to do with your victory. You will be victorious to the extent that you believe this to be true. If there is a shadow of a doubt that you can be separated from God's love by you, your actions, your sin, other people's opinions, or any outside source (such as demons), then you will falter. If you stand firm in the truth of God's love, if you know that you are adopted into the family of God, and if you no longer allow condemnation to speak to you, you will be more than a conqueror.

Romans Eight Living in the Spirit is as easy as first learning to play the piano, creating software, becoming a soldier at boot camp, or building a rocket to the moon. It doesn't come naturally or easily. It goes against our fleshly grain. Some naturally take it on. Others seem to struggle in the process. *It calls for a sense of desperateness out of a place of understanding we cannot do life on our own.* We have to come to the end of ourselves before reaching out and pulling in the Spirit of God. If we are self-reliant or rebellious or highly educated or affluent in worldly things, we may think we can master life independently. God allows us those choices, and He won't push us into making a decision, but He will do all He can to show us we need Him. He sent His Son to earth to die in place of our punishment for our wrong living, our sin, to prove His love for us. God understands our depravity. Our Father's will is that we kill, shut off, and destroy our fleshly ways to connect with the very same Spirit that was in Jesus while on earth. God shows us that the Spirit life is abundant and full. His plan and destiny for us in our journey here on earth is to share the Spirit with us so we can overcome any sin, so we are not condemned, and so we can fully understand the love God has towards us. Paul gives us great weapon verses to overcome anything that rises up against us, and he convinces us that *nothing* can come between us and God's love for us. As one practices the piano and becomes a concert pianist and as one educates themselves to create the needed software of our time it's a process. When soldiers are denied privileges and, in time, rise to become the generals of our country and when rockets were first designed to send our astronauts to the moon, we too can learn to live in the Spirit, but it's a process. It takes time, it doesn't happen overnight, but when we truly learn to live God's way, see God's love and empower ourselves with the Spirit of God, we can live an abundant, full life of love, with more to come—living in the *Storybook Fairy-Tale Reality of the Kingdom of God*!

My Prayer

Jesus, You, have given us everything we need to live an abundant life. We no longer have condemnation. You have empowered us with Your Spirit to live freely in You. But if we let our sinful nature control our thoughts, we think about sinful things which lead to death. But we are no longer governed by the sinful nature, and Your Holy Spirit now controls us. Lead us by Your Spirit, which leads to life and peace. We groan now for what is to come. We are empowered to pray by the power of the Spirit who lives in us. You know what we ought to pray and give us the utterances. We learn that we are more than conquerors through You, and nothing can separate us from Your love! In Jesus gracious Name. Amen

Write a summary of chapter 8.

*We do not have to live a life after our own ways, wills, and wants; we are not ruled by our silly, childish flesh anymore!
Or are we?
Why are we still stagnant and not changing? Could it be, we are acting as if we still owe a debt?*

Our Worship
What Would I Have Done / Jenn and Brian Johnson
https://www.youtube.com/watch?v=kEdB7lQJ-MM

Communion (feat. Steffany Gretzinger & Brandon Lake from Bethel Music) / Maverick City / TRIBL
https://www.youtube.com/watch?v=91hHwlYPqxE

CHAPTER 9

Living in Faith Part 2

Read the complete chapter of *Romans 9*

God's Sovereign Choice–Israel's Rejection of Christ

> *I tell the truth in Christ, I am not lying, my conscience also bearing me witness in the Holy Spirit, (Romans 9:1)*

My Thought

When we are in the Spirit, we cannot lie without being convicted, for the Holy Spirit is truth. As we are in Christ, we become a new creature, and the old ways of our old nature become uncomfortable. If our old ways do not become uncomfortable, then we are probably not living in the fullness of what Christ has to offer us.

Your Application

Are you waiting to get the complete gift God is offering you? He wants you to live in the truth and fullness of Christ. When you do, there will be truth in your life. You will live in the truth and will be set free. Practice living in Christ today. When you see old behavior, cut it off and live in the newness of your life in Christ. Better yet, write out what is keeping you from the fullness of Christ.

> *that I have great sorrow and continual grief in my heart. (Romans 9:2)*

My Thought

Why is Paul so grief-stricken? As we follow this chapter, we will realize that when Christ came into him, Paul truly walked into his *Storybook Fairy-Tale Reality* and wanted his fellow Jewish brothers to come along with him in this world.

Your Application

The real test of the newness of life in Christ, you feel for the lost. You don't just change the way you live. There is a change in the way you feel about others. You feel compassionate about others. You want them to know this beautiful God with whom you have become intimate. You want them to understand the plan of salvation, and you want them to live in the same *Storybook Fairy-Tale Reality* as the Christians of old and the ones living today. Help lead someone today into this world of favor, love, power, and authority.

> *For I could wish that I myself were accursed from Christ for my brethren, my countrymen according to the flesh, (Romans 9:3)*

My Thought

Paul was so serious about sharing the good news that he would have cut himself off if his fellowman would come to know Christ. How radical is that? Could we do that? Honestly, wanting to be cut off so others could come in? I think Paul knew that the mercy of God would save him from being accursed. Paul must have been praying for them or had argued with some of the Jewish non-believers. Paul must have had a passion for these men to "get it."

Your Application

How much passion do you have for your fellow man? Do you desire their salvation? If so, then you will be acting like Paul and telling everyone you know. If you do not feel this passion that Paul felt, why not ask God for more love.

> *who are Israelites, to whom pertain the adoption, the glory, the covenants, the giving of the law, the service of God, and the promises; (Romans 9:4)*

My Thought

This is who Paul was passionate about, those who pertained to the adoption of God, those who knew about the glory of God from the Old Testament stories, they were given the covenants of God through the giving of the law, they served God and had the promises of God. These people should have known God, but they got lost looking for Him in the wrong places. While the Promise was in their midst, they didn't recognize Him.

Your Application

Sometimes, you can be so busy looking for God and your expectation of Him that when He comes, you don't notice Him. You may be running to conferences to meet with Him, but He's right in your room waiting for you to pick up the Word and spend time with Him. We all want encounters with our God, but who are we to choose where they will be? The Israelites had put God in a box, and from their study of the Old Testament, they decided the Messiah would come as a conquering King. They missed Him because He came as an ordinary baby. Let today be an opportunity to have an encounter with your God. Open your mind to all encounters and events that come your way today. Did you see God in them?

> *of whom are the fathers and from whom, according to the flesh, Christ came, who is over all, the eternally blessed God. Amen. (Romans 9:5)*

My Thought

Christ came out of this Jewish race, the Promise of Abraham, our Father, and yet most did not recognize Him. Why? Again, we have to get this, people; we want to have an experience with Him when we set our time to go to church or set on our calendar a conference that looks good. People, Christ walked for three years of His ministry amongst the common people. Jesus was approachable (He still is today). The children were held back, and Jesus said, "Let them come to Me." The blind man was told to be silent, and yet Jesus stopped to heal him. Jesus is available to us every minute of every day. Do not wait. Open your mind to have an encounter with Jesus continually. He wants to be with you all the time, not just church events and conferences.

Your Application

Today, look at every opportunity to let Jesus be a part of your day, open your heart to see His Spirit in everyday things. Write what you noticed today as your mind and spirit were open.

Israel's Rejection and God's Purpose

> *But it is not that the word of God has taken no effect. For they are not all Israel who are of Israel, (Romans 9:6)*

My Thought

Not all people will accept God's plan of salvation through Jesus Christ, our Lord. Not all people of Israel are the chosen. Not all Gentiles will accept the call of God on their lives. The call is for all, but not all will answer.

Your Application

Today, in your own life, accept the call so you will be the adopted of God, now find others who are adopted but who haven't heard the call. Share your testimony.

> *Nor are they all children because they are the seed of Abraham; but, "In Isaac your seed shall be called." (Romans 9:7)*

My Thought

The seed of Abraham is spiritual and physical. Those who belong to the Spirit of God are the children of Abraham. There were two sons, Ishmael and Isaac. Ishmael was begotten by the hands of Abraham, Sarah, and Hagar. The three helped God produce a counterfeit promised son. Abraham and Sarah were unwilling to wait the length of time God had in mind for the coming of the miracle, promised son, so Sarah suggested Abraham have relations with Hagar, her maidservant. We know the story. It ended up that Abraham had two sons; one was a counterfeit promise (Ishmael) and, Isaac, the promised son. The son, Isaac, was in the lineage of Jesus. Paul is now saying to us, not all who come from Abraham will be his descendants; only those who accept the call of God on their lives will have Abraham as their father.

Your Application

There will be those you share the gospel with that will accept the call. Those who accept the promise of salvation will inherit Abraham's promise. Be encouraged today as you share the gospel; those who are called will come in! Also, write about a time you helped God with His promises to you. Have you ever created a counterfeit promise, an Ishmael?

> *That is, those who are the children of the flesh, these are not the children of God; but the children of the promise are counted as the seed. (Romans 9:8)*

My Thought

There will be those born of the Jewish race that will not be children of God. Only those of the promised are the real children of God. Those who accept Jesus as Lord and Savior will be children of God. This goes for the Jewish nation as well as all other nations.

Your Application

All who sit in our congregations are not children of God. There are those in the flesh who are not desirous of knowing God but only fulfilling a religious ritual. It's not for us to decide who is of God; it's for us to share this precious gift God has given us. We leave the judging to God, and we do our part to love. Today share your testimony and see the effect it will have on people.

> *For this is the word of promise: "At this time I will come and Sarah shall have a son." (Romans 9:9)*

My Thought

Our salvation, our family, came from an impossible task. Sarah couldn't have a son. When we are given promises that are impossible for man and only possible by God, get ready for a miracle! Remember that when a promise comes to you, if it's something you can accomplish, then it's of your own mind and strength. If what God has promised you is mind-boggling, then it's from God. God doesn't only do simple. He likes to impress on you His ability to take care of you and work wonders through you.

Your Application

Find the impossible today; is there someone you know who is sick and needs healing? Go pray and allow God to heal. Does someone need wisdom? Go and pray impartation of wisdom from God.

> *And not only this, but when Rebecca also had conceived by one man, even by our father Isaac, (Romans 9:10)*

My Thought

What's up with our foremothers who were unable to have children? What's up with barrenness? Sarah couldn't have children, and neither could Rebecca. Isaac had to pray for her barrenness to leave, and finally, after about 20 years, Rebecca had twins.

Your Application

Read about barrenness. Does God want to perform a miracle and allow the impossible through barrenness in your life? Is the reason for barrenness something to be used for God's glory? Is barrenness a curse? Can barrenness come from sin in your life? Check it out; this is a good study.

> *(for the children not yet being born, nor having done any good or evil, that the purpose of God according to election might stand, not of works but of Him who calls), (Romans 9:11)*

My Thought

Now, this is a verse that can seem unfair and unjust, but if you know your God, you can completely know that He is nothing of the kind. He is just, and He is kind towards all. Remember to see the whole picture of God when people begin to question His character.

Your Application

How is it that before the twins were born, God had already chosen who He would hate and who He would love? Settle this truth in your mind. Talk with someone wiser than you to see what this is all about. Remember, we never allow our circumstances to define who God is. God is the same through good times as well as bad. Always judge your circumstances with a loving, knowing eye towards God. Allow yourself to know He is good, He is love, and He only teaches what is best, all the time.

> *it was said to her, "The older shall serve the younger." (Romans 9:12)*

My Thought

The prophecy of the twins was the older Esau would serve the younger Jacob. Prophecy is a word from God that will come to pass because God knows the future and because He is God. It's pretty simple to understand it if you know who God is. God has traveled throughout time and space, and nothing is a surprise to Him because He has been there. So, He speaks a prophecy over the twins because He has already seen it come to pass. God is past, God is present, and God is future. We know Him as past and present because we understand past and present. It takes faith to know Him as the God of the future.

Your Application

Do you have any problem believing the God of the future? How can you create more faith (*Romans 10:17*)? Today read about God's character and let that settle in your heart and mind.

As it is written, "Jacob I have loved, but Esau I have hated." (Romans 9:13)

My Thought

Wow, harsh! Not if you know the future. If you see a man hungry for the things of the flesh and not interested in the things of the Spirit, then you can begin to understand the harsh words are only true words. In *Hebrews 12:16, 17*, Paul reiterates what he said in this verse: *See that no one is sexually immoral, or is godless like Esau, who for a single meal sold his inheritance rights as the oldest son (16). Afterward, as you know, when he wanted to inherit this blessing, he was rejected. Even though he sought the blessing with tears, he could not change what he had done (17).*

Your Application

How often have you seen God do something that didn't make sense but continued to believe in the truth of God's character? God is good. God is love. He only teaches us what is best. Today and every day, always stand up for God, not what you see. Stand for the truth that God always wants the best for an individual, and if it appears that He hates that individual, He does not; it's for a purpose. Read John 14:22-24. Does Jesus clear up the confusion of predestination? After praying, write out your thoughts about predestination and our God is the God of the future.

Israel's Rejection and God's Justice

What shall we say then? Is there unrighteousness with God? Certainly not! (Romans 9:14)

My Thought

God is not unjust or unrighteous, ever! We have to understand this. God's archenemy will portray Him as evil, selfish, and a monster. God is not that. We have to go back to the Gift He sent to us. God sent His only Son to be whipped, beaten, and crucified in such an undignified way, which speaks volumes of His deep love for mankind, us. We cannot mistake the great Gift He gave as anything but Love.

Your Application

Why do you think it's so easy to believe that God is unjust or unfair when bad things happen? What do you think about these verses? *Hebrews 12:22-29 But you have come to Mount Zion, to the city of the living God, the heavenly Jerusalem. You have come to thousands upon thousands of angels in joyful assembly, to the church of the firstborn, whose names are written in heaven. You have come to God, the Judge of all, to the spirits of the righteous made perfect, to Jesus the mediator of a new covenant, and to the sprinkled blood that speaks a better word than the blood of Abel. See to it that you do not refuse him who speaks. If they did not escape when they refused him who warned them on earth, how much less will we, if we turn away from him who warns us from heaven? At that time his voice shook the earth, but now he has promised, "Once more I will shake not only the earth but also the heavens" (Haggai 2:6). The words "once more" indicate the removing of what can be shaken—that is, created things—so that what cannot be shaken may remain. Therefore, since we are receiving a kingdom that cannot be shaken, let us be thankful, and so worship God acceptably with reverence and awe, for our "God is a consuming fire" (Deuteronomy 4:24).* Write your thoughts.

> *For He says to Moses, "I will have mercy on whomever I will have mercy, and I will have compassion on whomever I will have compassion." (Romans 9:15)*

My Thought

God chooses to whom He will pour out His mercy and His compassion. This can become a confusing verse if we don't understand the truth of it. I think Paul is (under the inspiration of the Holy Spirit) trying to brighten us up. He is setting forth an answer to an argument that will come from the intellects, so the Holy Spirit gives it to us first. God doesn't go around thinking whom He will show mercy or compassion to. God has been with all humanity, God has seen their thoughts, motives, and intent of their hearts, all humankind, so from the vast knowledge of His experience with each person, He now can proclaim that He will show mercy and compassion to the ones who choose Him. Is that a mean God or just a very knowledgeable, loving God! We serve an incredibly loving God, full of mercy and compassion. He will pour His love out onto those who choose Him.

Your Application

Today or any day, don't let arguments ever send you running. Stand firm on the knowledge that your God is good. Whatever one says against your God, you can say, "I don't know why, but I do know that He is a good God!" Who can argue about the knowledge you have of your heavenly Father? They can question you, but as you stand firm in your faith without wavering, they will see you mean what you believe.

> *So then it is not of him who wills, nor of him who runs, but of God who shows mercy. (Romans 9:16)*

My Thought

Mercy is from God and God alone. Mercy does not come from one who wills it, nor does it come from one who works for it. Mercy is from a just, righteous God who knows none of us deserve it. He passes out His mercy to those who accept the precious Gift of His Son.

Your Application

Research the word "mercy" in your Bible, in your concordance; google it, and do a word study today. How many scriptures can you find on mercy? Are there one or two that speaks to you? How about memorizing it?

> *For the Scripture says to the Pharaoh, "For this very purpose I have raised you up, that I may show My power in you, and that My name may be declared in all the earth." (Romans 9:17)*

My Thought

So, if we aren't confused enough about God's kind character, Paul throws in Pharaoh. Pharaoh is used to show God's power and name to be declared in all the earth. Again, let's remember we serve a God of the future. God saw Pharaoh's heart and the intent of his ways. Pharaoh was going to reject the truth of God, so God used this God-rejecting man as a tool to show His power through plagues. God was able to rescue His people even though a Pharaoh said, "No!" Man cannot say "No" to God's plan. Remember that.

Your Application

Has someone said, "No!" to you when you knew God said, "Yes"? Like Moses, God will show His power through your faith when you stand for what God said. The "No" will be turned to "Yes" so God's name will be declared in your life. God knows who His children are (*2 Timothy 2:19*). God will use those who are not His to rescue and prosper those who are His. Read *Exodus 7–11*!

> *Therefore He has mercy on whom He wills, and whom He wills He hardens.* (*Romans 9:18*)

My Thought

We need to get this. God will have mercy on those He knows will follow Him. God will harden His heart on those who choose to reject God's beautiful Gift. He has no other choice.

Your Application

Never doubt God's love for the whole human race. There are so many scriptures that show God's love for man, and He is not willing that any should perish. Many scriptures show God gave man a will to choose life or death. As sad as it seems, many will choose death so they can live their own lives here on earth. Silly and very sad as it is, the free will given to mankind allows God to know who loves Him for Himself. All God wants is to live the rest of eternity with those who love Him, really love Him. Today take the time to check out the scriptures on God's love and scriptures on free will. Share your findings with someone.

> *You will say to me then, "Why does He still find fault? For who has resisted His will?"* (*Romans 9:19*)

My Thought

Why can God find fault with us if He has decided what will happen to us? Again, the only reason God has chosen what will happen to us is that He is the God of the future and sees our motives, our thoughts, and our final decision to either love Him or reject Him. From that perspective, He can now make decisions on how to use us for His glory. He can treat us like He treated Pharaoh, or He can guide us like He guided Abraham. Both men brought recognition to God. One ended up in destruction; the other ended up gaining God's many blessings. Ultimately, it is our decision; then God decides how to use that decision for His glory because He will get the glory!

Your Application

Are you beginning to understand the weight of your decision compared to not only eternity but the here and now? Pharaoh thought he was in control, but in the bigger picture, he was only a pawn in the Lord's hand. He was plagued and finally destroyed by water because of his arrogance and pride. On the other hand, Abraham was obedient and lived a life of servanthood to God his Father, and was blessed with many riches, honor, and family; he was blessed and not cursed. It's up to you; then God will decide what He does with your decision. Study Pharaoh and Abraham in scripture and in history. Write a comparison paper on the two.

> *But indeed, O man, who are you to reply against God? Will the thing formed say to him who formed it, "Why have you made me like this?" (Romans 9:20)*

My Thought

The Creator of all humanity has allowed us to decide to love our Creator or reject Him. Then we question the very plans our Creator has for us. It seems crazy when you think about it, but we are such silly people thinking we are someone when we are creations from His hand. Our Creator gives us free will to choose, and then we get mad at Him for basing our lives on our own decision.

Your Application

Do you understand that you have free will to do whatever you want? Do you understand that from that decision, God will then use it for His glory? God is not willing that any should perish, but He won't make you love Him either. For those who choose to love Him, you are called into His family and reap tremendous benefits. For those who reject His love, they will reap the consequences of destruction. It seems so simple, and yet people decide death over life; so sad.

> *Does not the potter have power over the clay, from the same lump to make one vessel for honor and another for dishonor? (Romans 9:21)*

My Thought

We are lumps of clay. Can you see the sophisticated man or woman reacting to hearing they are lumps of clay? Ha! Anyway, what a way to bring us back to our commonality when we know that we all started as lumps of clay. So, the intricacy of our human body is a direct result of the Master Potter who can make anything out of nothing! We should be falling at His feet every day in adoration and amazement at how brilliant our Potter is. He has the power over us to make out of us what He so chooses. One lump He will make an Abraham, and the other lump He will make a Pharaoh! Why? Because He is unfair in choosing whom He will honor and whom He will dishonor? No! He chooses one for honor because that one honored Him by choosing Him. The other He makes for dishonor because, in the end, the dishonored one will never accept Jesus' sacrifice for his sin.

Your Application

You always, always have to give God the benefit of the doubt. He is just, good, loving, and so much more. When people begin to blame God for this and that, saying He is not fair, you must always remember His character above what mere man may say about Him.

He is to be honored, not questioned for what He does.

All humankind is unfit even to tie His shoe, yet He opens up the Holy of Holies and allows the misfits in. Nothing can be said about Him, except His is just, holy, and wise above all. Your Potter knows what He is doing; rest in that. Passionately believe the truth and reject anything that comes against His character. Read *2 Corinthians 4* for a fuller understanding of the mercy of God. Write what stood out to you.

> *What if God, wanting to show His wrath and to make His power known, endured with much long-suffering the vessels of wrath prepared for destruction,* (Romans 9:22)

My Thought

Pharaoh is an excellent example of what Paul is speaking about, so are Herod and Hitler. God displayed His power and His wrath on these men who rejected His love. Can you imagine God wanting to send these men to their destruction? Sometimes you cannot reform a person, so they will never get it. God knows and uses them to save and show His wavering loved ones what is to come because God is not willing that any should perish! Although, many will choose to reject Christ.

Your Application

There are vessels of wrath, vessels to be destroyed in your day and age. It is not for you to decide because only God knows who will make the final decision for good or evil. Your job is to continually portray God as good. Never question His goodness. Go over scriptures of His character and set them to memory.

> *and that He might make known the riches of His glory on the vessels of mercy, which He had prepared beforehand for glory,* (Romans 9:23)

My Thought

Abraham is an example. His decision to believe God, opened a way for him to be born for the glory and mercy of God. God foreknew Abraham would stand for Him and walk in obedience, so Abraham was created for the glory of God. Abraham was not an arrogant man thinking he could navigate his way through life. He was a teachable, humble, and giving man who knew he needed someone bigger than himself.

Your Application

There are those in your life that will receive the mercy and grace of our Lord Jesus Christ because they, like Abraham, are sure there has to be something more to life and something bigger than them. Be aware of those who seem to have a teachable spirit, be open to sharing with them the love of the Lord.

> *even us whom He called, not of the Jews only, but also of the Gentiles?*
> *(Romans 9:24)*

My Thought

Paul says in this verse, those God has called, the Jews and the Gentiles, that's all mankind. God is not willing that any should perish but know there will be those who do perish out of their own fruition. We are all given a chance to follow this excellent Path. Sad to say, many will not heed the call and will perish.

Your Application

You are called! What a wonderful time to just let that sink in. The Potter, the God of creation, the Highest Power of all, has called you. Think and ponder on that for a day or two or a lifetime!

> *As He says also in Hosea: "I will call them My people, who were not My people,*
> *And her beloved, who was not beloved." (Romans 9:25)*

My Thought

He came to set forth a family, but many of His original family (the Israelite Nation) rejected Him, so God decides to call those who are not His family (the Gentiles) into adoption. We may not be born into it nationally, but He adopted us into it through divine love. We are now His family. The Jewish nation despised the Gentile nation, we were not loved by them. We are cherished by the Father, who included us into His eternal plan. Thank you, Jesus!

Your Application

Have you ever felt left out? God will never leave you out. He is for the underdog and will always have room for you. Lift your head and rejoice; the King of Glory knows you and loves you anyway. Oh, so good! Read *John 10:16*, Jesus told his disciples about other sheep, who are they?

> *"And it shall come to pass in the place where it was said to them, 'You are not*
> *My people,' There they shall be called sons of the living God." (Romans 9:26)*

My Thought

A confirmation on the last scriptures, in the Old Testament, God foreknew that the Jewish people would reject Him, so He is already talking about bringing in the Gentile nation. That's us! We are on His mind; yes, He is in love with us and desired us from the beginning.

Your Application

You are desired and adored by the God of the Old Testament. So fierce and strict as He was, His mind was on you. The love of God is unfathomable. Just sit and savor in His love!

> *Isaiah also cries out concerning Israel: "Though the number of the children of Israel be as the sand of the sea, the remnant will be saved. (Romans 9:27)*

My Thought

Brothers and sisters, there will be the remnant of Israel, who will receive the salvation of Jesus. The Jewish people, because of unbelief, have chosen to be cut out. They are blinded until they recognize Jesus as their Messiah. A remnant will understand it, and we will be a part of their family, the bigger family of God. Oh, what a day that will be when we join together and rejoice over the grand master plan of our Father.

Your Application

Study a custom of the Jewish nation and talk with a Jewish brother today if you can and learn about him.

> *For He will finish the work and cut it short in righteousness, Because the LORD will make a short work upon the earth." (Romans 9:28)*

My Thought

As in Hosea's time, God will cut short His judgment on the earth. A thousand years to God are as a day (*2 Peter 3:8*). So, we have only been on the scene a few days, according to God. What seems long to us is short to God because He sees the beginning to the unending. The span of eternity versus the small fragment of time here on earth is minimal to God's understanding of time. It seems so long to us who are mere mortals, but to God, He is cutting the time short because of His mercy. His plan is awesome, and we must rejoice in His plans. He knows what He's doing when we are shrugging our shoulders, wondering what is going on. God has it all under control. What He started in the Garden He will finish, despite Satan putting a wrench in God's plans or us getting in the way! Rest in that.

Your Application

Do you ever begin to think it's taking too long? Remember this scripture and let it soothe your mind. He will finish the work; it's guaranteed. Read *2 Peter 3:8* and *Psalms 90:4*. Write out your thoughts.

> *And as Isaiah said before: "Unless the LORD of Sabbath had left us a Seed, We would have become like Sodom, And we would have been made like Gomorrah." (Romans 9:29)*

My Thought

Ah, if not for Jesus, the Seed, we would be destroyed like Sodom and Gomorrah. Doesn't that just touch your heart? If not for Him, we would be lost. His excellent plan for our lives is to give us a path to walk on, to know Him more. He is our way of escape. When the angels came to rescue Lot, the people of Sodom were not interested in being saved.

Your Application

Read the account of Lot in Sodom; if not for Abraham, Lot would not have been saved. Abraham interceded on Lot's behalf. Look at this scripture in *Genesis 18–19*. Write out what you can learn about making choices from this situation.

Present Condition of Israel

> *What shall we say then? That Gentiles, who did not pursue righteousness, have attained to righteousness, even the righteousness of faith;* (Romans 9:30)

My Thought

Faith is easier to accept when there is no law/religion involved. The Gentiles were not looking to be righteous. They recognized something different in Jesus and accepted Him more easily than the Jewish nation looking for a coming King/Messiah. The Jewish nation had a picture of what they thought He would look like, so they missed Him when He came. The Gentiles weren't looking, so when He came, it was easier to accept Jesus.

Your Application

Do you have expectations of Jesus? Do you think He should do things a certain way? When He doesn't, do you reject Him because He didn't do things the way you thought He should? Be careful not to put God in a box. Look at the Jews and learn a lesson.

> *but Israel, pursuing the law of righteousness, has not attained to the law of righteousness.* (Romans 9:31)

My Thought

Religion binds up. The Jewish people were introduced to the law and got caught up in the law. They did not understand that the law was the picture of Christ. They were looking so intently at the law; they missed the Law Giver. Many Jews today are still looking. The good news is that those chosen will see and become a part of God's Family.

Your Application

Don't let religion get in your way of seeing God. He is not small enough to be set in a box, so don't try. All scripture breathes God. Look for God in scripture. Do not look to scripture to prove God. He is the One who wrote the Book; there is no reason to prove the author of the Book. Get to know

Him through scripture, do not be religious about it. He desires a relationship with you. He is talking to you throughout the Book. Look for Him, and you will find Him (*Isaiah 55:6–9*).

Why? Because they did not seek it by faith, but as it were, by the works of the law. For they stumbled at that stumbling stone. (Romans 9:32)

My Thought

We will never find God through our good works. We can't work hard enough to ever be good enough to be righteous enough to be in His presence. Our Jewish family and we will stumble every time we try to enter into His presence by good deeds. Jesus said, "It is finished," as He took His last breath on the cross. So, He said it, we believe it, and it's settled. It is by faith, believing Jesus did it all, that we get to enter into an encounter with God. We believe what He says is true, and we, by faith, follow hard after Him.

Your Application

Do you seek hard after God? Are you pursuing Him? Are you working to get to Him? Are you trying hard to get His approval? You are approved by the sacrifice of Jesus on the cross. Faith is the avenue to get to your Father. Ask God to increase your faith today! Read *Hebrews 12*. What does this teach you about faith? Write it out.

As it is written: "Behold, I lay in Zion a stumbling stone and rock of offense, And whoever believes on Him will not be put to shame." (Romans 9:33)

My Thought

Why? Why would God lay a stumbling stone and a rock that would offend us? We are so easily moved by emotion. Look at the Jewish people when Jesus came into Jerusalem riding the privileged donkey, they praised Him and raised their voices to the King of kings, and yet a week later the same voices were screaming out vehement shouts of death as they yelled, "Crucify Him!" We need to be offended, and we need to stumble over the Stone. We need to be stopped in our tracks (like Saul being knocked off his horse) to be moved into a deeper understanding of what Christ did for us on the cross. It goes beyond reason and emotion. It only makes sense when we are tripped up and see through the eyes of our spirit. That's why He has to become a stumbling stone. It isn't that easy to accept; we have to be roused around to throw away our religiosity in order to replace it with His eternal plan. God, our Father, knew it had to be something more than a casual meeting, or we would be fickle like the Jews. We would call for Him to be King of our lives, and then when things changed, we would scream at Him to get out.

Your Application

How's your relationship with Jesus? Has He caused you to stumble? Has He offended you? If your answer is yes, then you are on the right path. Remember that Stone will either change you or crush you; it all depends on how you allow Him to affect you.

Romans Nine teaches us more about faith. It also shows us the passionate side of Paul. He so longed for his fellow Israelite to understand that Jesus was the Messiah he was willing to be cursed to death, cut off from Christ! In this chapter, we see that not all of Israel's people were God's children, but only those who responded. It is the same with the Gentiles. Through foreknowledge, God has chosen a remnant that will be His children. God appoints some to love and some to hate. He used Pharaoh as an example displaying Father God's power and spreads His fame throughout the kingdom. "So unjust," we call out. Only if we do not understand who God is. He is merciful, kind, loving, the just Judge, and all that is good. Why would He want to create anyone to destroy? He doesn't. He sees our future decisions, and He knows what we will choose. With that knowledge, He then displays us for His glory or demonstrates His power through the pharaohs of the world.

My Prayer

In the Old Testament, God, You speak of plans for the Jews and Gentiles to become part of Your family. We, who are Gentiles, may have thought that we were an afterthought after the Jews rejected Your Son, Jesus as their Messiah. We see in this chapter we were part of Your plan from the beginning! Paul understands the need to reach his Jewish brothers and so longs for them to get it; he says he would give up his salvation in order that the Jewish nation would come to know You, Jesus. Paul shows us what it looks like to have a passion for souls; unbelievable! As we go further into chapter 9, we see Paul explaining the justness of You, Father, in that You chose some for good and others for evil. In each case, You are still displaying Your glory and rightness. Why You would choose some for glory and others for judgment is confusing until we see that God, You, are the God of the future, and You know the intent and purpose of people's hearts. Father, You, are Sovereign and what You do is just. Always! In Your just Name. Amen.

Write a summary of chapter 9.

Why?
Why would God lay a stumbling stone before us
and a rock that would offend us?
It goes beyond our reason and emotion; it
only makes sense when we see
through the eyes of our spirit.

Our Worship
Wait On You / Elevation Worship & Maverick City
https://www.youtube.com/watch?v=K3TYG7Q_fj4

CHAPTER 10

Living A Question

Read the complete chapter of *Romans 10*

> *Brethren, my heart's desire and prayer to God for Israel is that they might be saved. (Romans 10:1)*

My Thought

Paul is talking with the Christians in Rome whom he has never met. He is restating to the Romans how much he desires his fellow Jews to receive Jesus as Messiah. Paul had been called to the Gentiles, kings, and then Israel, as we see in *Acts 9:15*, but his heart was for his fellow brothers. He so desired the Jewish people to understand that Jesus was the Messiah they were looking for. Sometimes prayer is the only thing you can do with your family, prayer, and being a silent example of Christ. God sends others to minister to our family members quite often and sends us to other people's family members.

Your Application

Are you concerned about a loved one? Leave them with Jesus. He knows your heart's desire. He will send someone their way to minister to them. Sometimes people just don't understand it, and the best thing you can do for that person you love is to follow Paul's example: love them and pray for them. Why don't you do that right now for someone you love and desire to see saved, and today, find someone outside your family who needs a good word spoken to them? You might just be the answer to someone else's prayer!

> *For I bear them record that they have a zeal of God, but not according to knowledge. (Romans 10:2)*

My Thought

The Jews were religious, they were zealous for the things of God, but they missed the Door (Jesus) of salvation, the coming Messiah, because they decided how He would come. Jesus stood before them, yet they had spiritually blind eyes and were unable to see Him. They lost focus and concentrated more on the letter of the law and missed the fulfillment of the law. They were looking for a conquering king. He came as a helpless baby. They missed Him.

Your Application

Do you miss Him? You may ask how? Are you religious? Have you set boundaries on what your Savior can and cannot do with your life? Do you follow rules and regulations over faithfully following God? Has He asked you to do something, but you didn't even hear because it was outside the perimeters of where you think God would be? Break religion; it binds up and stifles the spirit. Today go outside your boundaries of religion and do something you have never done before.

> *For they being ignorant of God's righteousness, and going about to establish their own righteousness, have not submitted themselves unto the righteousness of God.* (Romans 10:3)

My Thought

The Jews established what they thought was righteous, so when Christ's righteousness came and did not look anything like theirs, they rejected His! Sad to say, we do the same thing, especially those who grew up in the church. Rules and boundaries set by our church fathers led us down a slippery slope to find ourselves in ropes of religious bondage. We cast judgment on others who do not live within the limitations of our regulations. Doesn't that sound terrible? Even as I write it, it does not sound like the promised liberty and abundant life that Christ promised all who followed Him. How did we get so far off track? How did the Jews lose sight of their coming Lord, not even able to recognize Him? He comes unexpectedly to unexpected places. He still does that today. Jesus shows up in villages of unknown places and sets fire in the hearts of those who willingly accept His message. He shows up in hospitals in remote areas that no one has even heard of and heals the sick. He shows up on campuses through radical people who have lost all religious pretense and just love God with all their heart.

Your Application

Where is God showing up? Is He in your bedroom, in your school, your workplace? Where is God showing up? Be alert and look for Him today without religious limitations; let Him show up and show off!

> *For Christ is the end of the law for righteousness to every one that believes.* (Romans 10:4)

My Thought

When Jesus Christ came to this earth as a Person, He fulfilled and finished the law of righteousness through His death and resurrection. Now it's up to us to believe; if we do, the end of religion is ours: no more rules, no more regulations, and no more boundaries as we know them. There is one commandment, no, two: Love God with all your heart and love your neighbor. It sums up what Christ came to do. All the Old Testament laws were saying the same thing: "Be considerate!" but in an unattainable way. Christ entered to complete the law, break the bonds of religion, and give us abundant life filled with liberty, and yet some still walk in the law of righteousness. Why?

Your Application

Are you free? Have you believed and received the end of religion? Are you able to love your Lord freely and live in the *Storybook Fairy-Tale Reality of the Kingdom of God*? If yes, great—continue; if not, why not? What is stopping you? Ask God if you are still carrying a religious spirit. Ask God how to get rid of it. Read the book of *Galatians*.

> *For Moses describes the righteousness which is of the law, that the man which does those things shall live by them (Leviticus 18:5). (Romans 10:5)*

My Thought

Paul will take us through several scriptures to prove his point about the law and how we need to listen to the Law Defender (Jesus) and see how He made a way for us. In *Leviticus*, it says if your righteousness comes from the law, to live, you have to follow all the law. Impossible! *For the person who keeps all of the laws except one is as guilty as a person who has broken all of God's laws. For the same God who said, "You must not commit adultery," also said, "You must not murder." So if you murder someone but do not commit adultery, you have still broken the law. (James 2:10, 11)*

Your Application

Do you set unrealistic expectations for yourself or others? Righteousness by the law is religion. List areas in your life where you see signs of a religious spirit. Again, break the religious spirit off of you today and live by Jesus' grace by simply confessing and accepting His forgiveness. Ask Jesus how to live daily by His Spirit.

> *But the righteousness, which is of faith, speaks on this wise, Say not in our heart, Who shall ascend into heaven? (Deuteronomy 30:12) (that is, to bring Christ down from above:) (Romans 10:6)*

My Thought

The righteousness of faith is quite different from the righteousness of the law. The law expects you to keep all the commandments on your own. The righteousness of faith is satisfied with the works of Jesus when He came down from heaven and lived on earth. The righteousness of faith allows you to live freely under His covering because all requirements were completed. It's like someone coming in, taking our place, and completing our final exam for us, passing with flying colors, and now we have passed from the confinements of the school into the liberty of life.

Your Application

Have you accepted the righteousness of faith, knowing that you are no longer under the tutelage of the law, but now grace and freedom are your teachers? That is what our Lord is trying to tell us through Paul. Accept that you no longer have requirements to fulfill, only the debt of love. Love on your Lord today and spread His love to someone.

Or, Who shall descend into the deep? (Deuteronomy 30:13) (that is, to bring up Christ again from the dead.) (Romans 10:7)

My Thought

The righteousness of faith sent our Lord to the depths of death. The punishment for us, He took on, that we might have life. Why do we then set ourselves back in a prison of religion? God, our Father, must shake His head at our foolishness. The price being paid, we still linger in limbo because we try to live in our own righteousness.

Your Application

List ways you live in your own righteousness. What are things that you do that are religious? Do they make you more righteous, or do they lay a heavy burden on you? Read *Matthew 11:30*, ponder on it and set it to memory.

But what saith it? The word is nigh you, even in your mouth, and in your heart: (Deuteronomy 30:14) that is, the word of faith, which we preach; (Romans 10:8)

My Thought

The Word of faith is close to you, as close as your mouth and heart. It is a Word given to you from the beginning. In every one of us is a God voice that calls our name to share in His heritage. He has called, and it is up to us to respond. How do we hear the call? *Psalms 46* tells us to *"be still and know that He is God,"* amid catastrophes. It is up to each of us to be still, no matter where we are, and hear Him. He has promised to be near, so we need to be still and listen if we are not hearing Him.

Your Application

How often are you quiet, to hear the Lord speak to you in your heart? Take time today to be still. Read *Psalms 46* in its entirety and meditate on it. Ask for an encounter with your God.

That if you will confess with your mouth the Lord Jesus, and will believe in your heart that God hath raised him from the dead, you will be saved. (Romans 10:9)

My Thought

How does the righteousness of faith work? Confess and believe. Confess with your mouth out loud that Jesus is Lord of your life and believe in your heart that God raised Jesus from the dead, then you are saved from destruction. We are all headed for hell because we deserve it, but we can turn towards heaven by confessing Jesus and believing God! Amazing, I know! Our Father takes all the work out and only asks us to believe. Oh, yes, there is work to be done as we mature in our salvation, but in receiving salvation, there is only believing, no works involved at all.

Your Application

Do you work for your salvation, or are you just doing what scripture says—confess and believe? Consider for a moment what you do believe about this. Reconsider the price paid for you to only have to confess and believe. Doesn't it just make you want to give Him a colossal hug today? Hug someone as if they were Jesus!

> *For with the heart man believes unto righteousness; and with the mouth confession is made unto salvation. (Romans 10:10)*

My Thought

The heart and the mouth are the two objects God uses for us to receive salvation. Let's ponder for a moment: why? If He said with the feet, we walk into salvation, or with the hands, we work for salvation, we would gain the partial credit for work. The heart is the emotional part of our being. It takes faith or significant evidence to believe, so God set the heart to be part of our salvation. It says in *Luke 6:45*, *"Out of the abundance of the heart the mouth speaks."* Thus, the connection of heart and mouth. God is stating if our heart believes, our mouth will indeed confess it. Out of the abundance of the heart will flow out of our mouth, the truth of what we believe.

Your Application

Have you listened to yourself lately? What is your heart believing? What are you saying around others? Does it sound like you believe, or are you betraying yourself with your words? Take inventory of your heart. What's in there right now? Do you need to be washed over by the truth once again and walk in the righteousness of faith rather than the righteousness of the law? Confess and believe!

> *For the scripture says, whosoever believes on Him will not be ashamed (Isaiah 28:16). (Romans 10:11)*

My Thought

If we believe in Jesus, we will not be ashamed. Paul is dedicated to the scriptures of the Old Testament. He brings quite a few Old Testament verses in *Romans 10*. We, too, need to use scripture to make our case for others.

Your Application

If you believe in Jesus, then why not take scriptures to memory and use them next time you have a chance to share your faith.

> *For there is no difference between the Jew and the Greek: for the same Lord over all is rich unto all that call upon him. (Romans 10:12)*

My Thought

God, our Father, does not differentiate between races. He is open to receive all who come calling on Him. He has so much love and wants to give it away to those who choose Him.

God is wealthy in His love towards His children, He is not going to run out. He has lots of love to go around.

We are one big happy family of all nations, tribes, and languages!

Your Application

Do you differentiate between people? Do you judge people? Your Father does not want that kind of behavior in His kingdom. All are welcome, and He is training you to be accepting of all people. If you have a problem with a particular race or type of person, talk with your Father today and ask Him to show you His thoughts about them. Open your heart to the Holy Spirit and ask for more love.

For whosoever shall call upon the name of the Lord shall be saved (Joel 2:32). (Romans 10:13)

My Thought

Paul quotes Joel. Anyone who calls on the Lord will be saved. What good news that is for all of us, Jesus gives us a nonexclusive family. Open to all who will believe in their hearts that God raised Jesus from the dead and confess with their mouths Jesus Christ is Lord. Seems so simple, yet how many through the ages have stumbled over this simple belief?

Your Application

Why do you think this is such a hard pill to swallow? Why has God made it so simple to enter, and yet so many are confused, many are angry at what God asks of them? Take a closer look today at the values people around you put on God's ways. Do you think they understand the simplicity of entering into God's *Storybook Fairy-Tale Kingdom*?

How then shall they call on him in whom they have not believed? And how shall they believe in him of whom they have not heard? And how shall they hear without a preacher? (Romans 10:14)

My Thought

Paul, the missionary, will now go into his soapbox statements. He has brought us to see how easy it is to enter into the family of God, but he also makes an excellent four-point message: without a preacher, they will not hear; without hearing, they will not believe, and without believing, they will not call on Him. Each of us must share the good news of Jesus Christ in our own way every day. We must open our minds and hearts to readily speak the good news. If it's by simply smiling on gloomy days or sharing an encouraging word to the person you most dislike, or blatantly sharing the gospel of Jesus Christ to a stranger, it must be done for the sake of love. It can be done naturally supernatural as we depend on the Holy Spirit to direct our lives.

Your Application

What will you do today to walk out the three steps that Paul insists needs to be done in order to complete the family? Open your heart today to what the Spirit wants you to do. Drop all agendas of what you think it might look like and play a game with the Lord and let Him lead you into the joys of sharing your salvation with other kingdom members not yet calling on His name because they haven't heard so they couldn't believe! Increase the family of God today by opening your heart to others.

> *And how shall they preach, except they be sent? as it is written, How beautiful are the feet of them that preach the gospel of peace, and bring glad tidings of good things (Isaiah 52:7)! (Romans 10:15)*

My Thought

The fourth part of Paul's soapbox message is that no one will preach unless sent. So, let's check out Jesus' last words to His disciples and His family (that's us): He said to them, *"Go into all the world and preach the gospel to everyone,"* (Mark 16:15). We have been sent to preach the good news to everyone. So maybe some of us don't preach as well as others, that's okay. Let's check out the Greek word preach: Kerusso, which means proclaim, herald, or preach…so if we are not into preaching, then we can be proclaiming or heralding. The most important thing is that we are not keeping our lamps under a bushel (Matthew 5:15) but sharing what we have with others. In so doing, we are bringing our joyful message of peace to those ready to listen and we are inheriting a crown. *(For what is our hope, our joy, or the crown in which we will glory in the presence of our Lord Jesus when he comes? Is it not you? 1 Thessalonians 2:19)*

Your Application

It may be hard for you to share with others about your God because maybe you haven't done it lately or at all. The way to begin is to know what you believe. Write out what you believe in simple statements. By going through this study, you are sure to learn more about what you believe. As you set your beliefs into simple statements, now begin to share what you believe with others. You didn't ride a bike with ease the first time you got on (unless you are like my daughter, Ashley; a story for another day); it took a while, but soon you were peddling with confidence. The more you share what you believe, the easier it will get, and before you know it, you will be proclaiming it to the multitudes.

> *But they have not all obeyed the gospel. For Esaias saith, Lord, who hath believed our report (Isaiah 53:1)? (Romans 10:16)*

My Thought

Not all will obey, not all will respond, and not all will think of us as preachers with beautiful feet. That is not our concern; we are to be obedient in sharing and let God deal with each person's response. If someone rejects our words of truth, then we are to keep sharing with others. God will deal with the one who rejects Him. For some reason, not everyone will believe. It's imperative that we continue to share our good news until He comes back. We must get used to communicating with anyone who will listen.

Your Application

Have you been rejected by someone while sharing the good news? (Remember, it isn't you they are rejecting. It's Jesus.) Hold firm to what you believe and do not waiver in your faith. Read the account of Joseph's life in *Genesis 37, 39–50.* Write about the many times he was rejected, and yet he continued to share the good news. He kept his integrity and helped save the remnant of Abraham and all the peoples around Egypt.

So then faith cometh by hearing, and hearing by the word of God. (Romans 10:17)

My Thought

To increase our faith, we must hear the Word of God. For others to increase their faith, we must share the Word of God. The Word of God is not a list of dos and don'ts. It is living and active. *Sharper than any double-edged sword, it penetrates even to dividing soul and spirit, joints and marrow; it judges the thoughts and attitudes of the heart (Hebrews 4:12).* It is so important that we understand how necessary the Word of God is in our individual lives. We cannot receive the Word of God on a once-a-week or bi-weekly basis; we will starve. We have to develop a desire to be in the Word daily so we can receive our dosage of faith to continue in our relationship with our Father. The Word is active and living to grant us a deeper understanding of who our Father is. The Word is powerful to bring down strongholds set up against us. The Word is God, so if we want to know God, we need to be in the Word.

Your Application

Honestly, how often do you read the Word? This is a question between you and God. It's hard to start a new habit if you have never been a disciplined reader. Still, I guarantee if you set time aside daily to read your Word, you will gain a great deal of satisfaction and contentment in your life, with many more benefits of knowing God better.

But I say, Have they not heard? Yes verily, their sound went into all the earth, and their words unto the ends of the world (Psalm 19:4). (Romans 10:18)

My Thought

There will be a time when all will hear. *"The trumpet will sound and the dead in Christ will go first and then we which remain will be caught up with them in the sky and we will forever be* with the Lord," (*1 Thessalonians 4:16–17*)! Until that time, we must share the good news of the gospel of Christ!

Your Application

Consistent sharing is essential. Does that mean you have to be talking all the time? No. You can share the gospel by your good deeds. Why not do something today that shows the love of Jesus without words.

> *But I say, Did not Israel know? First Moses said, I will provoke you to jealousy by them that are no people, and by a foolish nation I will anger you* (Deuteronomy 32:21). (Romans 10:19)

My Thought

How did Israel miss the Messiah? Paul goes right back to his opening statements. He really does love His Jewish brothers. Then Paul rests in the scriptures. In *Deuteronomy*, Moses foretells that the Jews would be jealous of us, we (the saved Gentiles) would provoke them to anger because we believed in Him whom they rejected. Paul looks to scripture throughout this chapter and sees the faithfulness of God's Word. Paul saw that the Old Testament spoke of the Jewish nation missing out on the Messiah. The scripture told Paul a new breed of people would become God's family. Paul could rest in God's Word to be true.

Your Application

Is there something going on that is causing you to wrestle with the sovereignty of God? Do you question some events in your life or wonder why people don't understand it? Rest in the scriptures and know God is faithful to set all things in their place in the proper time (*Ecclesiastes 8:5, 6*). Today put the things you do not understand into the loving hands of your Father and find the peace and joy He has for you.

> *But Esaias is very bold, and saith, I was found of them that sought me not; I was made manifest unto them that asked not after me* (Isaiah 65:1). (Romans 10:20)

My Thought

Paul is now expressing the fact that God called us. We didn't seek Him, nor did we ask for Him. He just picked us to be the objects of His affection so He might make the Jewish nation jealous so that they would come back to Him. Does that mean God is using us to bring about His original choice? Yes, and aren't we glad. We were the objects of His affection; we receive the same inheritance as the Jewish nation and the same inheritance as Jesus, that ought to be good enough for us to be satisfied. He used a foolish nation to confound a self-thought wise nation.

Your Application

God uses the foolish things of this world to confound the wise (1 Corinthians 1:27); remember that next time you're feeling foolish. God sought you out, and God made Himself transparent to you. Many of the Jewish people today still do not believe. Take time today to pray with the same passion as Paul for their salvation.

> *But to Israel he saith, All day long I have stretched forth my hands unto a disobedient and gainsaying people (Isaiah 65:2). (Romans 10:21)*

My Thought

Ouch! The Word hurts sometimes, but truth is truth. We must accept the bruises the Word brings our way to make us better people. One day the Jewish remnant will believe, but for now, many are disobedient and in it for what they can gain.

Your Application

Where is the Word hurting you? Conform to the Word so that your character can be a light to those around you. Today be honest with yourself and allow the Word to hurt a bit. Read *1 Corinthians 13*. Where are you at regarding love? Don't try harder. Surrender more to the encounters of Jesus. Be still and know He is Father God, and He will supply all things to you.

Romans Ten Paul reiterates the need for Israel's salvation. They knew the law (rules and rituals) according to the Old Testament. They missed the fulfillment of the law. Paul sees their situation plainly, for he was once like them, living religiously in the law of Moses. Paul saw the truth, with his eyes open to who the Messiah was, he now longs for them to see Jesus in the same light. Paul believed with his heart and confessed with his mouth that his righteousness came from Jesus, not the law. Most of Israel would not see it that way. They rejected Jesus, so God went to the Gentiles, all planned before the foundation of the world, to make His people jealous to receive Him as the Messiah. God said to Israel, *"All day long I have stretched out My hands to a disobedient and contrary people"* (*Romans 10:21*). A sad ending, if it were the end. God, our Father, has a plan to bring His people back into the fold. As with each of us, if we wander off, God has a plan to bring us back to the truth of who He is and reminds us how much we need Jesus, for our righteousness comes from Him!

My Prayer

If we confess You, Jesus, as our Lord and believe in our hearts that Father, You raised Jesus from the dead, we will be saved! All who trust in You will not be disgraced. We, the Jews and the Gentiles, are all the same in Your eyes. We all have You as Lord. You give generously to all of us who call on You. How can we call on You unless we believe, and how can we believe unless we hear, and how can we hear unless we are told, and how can we be told unless someone is sent? So, the scripture says, *"How beautiful are the feet of messengers who bring the good news"* (*Romans 10:15*)! Send us, Lord. In Your saving Name. Amen.

Write a summary of chapter 10.

It may be hard for you to share with others about your God because maybe you haven't done it lately or at all. The way to begin is to know what you believe. Write out what you believe in simple statements. By going through this study, you are sure to learn more about what you believe. As you set your beliefs into simple statements, now begin to share what you believe with others. You didn't ride a bike with ease the first time you got on (unless you are like my daughter, Ashley, a story for another time!), it took a while, but soon you were peddling with confidence. The more you share what you believe, the easier it will get, and before you know it, you will be proclaiming it to the multitudes.

Our Worship
Promises (feat. Joe L Barnes & Naomi Raine) / Maverick City Music
https://www.youtube.com/watch?v=q5m09rqOoxE

CHAPTER 11

Living in Understanding

Read the complete chapter of *Romans 11*

> *I say then, has God cast away His people? Certainly not! For I also am an Israelite, of the seed of Abraham, of the tribe of Benjamin. (Romans 11:1)*

My Thought

God continues to love the Jewish Nation. They are His heart, His children, His country. He will not cast them away just as you would not deny a family member who is not living up to God's standards. We don't just throw people out; we love people back into their rightful place in the family. God has a plan for the Jewish nation that will call His children back to Him.

Your Application

Have you written off someone today? Are you still holding a grudge from months or even years back? Today open your heart to your Father God and ask Him to supply you with the love and forgiveness to let go of the memory. To grow in the Lord and live in the *Storybook Fairy-Tale Reality*, you must live according to God's standards. Read *Mark 11:25*. Live *Mark 11:25*. If you don't know how, ask God to help you, call or visit a friend who can help pray you through to victory. Victory is yours today. Don't wait to forgive; it's a waste of your precious time.

> *God has not cast away His people whom He foreknew. Or do you not know what the Scripture says of Elijah, how he pleads with God against Israel, saying, (Romans 11:2)*

My Thought

God already knew before He created Adam and Eve, and before He established His nation, Israel, they would reject His Son. Elijah was so upset with Israel that he pleads with God to punish them. Elijah saw their rebellion and wanted God to destroy them for not listening, and yet God knew beforehand and already made a way of escape for them. Such love of the Father! He is that way towards us as well. He loves us, He sees our rebellion and foolish ways, and yet, in our worst state, He planned for His Son to rescue us from ourselves. What an amazing God we serve!

Your Application

Do not have the eyes of Elijah, who could not see beyond his pain. He could not see what God had in store because he got in the way. He could only see from his point of view. Your point of view is not clear. You can only see so far, then it gets blurry. Today ask God to allow you to see that brother or sister that you don't get along with from His point of view. Open your eyes to see past you and into the perspective of your loving God. Read *Mark 9:38–41*; write what the scriptures mean to you. What was God trying to tell His disciples?

> *"LORD, they have killed Your prophets and torn down Your altars, and I alone am left, and they seek my life"? (Romans 11:3)*

My Thought

Okay, here is Elijah, in an exhausted state of mind. He is worn out and spiritually empty, so he believes what he is saying is true from his perspective. Let's look at the reference and see if it is. In *1 Kings 19:9–14*, we see that Elijah was running on his own strength, and we find him hiding in a cave, so God shows Himself to Elijah. In verses, 15–18 God also shows His plans to Elijah and the complete truth. Elijah said, *"Lord they have killed ALL the prophets..."* yet in *1 Kings 18:4*, Obadiah had taken a hundred prophets and hidden them in two caves. Elijah felt alone, therefore he spoke it as truth. His feelings were not the truth, but he believed them to be. God will show us the truth; are we listening? God uses our brother Elijah to show us an example of what not to do after partnering with God in some great act.

Your Application

Know that your feelings are not always right. You must not rely on what you feel; it will lead you into saying things that are not true, especially when you are exhausted. Read *1 Kings 8–9* to understand why Elijah felt the way he did. Also, read what Jesus often did to restore His spiritual self: *John 6:15, Matthew 14:23, and Luke 5:16.* He went into the Father to go out to minister, then back into the Father to go out, to go in to go out to go in. Always end with going back into the Father!

> *But what does the divine response say to him? "I have reserved for Myself seven thousand men who have not bowed the knee to Baal" (1 Kings 19:18).* (Romans 11:4)

My Thought

God is so awesome. He didn't get caught up in the fact Elijah lied, He just spoke the truth. He knows the insecurities of man. He isn't shocked or angered by our sins, folks. He just kindly tells the truth to Elijah. I love that! How many times do we hear parents getting so mad that their child has lied instead of stating the truth first? What a perfect example of God's parenting! "Elijah, son, I have seven thousand men. You are not alone!" God spoke divinely to His son what he needed to hear.

Your Application

God will speak to you the same way. You may talk about 'feelings' that are not true. Your Father will speak the truth to you in a loving, caring manner. Not only that, but God also showed Himself to Elijah when he was in the depths of despair. Look for God when you are hiding or not feeling so well. He will show up for you too! Today, if you feel a bit down, how about reading some truth: *Matthew 11:28-30.*

> *Even so then, at this present time there is a remnant according to the election of grace. (Romans 11:5)*

My Thought

Back to the Jewish nation, there is a remnant! Our Jewish brothers and sisters are out there. Some already get it, and some will understand Jesus is the Messiah very soon. We who do believe in Jesus must pray for their salvation. It pleases the Father's heart that we come together in unity to acknowledge His Son.

Your Application

Do you pray for our Jewish brothers and sisters? Let that be a part of your daily prayer. Today open your heart to pray for the lost. Share your faith today with someone.

> *And if by grace, then it is no longer of works; otherwise grace is no longer grace. But if it is of works, it is no longer grace; otherwise work is no longer work. (Romans 11:6)*

My Thought

It is grace that gives us the Promise. We did not do anything to deserve it. There are not enough works for us to do to receive such a priceless Gift as our Savior. Paul is so clear; it is Jesus, period. Nothing else can be added to this. Our efforts are futile. Our works are ineffective. Our credit for receiving Jesus is zero! It was all Jesus, nothing but Jesus, and that is all we can say about this. Why is it so important to Paul and our Father that we get this? We are selfish children, and if there is any credit that can be had, we will find it. We read our Bible, fasted, and prayed for two weeks, so therefore God loves us. No. We were selfish, sinful, and prideful all the time; in spite of that, God loves us! Yes, no works can give us this, only a perfect, incredible, everlasting, and unlimited love from a Father who wants a relationship with us. He did it all. All we have to do is accept it. Believe and receive.

Your Application

Are you taking any credit for your righteousness, right standing before God? Repent and move into the freedom of knowing you are loved in your worst state, and there is nothing you can do about it. Today, rest in that perfect love and hang out with your Father; it will make Him so happy!

> *What then? Israel has not obtained what it seeks; but the elect have obtained it, and the rest were blinded. (Romans 11:7)*

My Thought

There are a few Christian Jews that understood, like Paul, the apostles, the others who believed, and received in *Acts*. A continued few receive Jesus as the Messiah, but of all, most were blind. There will be a day when all who are elected will come to the saving knowledge of Christ Jesus. When that happens, the Father will see the completeness of His plan. As it is in heaven, it will be on earth! What a day of rejoicing that will be, when we all see Jesus; we will sing and shout the victory!

Your Application

God doesn't fear the state of His Jewish nation, nor does He condemn them. He rests in the plot of heaven and the timing of His plan and knows it will all come to pass. So, do not fret over an unsaved loved one. Just love them, and in the timing of our Father, it will all come to be. What does worry do for you? Nothing! What does faith do for you? You live in peace and freedom, knowing God has it all in His hands. Just pray for that loved one with passion, have compassion towards them, and rest assured God's will, will be done!

> *Just as it is written: "God has given them a spirit of stupor, eyes that they should not see and ears that they should not hear, to this very day" (Deuteronomy 29:4; Isaiah 29:10). (Romans 11:8)*

My Thought

The Israelites were into the laws of Moses and kept them to show their elite status. They were so focused on the law that they missed the fact the law was just a shadow of the coming Messiah. The Fulfillment of the law showed up, and they missed Him. Anyone looking for Him would have found Him (e.g., the disciples, Simeon, Anna, even Nicodemus) by remembering what Old Testament scriptures said. The Jewish people saw all the miracles in Egypt and the desert, yet they still couldn't see who was right in front of them. They did not understand; their eyes were blind, and their ears deaf to the things of God. Before we get carried away about how the Jewish nation missed Him, we too can be the same way. We can see the miracles of God, we can know His faithfulness, and when hard times comes our way, we too, like our Jewish brothers and sisters, are without understanding. We have ears that do not hear and eyes that do not see.

Your Application

Has God given you a spirit of stupor today? Are your eyes not seeing and your ears not hearing? Look into scripture today and find Jesus. Let the scripture talk to you in the voice of God. The Word is active, alive, and breathing out Jesus. Do not let the Word escape you by just reading it out of duty or curiosity; find Jesus in scripture today.

And David says: "Let their table become a snare and a trap, a stumbling block and a recompense to them. (Romans 11:9)

My Thought

David is talking about the Jewish people. What is their table? A table is a sign of eating and fellowship. It could be the altar of God, or it could mean their daily bread. Whatever it represents, the Holy Spirit, who knows all things, inspires David to write an imprecatory (praying a curse or punishment) psalm towards the Jewish people who reject Christ. When we live this life as though eating, drinking, and being merry is all there is, we curse ourselves. When we put more stock on this life here and now and less on the times to come, heaven, then we set up for ourselves a snare, a trap; we stumble on the very life we are living because we think what we see is all-important. We will be recompensed for how we lived this life.

Your Application

How often do you allow the blessings of God to become a snare? Do you see the benefits and gifts of God as something you own? Do you take the blessings of His presence for granted? Check out your attitude. Compare it to the Jewish people who took advantage of their blessings and didn't even see their Messiah. Today tell Jesus that you know He exists, and He has given you all good things. Read *James 1:17*, write out what it means to you. Write a prayer of thanksgiving to Jesus and write out who He is to you. Acknowledge that He is the Messiah that has come, and He is the One whom you wait for, to return a second time!

Let their eyes be darkened, so that they do not see, and bow down their back always" (Psalm 69:22, 23). (Romans 11:10)

My Thought

The imprecatory Psalm continues to show the consequence of rejecting Christ. They do not see what is right before them, and they are bowed down with the burden of looking for the Messiah, who has already come. Unbelief is a great evil. It's like seeing but closing your eyes to the evidence of the reality of the Person you are looking for. It's like being burdened with the "ever searching" for the Person who was promised. The Messiah has come, and yet our Jewish brothers and sisters are still looking. Can we be guilty of this? Although we know Jesus is the Messiah, do we hear Him tell us something and ignore it because we'd rather not do it? Do we close our eyes to the sorrow of the world or look the other way? How are we any different when we reject His will for us?

Your Application

Take a hard look at yourself today. Are you like your Jewish brother or sister whose eyes are closed to the goodness of Jesus? Do not curse yourself today by closing your eyes to the calling and blessings of God. Acknowledge that you have a purpose right now, look to Jesus for the things He wants you to do. You are here for a reason; ask Him, then live it out. Take time today to be quiet before the Messiah, look at Him, and listen to Him. He has good things to say.

> *I say then, have they stumbled that they should fall? Certainly not! But through their fall, to provoke them to jealousy, salvation has come to the Gentiles.* (Romans 11:11)

My Thought

What? God is attempting to make the Jewish nation jealous because of the Gentiles? God's plan is perfect. He knows what He is doing. He calls His own, but His own accepted Him not, so He calls out to the Gentile nation without law or knowledge, and many received. The Jews looked down on the Gentiles, so God used the very people whom the Jews thought were an inferior race to become the family of God. The One the Jews rejected will come back for His chosen people, but for now, it's the time of salvation for the Gentiles.

Your Application

Do you consider God unfair if He calls the Ted Bundys of the world to salvation? Have you decided in your heart who can and who cannot be saved? Be careful. Today consider your theology, is it up to date with God your Father, or are you still living by the world's standards? God is not willing that any should perish. Read *Luke 23:39–43*. Write out your thoughts. Look up who Ted Bundy is, write out your opinion of the end of his life.

> *Now if their fall is riches for the world, and their failure riches for the Gentiles, how much more their fullness!* (Romans 11:12)

My Thought

The coming home of the prodigal was incredible. The son left the father with all his inheritance, yet the father gave him more when he came home. The Jewish people have great things to look forward to. God, the Father, is ready to lavish His love on His people on the day of their return! They rejected Jesus, and the Gentiles were given a chance to choose to decline or receive Him. Although there are Christians who are Jewish, when that time in church history is over, the Jewish nation will be given another opportunity to receive their Messiah! The fullness of the family of God will be complete, and we will live happily ever after. Until then, we must pray in as many lost souls as possible and share the gospel of Jesus Christ.

Your Application

Is your heart concerned about the lost, the fallen, and the failed? You are to have the heart of God, and His heart was that none would perish. Today, ask God to lead you to someone who is lost, release the truth of the love of God on them. Read *Acts 8*.

> *For I speak to you Gentiles; inasmuch as I am an apostle to the Gentiles, I magnify my ministry,* (Romans 11:13)

My Thought

Paul was called to be an apostle to the Gentiles, to kings, and his Jewish brothers and sisters. Paul had more grace over his Gentile ministry than he did over the Jewish nation. He had far more converts in the Gentile regions than he did with his own race. So, Paul says he will call attention to his ministry to the Gentile nation if it helps lead his descendants to Jesus.

Your Application

Again, sometimes you have to focus on what God has put before you and leave your real concern, the lost ones of your own family, to Jesus. Today write out all your family and friends who are not saved yet, put them between the pages of your Bible, and believe for their salvation.

> *if by any means I may provoke to jealousy those who are my flesh and save some of them. (Romans 11:14)*

My Thought

Paul believes in the elect of God, so he states that some of them will be saved. Paul is also stating with God his intentions of making the Jewish people jealous by extending his hand towards the Gentiles. He does what he can and leaves the rest to God.

Your Application

Sometimes, you have to leave the one you love alone, in that you do not harp on them anymore about being saved. You just go on speaking to others about the goodness of God, you share your testimony with others, and you create an atmosphere of "jealousy" (leaving your loved one alone) and focusing on others whom God puts in your path and leave the ones you love to God. Just love those in your inner circle who don't know God and let God do the work of saving them. Learn from Paul. Today do something special for your loved one without mentioning anything of God. Read the book of *Esther* and let it be an example to you. Count how many times God was mentioned in *Esther*!

> *For if their being cast away is the reconciling of the world, what will their acceptance be but life from the dead? (Romans 11:15)*

My Thought

God cuts the Jewish nation off the Vine and grafted in the Gentiles, so a chance would be given to enter the *Storybook Fairy-Tale Kingdom* and be reconciled to Father God. If God made a way for us to come into sonship who were not His chosen race, how much more will God make a way for the Jewish nation to once again, with eyes wide open, accept His generous offer to live in Him. We should never decide God is finished with a person because they have gone too far. God's grace reaches beyond our imaginations. God's grace is a wonder to be admired but never understood!

Your Application

Have you given up on someone? Check out the scripture again. God does not give up on His people. Neither should you. Keep on praying and believing that God's grace can graft back in the one you think is hopeless. God specializes in impossible things. Today, praise God for being so gracious and then say a prayer for someone that the Spirit puts on your heart. Look up the word, "grace," and write its meanings. Write what you are thankful for about grace.

> For if the first fruit is holy, the lump is also holy; and if the root is holy, so are the branches. (Romans 11:16)

My Thought

This Vine, which is Jesus, is holy; therefore, the whole of the Vine, the roots, the branches, the fruit, and the clump of the Vine are all holy. The Vine is complete in and of itself. Anything added to the Vine is holy not because the branches are holy but because they have been grafted into holiness. Once touched by the Vine, we become holy because we now belong to Jesus, and He is holy. A fine concept to bring to the table next time shame wants to wrap itself around us. We are holy, not when we are perfect, but we are holy when we accept Jesus and separate ourselves from our sins. Jesus and holiness become connected to us. "Be holy as your heavenly Father is holy," (Matthew 5:48).

Your Application

Holiness is not a spooky word, and it's not a "holier than thou" word; holiness is being separated from the world, your flesh, and sin. Holy is wholeness. It's simply saying, "I accept Jesus, and I am going to spend the rest of my days knowing Him. I am not interested in the things of this world anymore, and my flesh can take a hike because I'm happily connected to my Master Jesus."
Read some scriptures on holiness and get a better idea of what it means. *1 Peter 1:15, 16; Leviticus 20:26;* check a few more. Write an essay on what you thought holy meant and what it means to you now.

> And if some of the branches were broken off, and you, being a wild olive tree, were grafted in among them, and with them became a partaker of the root and fatness of the olive tree, (Romans 11:17)

My Thought

In the description of the Gentile race, some of the Jewish branches were broken off because of unbelief, so some of the wild olive tree branches (us) could be grafted in among the Jewish branches. The two nations become one in Jesus. We eat of the fullness of Jesus' inheritance. *Ephesians 2:11 Therefore, remember that formerly you who are Gentiles by birth and called "uncircumcised" by those who call themselves "the circumcision" (which is done in the body by human hands)— 12 remember that at that time you were separate from Christ, excluded from citizenship in Israel and foreigners to the covenants of the promise, without hope and without God in the world. 13 But now in Christ Jesus you who once were far away have been brought near by the blood of*

Christ. 14 For He Himself is our peace, who has made the two groups one and has destroyed the barrier, the dividing wall of hostility...

Your Application

You are a part of a great big, wonderful family. We squabble, fight, get jealous, do silly things to hurt each other, but we also share an inheritance, we love, we sing, and we look forward to our "Coming King." That's what a family does, but you are part of this crazy family. Reach out to someone today and share a bit of your family history and your kingdom Family history.

do not boast against the branches. But if you do boast, remember that you do not support the root, but the root supports you. (Romans 11:18)

My Thought

This is a great scripture to remember when getting ready to brag about anything we do. We do not support the root system. Our gifts, our abilities, our treasures all come from the Father in heaven. He supports everything in us. He supports us. We don't have any bragging rights when it comes down to it. It's all Him. It always has been, it always will be. When we realize we are grafted into the Vine and the Vine supports us, and without the Vine, we are nothing, we then change our opinion of ourselves and the Vine. We move and breathe and have our being because of the Vine. So, when the other branches are hanging out with us, we have nothing to boast about since we are all here because of the sacrifice of Jesus Christ

Your Application

Whatever floats your boat in boasting, God has just sunk it because there is no boasting allowed in the kingdom. You are to give homage to where it is due. Jesus, our King, is the One to whom we can and must boast about, always. Today in your travels, boast of the goodness of your Lord.

You will say then, "Branches were broken off that I might be grafted in." (Romans 11:19)

My Thought

The truth is branches (Jews) were broken off because of unbelief, and we (Gentiles) are grafted in because of faith. Others lost out, and we won a place in the kingdom. Chosen by Jesus, we rule and reign. We need to realize the significance of this. We took the place of others that could have remained on the Vine. We belong to a royal priesthood. Our roots are of royalty and holiness.

Your Application

Take time today and realize who you are. Ponder how you got here and be thankful that you are a grafted-in branch. Read *John 15* and write an essay on being a branch in the Vine.

Well said. Because of unbelief they were broken off, and you stand by faith. Do not be haughty, but fear. (Romans 11:20)

My Thought

Most of the Jewish nation was broken off the Vine, why, because of unbelief. It happens to be a trait of theirs. Moses was held back from the Promised Land because of unbelief. The Israelites went into captivity because of unbelief and disobedience. The Jewish nation missed Jesus because they didn't believe He was the Messiah. We believe by faith that Jesus Christ is the Son of God, and because of that faith, we are grafted into the Vine. Don't think we are so great in our faith but stand in awe that if God can cut off His people, He will not stop in cutting us off as well, if we stand in pride, thinking it's us that got us here.

Your Application

Humble yourself, stand in awe of the One who got you where you are at today. Know that God is not a respecter of people. He will give to His Son those who bow low and recognize how great Jesus is.

> *For if God did not spare the natural branches, He may not spare you either. (Romans 11:21)*

My Thought

That's a strong word for those who use cheap grace. "I can do whatever I want to do; I am saved." Really? This scripture tells us that if Father God didn't spare His own natural family, He won't always contend with us if we continue to cheapen His grace with our sinful ways. Grace carries authority with it; if you use it for your good, you can end up losing it.

Your Application

If you are a policeman and you flash your badge around every time you want to get places for your good, it will get around that you are neglecting your authority, and eventually, it will be taken away. The same is true with your salvation. If you think grace is your cover and you use it each time you willfully sin, there will be a day grace won't spare you. Be cautious that you appreciate the gift of grace. God isn't threatening you with grafting you out; He is a loving Father, and He's warning you, "If I didn't stop at taking out my own because of their unbelief, I wouldn't stop at taking you out because of pride."

> *Therefore consider the goodness and severity of God: on those who fell, severity; but toward you, goodness, if you continue in His goodness. Otherwise you also will be cut off. (Romans 11:22)*

My Thought

The character of God is stated here. We must realize He is good, and He is severe. He is love, and He holds wrath. He will rescue, and He will destroy anyone holding onto sin. He is gentle, and He is harsh. To those who are married to sin, God will destroy them both. To those who love His Son, God pours out His goodness on us. Here's the thing: if we discontinue loving His Son, God will cut us off. He's not kidding. God is not Santa Claus, just passing out gifts. God has come to give us Jesus, and how we treat His Son is how He will treat us (*Matthew 21:33-46*). He is good and wants to share His goodness with all who hold His Son up as King/Messiah; to all else, they will be cut off the Vine and cast into the fire.

Your Application

Please, understand that God is not a force to be reckoned with; you do not want to be a sinner in the hands of an angry God. You need to understand that God is not playing games here but that He is searching for those who will adore His Son. He wants to start a family who lives eternally and is looking for those who want to live forever, worshiping, loving, and living with King Jesus. Read *Deuteronomy 32:28-47* and *Isaiah 66:4*; what is God's character here? Does it seem like God is not playing games? Is He justified in His actions? What is God telling you today? Read *Matthew 21:33-46* and write down your thoughts.

> *And they also, if they do not continue in unbelief, will be grafted in, for God is able to graft them in again.* (Romans 11:23)

My Thought

Paul is actually happy to write this verse. He so longs for his fellow Jews to get it and be grafted back into the True Vine. God can graft back into the Vine that which He took out. God is excited to bring back into the family those that were there in the first place. He desires that all come into the family, for He is not willing that any should perish. Hell was never intended for humanity, only Satan and his followers. Those who did not believe, but have a change of mind and heart, will be grafted back in and saved from hell.

Your Application

Are you thankful to be grafted into the Vine? Pray for those who are grafted out to believe and be brought back into the family. Read *Isaiah 60* and report on your findings. What is God's character in verse 10?

> *For if you were cut out of the olive tree which is wild by nature, and were grafted contrary to nature into a cultivated olive tree, how much more will these, who are natural branches, be grafted into their own olive tree?* (Romans 11:24)

My Thought

The Jewish nation will return home to their Father and His Son. The chosen generation will finally drop their unbelief, their eyes will be opened, and they will openly acknowledge their Messiah. What a great day that will be.

Your Application

Pray for peace for Jerusalem (*Psalms 122:6*). Ask Father to quicken His time to come and take us all unto Himself. Until that time, be assured that Jesus' name will be spoken of throughout the nations. Take some time today and learn about the return of the Jews to Israel.

> *For I do not desire, brethren, that you should be ignorant of this mystery, lest you should be wise in your own opinion, that blindness in part has happened to Israel until the fullness of the Gentiles has come in. (Romans 11:25)*

My Thought

God set a time for the Jewish nation to understand His plan of salvation and accept the prophetic words pointing towards their Messiah, Jesus. After that time was up, God set the Gentiles' time into motion to believe and accept Jesus by faith, which is called church history. This time will come to an end when the rapture takes place (1 *Thessalonians 4:16–18, Revelation 1–4*), and it will once again be time for the Jewish nation to recognize their Savior (*Revelation 4–22*). It's important as citizens and children of the family of God that we know the signs of the times. It is our heritage, and we must learn it and not be ignorant of our family lineage and culture.

Your Application

Read up on all you can to understand the Lord. The scripture was given to us to know God more. We are also gifted with many sons and daughters of the faith that express God's heart so well. Dig deep into their wells of knowledge, never stop learning about the things of the Lord, these efforts will remain forever.

> *And so all Israel will be saved, as it is written: "The Deliverer will come out of Zion, and He will turn away ungodliness from Jacob; (Romans 11:26)*

My Thought

Does this mean all who are of Jewish descent will be saved? No: *In other words, it is not the natural children who are God's children, but it is the children of the promise who are regarded as Abraham's offspring. (Romans 9:8)* It says all who are Jews are not children of God, but only those who are of the promise. It does mean all who are predestined will be saved. The Deliverer, Jesus, will cleanse unrighteousness and save the tribes of Israel.

Your Application

Name the twelve tribes/sons of Jacob/Israel and tell something of each tribe.

> *For this is My covenant with them, when I take away their sins"* (Isaiah 59:20, 21).
> (Romans 11:27)

My Thought

God has promised to take away their sins and deliver them. God's promises are yes and amen (2 *Corinthians* 1:20), so we can be confident that if it's here in scripture, that is what will come to pass.

Your Application

If God has given you a promise, hold on to it, and don't let doubt or circumstances cause you to waiver. What promise has God given you? Write it out and paste it where you can see it.

> *Concerning the gospel they are enemies for your sake, but concerning the election they are beloved for the sake of the fathers.* (Romans 11:28)

My Thought

Confusing—they are enemies, and they are beloved. The Jewish nation is an enemy to God because of disbelief in the Messiah, so for our sake, they became enemies to graft us into the family. On the other hand, they are beloved for the sake of Abraham, Isaac, and Jacob. The promise God gave to them will be fulfilled.

Your Application

Read *Revelations* 7 and 14. Who are the 144,000?

> *For the gifts and the calling of God are irrevocable.* (Romans 11:29)

My Thought

What God sets into motion, no one is capable of stopping. Hear this loud and clear. No demon, no angel, no man, and no force can stop what God says will be. There will be scoffers; there will be mockers, and there will be deceivers, but it does not take away the truth of God's Word. It only enhances it. Why are so many angry at something if there were no truth to it? It would be ignored and left for nothing. God's gifts that He has given to you are irrevocable, and His calling He has on you is unchanging. We must recognize that what God has given us and where He has called us will come to pass, so why fight it. Give in to this Most Holy God and allow what He has destined to come sooner rather than later.

Your Application

Do you know the gifts God has given you? Do you know that you are called for such a time as this to do something wonderful? If the answer is no, then search until you know; ask the Holy Spirit to reveal these things to you. Read *Proverbs 25:2*. Read *Psalms 139*. Read *Jeremiah 29:11*. Read *1 Corinthians 12:7–11*.

> *For as you were once disobedient to God, yet have now obtained mercy through their disobedience,* (Romans 11:30)

My Thought

Mercy, we cry mercy, for those who are disobedient, that they would have time to repent and be saved, even as we have received mercy and are saved. There are many perishing because we have not shared the gospel. The Good News is so important. We must register in our beings that one of our sole purposes here on earth at this specific time is to share the good news of Jesus Christ. Jesus' last words to the church were: *"…But you will receive power when the Holy Spirit comes on you; and you will be My witnesses in Jerusalem, and in all Judea and Samaria and to the ends of the earth"* (Acts 1:8).

Your Application

Check out these places: Jerusalem, Judea, Samaria, and the ends of the earth. What do the names mean? Where are they, and why are they important enough for Christ to mention them? What does "witnesses" mean in this passage? Do a verse study and show what you find.

> *even so these also have now been disobedient, that through the mercy shown you they also may obtain mercy.* (Romans 11:31)

My Thought

Mercy is a beautiful word, and God does show it quite frequently. Again, the concept of disobedience of one group allows acceptance to another. So, when the accepted group receives mercy, the Jewish people in time might obtain mercy for their disobedience, knowing for their sake we are saved. We are indebted to the Jewish nations, and for that, we should be grateful and connected to them emotionally and spiritually.

Your Application

How are your feelings towards the Jewish nation now that you understand their part in granting your salvation? Deepen your roots by understanding more of their culture. Study their festivals and ceremonies and write out the ones that impressed you the most.

> *For God has committed them all to disobedience, that He might have mercy on all.* (Romans 11:32)

My Thought

All have sinned. All have come short of the glory of God. The Jewish nations didn't reach the finish line; they got off track and disobeyed the truth. The good news is, all that disobeyed can all have mercy. His mercies are new every morning (*Lamentations 3:22–23*), great is His faithfulness, where sin does abound grace does abound even more (*Romans 5:20*).

Your Application

Take a moment to understand the generosity of the Lord, your God, whose loving-kindness leads us to repentance (*Romans 2:4*). Oh, what a great God we serve. Now, you can see why Paul writes the next few verses. Take a moment while you read it and allow your spirit to align itself with His Spirit…

> *Oh, the depth of the riches both of the wisdom and knowledge of God! How unsearchable are His judgments and His ways past finding out! (Romans 11:33)*

My Thought

No one can fully know or understand our God. He is the Bright and Morning Star, and He lavishes His love on us; He is the Just Judge, our Counselor, Prince of Peace, our Stronghold, our Tower whom we run into and are safe. He punished our sin with His own body and separated us from our sin as far as the East is to the West! He is the First and the Last, the Beginning and the End, we do not need to fear for He is always near us, He is good, He is love, and He only teaches us what it best. That is only a shadow of who our God is; we will never truly understand our God until we see Him face to face!

Your Application

Look up descriptions of Jesus and God, our Father, and write them out. Carry it along with you on your phone, in your wallet, purse, or backpack, whatever you bring with you wherever you go. When you have downtime, instead of looking at social media, go over who your God is. Refresh and encourage your soul. It pays eternal dividends!

> *"For who has known the mind of the LORD? Or who has become His counselor?" (Isaiah 40:13; Jeremiah 23:18) (Romans 11:34)*

My Thought

When mockers and scoffers try to dissuade you of your Father, use this scripture to stand against their sway and use it as an arsenal toward the enemy. God's mind is far beyond the smartest of our most intelligent people who have ever been born. No one can counsel our God. He is all wisdom. He has all the answers, and He solves all problems. The mind of God is beyond our small frame, but in all that He is, He loves us. We are His children.

Your Application

Say your scriptures of description out loud. Listen with your ears who God is. Let it settle deep into your soul. The more you know Him with your mind and heart, the more you will be involved in the *Storybook Fairy-Tale Reality of the Kingdom of God.*

> *"Or who has first given to Him and it shall be repaid to Him?" (Job 41:11) (Romans 11:35)*

My Thought

God does not owe humanity anything. God has always been. Everything we have was given to us from God. He is the First and Last, all eternal. He does not need to repay anyone for anything. Everything He has is His. Everything He has, He has given it out of love to us. He longs for a relationship with His created beings. No one gives to God first that he should repay God. He is the everlasting Giver. We owe God. We owe Him a debt of gratitude that we cannot even repay.

Your Application

You are never in a shortage or famine when you live with your Father. He said he would supply all your needs according to His riches in glory (*Philippians 4:19*). Next time you're feeling a bit in need, go to the bank of His Word and fill up on His promises.

> *For of Him and through Him and to Him are all things, to whom be glory forever. Amen. (Romans 11:36)*

My Thought

Amen to our God, who gives us all things that are His. All glory and honor and blessings and praise will be raised to our Lord, *Revelation* tells us. Once we fully see the plan of our good God, we will bow at His feet. We will be amazed at how all things were working out for us to have an eternal home with Him and how all things were working for His glory.

Your Application

Rejoice today that your name is written in the Lamb's Book of Life. Write out a prayer of praise of your own to tell your Father how much you love Him.

Romans Eleven develops our understanding of God's relationship with Israel. It shows us God has not rejected Israel. In His kindness and grace, undeserved favor, God has remained faithful. This is God's character no matter what else we may hear or see. We base all of whom God is on His Word. He is good, He is love, and He only teaches what is best. God made salvation available to the Gentiles to entice His people to come into covenant with Him. Paul was an apostle to the Gentiles; he wanted the Jews to be jealous of what the Gentiles had, a relationship with their Messiah. He longed for the Jews to see that since they were cut off the Vine, their return would be that much sweeter!

My Prayer

Jesus, You, are not willing that any should perish, You long for all to come to You. The plans You have for all humankind are good. Please open the eyes of our Jewish brothers and sisters so they may understand who You are. You are their Messiah, and You love them. Lord, could You bring salvation to those we love who have left You or never met You? Could You bring them to a saving knowledge and acceptance of who You are? Thank You for all You will do and all You do in Your mighty and gracious Name. Amen.

Write a summary of chapter 11.

What God sets into motion; no one is capable of stopping it.
Hear this loud and clear.
No demon, no angel, no man, and no force can stop
what God says will be.
There will be scoffers, there will be mockers,
and there will be deceivers,
but it does not take away
the truth of God's Word.
It only enhances it,
because why would so many be so angry at something
if there were no truth to it.

Our Worship

For the Cross / Brian and Jenn Johnson
https://www.youtube.com/watch?v=VMrTj5Vg2k4

CHAPTER 12

Living a Reformed Life

Read the complete chapter of *Romans 12*

> *I beseech you therefore, brethren, by the mercies of God, that you present your bodies a living sacrifice, holy, acceptable to God, which is your reasonable service.* (Romans 12:1)

My Thought

Paul strongly suggests that we present our bodies as a <u>*living sacrifice*</u> to God. We are to give our whole selves, flesh, and spirit, and soul to God. What is holy and acceptable, our bodies only? Nope. What is holy and acceptable is the sacrifice we give to God, our bodies, our flesh, our desires, our plans, and agendas. We offer up our spirits to God as a living sacrifice, which is a reasonable thing to ask. It is a service we can decide to do. It is reasonable because of what God did for us through Jesus Christ.

We were spared death on Christ's behalf.

Now, with that in mind, we give our bodies, alive, as a sacrifice, and that sacrifice will be holy and acceptable to God. The only way we can offer ourselves as a living sacrifice is as God gives us the ability... "*by the mercies of God...*" So even in offering our bodies, it's entirely because God provides us with the ability to do it. We just have to be willing.

Your Application

How do you offer your body as a *living sacrifice*? The Old Testament sacrifice was slain, blood-drained, and put on the altar to be consumed by the fire. How do you do that and live? Jesus Christ was slain on our behalf. His blood was drained from His body, so what is left for you to do? Let the fire of the Holy Spirit guide you daily. No longer do you call the shots, but you willingly allow the Spirit of God to decide for you what will happen to your life. Your agenda is burned up at the altar, and you take on the incredible destiny God has for you. Through surrendering your will to Him, reading His Word, and speaking to Jesus every day, you alter your life to follow Him; that is what a living sacrifice looks like. Are you ready?

And do not be conformed to this world, but be transformed by the renewing of your mind, that you may prove what is that good and acceptable and perfect will of God. (Romans 12:2)

My Thought

When Christ came to the earth to declare the kingdom of God, He came up against the pressure to conform to the religious leaders' ways. He came to break the rule of man and show a new way. We are conflicted every day to choose to live by the world's standards or to live by the kingdom of God. They are exact opposites. The world says take care of yourself, get ahead no matter the cost and do it your way. The kingdom tells us to have no other gods before us and look out for our fellow brothers. Our mind and heart are the keys to which way we will follow. If we have made ourselves a *"living sacrifice,"* then we are no longer our own, and the renewing of our thinking is transforming us. We don't think the old way anymore; we are thinking about God and listening to Him. When you renew your mind to think about and follow after Jesus, then you show the good and acceptable and perfect will of God.

Your Application

Renewing your mind is hard. Renewing your mind is the key! Do you want the good and acceptable and perfect will of God in your life? Work at renewing your mind. Meditate on His Word, actively know what you are thinking, and learn to pray/talk to God without ceasing.

Serve God with Spiritual Gifts

For I say, through the grace given to me, to everyone who is among you, not to think of himself more highly than he ought to think, but to think soberly, as God has dealt to each one a measure of faith. (Romans 12:3)

My Thought

Paul, through God's grace and his own experience, is saying to all of us, "Don't think too highly of yourself." Paul, when he was Saul, being a Pharisee, persecuted the Church of God and killed the saints for their faith in God. Saul thought too highly of himself, standing in place of God, to decide who would live and who would die. Paul is warning us not to go to that place of judgment, not to think of ourselves better than anyone else. Paul tells us to think seriously about who we are in Christ. We need to remember verse one of this chapter; we offer ourselves as a continual *living sacrifice*. We can no longer think of ourselves as better than others. We must see others as Christ did. He loved them so much. He bled and died for them, as well as us. God has given each one a measure of faith. God has given each one of us a place in Him. We should rarely think of ourselves and be transformed by renewing our minds to have our thoughts conformed to His thoughts.

Your Application

Training our minds to have thoughts towards heaven and not all about us is essential and our mentality should be to help others when we have the grace and faith to do so. Learning to live in our *Storybook Fairy-Tale Reality of the Kingdom of God* will help us. When you think of living in a kingdom world within this world, you learn to live by the kingdom's rules of love. What would that look like to you? Write your thoughts.

> *For as we have many members in one body, but all the members do not have the same function, (Romans 12:4)*

My Thought

Everyone is not going to do the same thing, but we all belong to the same kingdom. Our loyalties lie with Christ, and our abilities are set from heaven to further the kingdom. As we have our eyes on Jesus, we are able to serve in the capacity to which He has called us, which is different from what He has called our fellow brothers and sisters. We each have a particular gift given to us, and we must be responsible to serve our Father in the gift He has given us. We must be concerned that we do exactly as the Father has directed, even when it is different from others.

Your Application

Follow God in your gifts and services. Do not follow man. God will direct you in what to do. As in a symphony, you will play your own instrument, but as the Body of Christ each plays their part; it's a symphony of sweet music to our Master's ear. Your desire is for our Master to be pleased with what you do.

> *so we, being many, are one body in Christ, and individually members of one another. (Romans 12:5)*

My Thoughts

There are so many of us forming one Body in Christ, and we are all part of each other. We are individuals who are to be one in Christ. This is where the renewing of the mind is ever so necessary. We can get caught up in looking at what someone else is doing in the kingdom and become so distracted that we don't do our part; or we feel our position is minuscule to others who seem to be doing so much more. We need to realize as we renew our mind that what we are called to do, be it seemingly small or large, is precisely what the Father has asked us to do. We must do it to the best of our ability. Individuals who become one is a kingdom phenomenon that can only be explained in Jesus' death, burial, and resurrection. It's only as One gives up His life for many that many can become one in Him.

Your application

As you daily believe that Jesus wants you to be an individual who submits to Him (you are a *living sacrifice*) and not only to Him but to one another in the kingdom, you will be part of this unity. Looking out for others is a high priority in the kingdom. Practice that today.

Having then gifts differing according to the grace that is given to us, let us use them: if prophecy, let us prophesy in proportion to our faith; (Romans 12:6)

My Thought

The symphony is an excellent example of this verse, having different instruments according to what talent we each have, then we use them to create beautiful music together. If we are gifted in the saxophone, we play the saxophone to the best of our practiced ability. We in the Body of Christ have different gifts. We must use our gifts that are given to us to the best of our practiced ability. Spiritual gifts need to be practiced; just as musical instruments need to be.

Your Application

First of all, what are your gifts? If you do not know, ask God and your leaders. Once you know your gifts, practice it. Use it. Learn how to further the kingdom with your gifts. The kingdom needs your gifts. Don't covet another's gift. Improve your gifts. Read *1 Corinthians 12*. Take the spiritual gifts test: https://giftstest.com/test

or ministry, let us use it in our ministering; he who teaches, in teaching; (Romans 12:7)

My Thought

For example, if one plays the piano, then play it. If one plays the drums, then drum. In other words, what God has given us the spiritual ability to do, do it. We can't just sit on our gifts; if we did, there would be no music, no unity. We have to use our gifts for the furtherance of God's kingdom.

Your Application

Are you a prophet? A minister (one who loves to serve others)? A teacher? Do you naturally exhort or encourage? Are you a giver? Are you a leader? Do you show mercy? Whatever your gift, use it as if you are serving the Lord. Use your gift wisely and often.

he who exhorts, in exhortation; he who gives, with liberality; he who leads, with diligence; he who shows mercy, with cheerfulness. (Romans 12:8)

My Thought

Each gift, like a symphony and its instruments, adds to the fullness of the Body of Christ.

Your Application

Today, use your gift to help someone. Write about it.

Behave Like a Christian

> *Let love be without hypocrisy. Abhor what is evil. Cling to what is good.*
> *(Romans 12:9)*

My Thought

God needs our love to be real. We can act like we love someone and then talk about them behind their back. God is telling us to love genuinely. How? As we renew our mind, as we daily bring our bodies as a *living sacrifice*, we begin to understand that holiness and purity come from leaving our old thought life and our old ways at the cross. When we renew our minds, every day we become more like Jesus and less like us.

Your Application

Today, practice renewing your mind. Ask God for the Mind of Christ (*1 Corinthians 2:16*) and the Heart of God (*Acts 13:22*). Ask Him for the Fruit of the Spirit (*Galatians 5:22–23*) and the gifts of the Spirit (*1 Corinthians 12*). Write the scriptures out and meditate on them.

> *Be kindly affectionate to one another with brotherly love, in honor giving*
> *preference to one another; (Romans 12:10)*

My Thought

Not thinking too highly of ourselves brings us the ability to prefer others over ourselves. Being kind is a character trait of our Lord.

> *As we hang out with Him in the Word and in prayer,*
> *we tend to become kind-hearted.*
> *Brotherly love with kindness is intense love.*

Your Application

Look up David and Jonathan's love in the Old Testament. Jonathan gives us a perfect example of this scripture. Write out your thoughts.

> *not lagging in diligence, fervent in spirit, serving the Lord; (Romans 12:11)*

My Thought

Let us not be lagging in our pursuit of the Lord. Don't let a day go by without diligently seeking His face. As we are fervent in our spirit to seek after the Spirit of the Lord, we will be serving the Lord.

Your Application

There is great reward in seeking the Lord. Take each day as an opportunity to know Him more. Diligently seek to know Jesus and with that fervently serve the Lord daily. You will never regret the times you do.

> *rejoicing in hope, patient in tribulation, continuing steadfastly in prayer;* (Romans 12:12)

My Thought

As we daily rejoice in hope (the expectation of coming good), as we are patient in tribulation and as we continually stay steadfast in prayer, we will become the warriors God intends us to be. Being a Jesus follower is not an easy or simple undertaking. It is usually a broken person who comes to Jesus; we need a Savior, but it takes a person of courage, boldness, and tenacity to decide to keep following Jesus. Many people call themselves Christians, but a real follower of Christ is willing to live out *Romans*, chapter 12. Not an easy pursuit, but well worth the energy. Knowing Christ, really knowing Jesus, and having His Spirit in us, helps make *Romans 12* a doable chapter. Without the knowledge of Jesus and His Spirit, it's not likely a person can rejoice in hope or be patient in tribulation or even stay steadfast in prayer; ask the disciples of Jesus.

Your Application

What did the disciples do when Jesus was arrested (*Mark 14*)? Check it out. Then look at how they endured tribulation after Jesus' ascension. Look up and write out how each of the 11 disciples died. It's amazing the transformation they each had. They finally believed what Jesus was saying to them in the three years He walked with them. After Jesus' Spirit of truth came in them, they didn't scatter; now, they were willing to die for Him.

> *distributing to the needs of the saints, given to hospitality.* (Romans 12:13)

My Thought

A mirror is given to us in verses 10–21. These verses reflect our Lord while on earth, and the verses give us an example to live by. We are to see the needs of our fellow brother and sister in Christ and be hospitable whenever necessary.

Your Application

Take these first twelve verses and memorize them and set them as Christ's standard of how you should live. Dedicate your life to living them.

> *Bless those who persecute you; bless and do not curse.* (Romans 12:14)

My Thought

Ouch! This may be a hard verse to swallow, but Jesus isn't just saying this is a good thing to do if you can. He is saying, as He did on the sermon on the Mount, to live this verse. Those who persecute you are to be blessed by you, not cursed. When you curse those who persecute you, you are only showing what is inside of you. You still have your flesh (remember *living sacrifice*?) acting out its ugly self. When Christ was persecuted and wrongly accused, He spoke not a curse but a blessing. What came out of His mouth showed what was in His heart, purity, and holiness. We need to learn to fill our hearts with God so that when we are persecuted, we too can bless and not curse.

Your Application

Out of the heart the mouth speaks. If you are cursing those who persecute you, then it is a "you" problem, not a "them" problem. Ask God today to show you your heart. Does it need to be cleansed and renewed? God will happily change your heart if you are transformed by renewing your mind/ thoughts (prayer and studying the scripture). Read *Matthew 5–7* in one sitting. What stood out to you?

Rejoice with those who rejoice, and weep with those who weep. (Romans 12:15)

My Thought

How often do we rejoice when others lose things, and we weep when others get ahead? Jesus said, as you prefer your fellow brother and sister, we will weep with those who weep because our compassion and mercy will be like His. Jesus said we will rejoice when others get ahead because we will prefer our neighbor above ourselves. Think of what a beautiful world that would be. It will be one day!

Your Application

Why don't you take a look at your attitude? Do you get angry or even weep silently when others get ahead? Someone else got a raise and you didn't? Do you silently rejoice when bad things happen to someone you think had it coming? Look up the word *Schadenfreude.* Again, it's time for heart surgery. God will change your heart if you are transformed by the renewing of your mind through the scriptures. God has a method to His madness or really what we think is madness. He wants us to be unlike the world and more like Him.

Be of the same mind toward one another. Do not set your mind on high things, but associate with the humble. Do not be wise in your own opinion. (Romans 12:16)

My Thought

As we renew our minds, we can be of the same mind towards one another. As we each seek to know Jesus, be filled with the Spirit, and lay our lives down as a *living sacrifice*, we can be of the same mind. As we walk in this way, we can easily not set our minds on high things. We are no longer interested in getting ahead; we now want to know how we can help others get ahead. We are not interested that others hear our opinion, but we want them to hear and understand God's truth! What a beautiful world this could be if we each learned to live this way.

Your Application
Today, listen to yourself. Really listen. Do you cause strife, being opposite of what others are saying? Do you set your mind on higher things? Do you want to hang out with the humble? Are you always quick to give your opinion? Just take a mental test on how well you live verse 16; if you pass, excellent. If not...do you think it's time to walk out verses 1 and 2?

> *Repay no one evil for evil. Have regard for good things in the sight of all men.*
> (Romans 12:17)

My Thought
The character of a person sits in this verse. If we can repay good when evil is done to us, then we have learned a great deal of Jesus Christ and His life. We have learned why He came and for whom He died. This is a tough thing to ask of anyone, yet Christ does not ask it without showing us how to live it. He paid for that evil that we are not to repay. He paid with blood, wounds, and allowing Himself to be unjustly punished for something He never committed. The evil done to you and me, the evil you and I have committed, is covered with His blood. Now He asks you, and He asks me, can you not repay that evil because I have already taken it on My Body? Oh, if we could only understand this concept, we would live so differently.

Your Application
Today, let go of revenge. Have regard for good things for this person. Impossible in your own strength but re-read the crucifixion and see how Jesus responded to His accusers. Jesus is an amazing example, but not only an example; He took that evil done to you and put it on Himself. Jesus is telling you, don't repay that evil because it's covered, now let go. As you do, He settles your heart with His peace.

> *If it is possible, as much as depends on you, live peaceably with all men.*
> (Romans 12:18)

My Thought
Ah (with a chuckle), as we understand the last verse, we can understand how Paul asks us to live at peace with all men. We can do our part to live peaceably with all when we know the cross.

Your Application
Who is under your skin right now? Who bothers you and irritates you? Place them under the blood and forgive them and live at peace. Is it really that simple? Yes, it is. Just do it. Write about it.

> *Beloved, do not avenge yourselves, but rather give place to wrath; for it is written, "Vengeance is Mine, I will repay," says the Lord. (Romans 12:19)*

My Thought

We think finally, you are speaking my language, "Get them, God!" Paul is telling us not to repay evil for evil. Here in this verse, Paul says, don't avenge yourselves. He is telling us that God will repay. How will He repay? In love. God will forgive the person who has done us evil. God will welcome this person into His kingdom. Not a good thought, right? Well, God is not willing that any should die, not even the one who did evil to us. However, God will not make anyone accept His Son, Jesus. Those who have done evil to us—if they decide to walk in the way of the world, choosing not to believe in the Son of God—their consequence will be eternal damnation.

Your Application

When you look at it that way, you still may be saying, "Good, they deserve it!" Okay, you are right, they do, but so do you. God loved us while we were in sin. We all deserve eternal damnation, but God made a way for all of us to reconcile to Himself. You must understand this if you are to free yourself from the evildoer. God wants you to be free, and God wants you to let go and live at peace. How? Look at the next verse!

> *Therefore "If your enemy is hungry, feed him; If he is thirsty, give him a drink; For in so doing you will heap coals of fire on his head (Proverbs 25:21, 22)."* (Romans 12:20)

My Thought

Finally, God is thinking our way. If we do all this kindness towards our enemy, then God will pour fire on his head! Great, we can understand that language. Feed our enemy, give him a drink, and in so doing, we will harm him by heaping coals of fire on his head. Do we get to harm our enemy? Does God mean to sincerely give our enemy food and drink? Can we answer that question?

Your Application

Forgive, and you will be free to do to your enemy what God asks you to do. Be transformed by the renewing of your mind. Look up what "coals of fire" meant in the Old Testament (https:// dailygoodies.wordpress.com/2010/01/04/heaping-coals-of-fire-a-figure-of-speech/). You might be surprised. Write about it.

> *Do not be overcome by evil, but overcome evil with good.* (Romans 12:21)

My Thought

If we are evil like our enemy is evil, how are we any different? But if we feed our enemy and give drink to our enemy, we have overcome our hateful retaliation, and we have overcome the evil done to us by our enemy with God's goodness. The basic need of all people, good or evil, is love and nourishment. God is saying when we renew our mind, as in verse 1, then, and only then are we able to be mature enough in Christ to see God in all that touches us, even when evil men and women do us wrong. We can live at peace, for we know God is looking out for us.

Your Application

Try it today. What do you have to lose?

Romans Twelve tells us to give our bodies over as a *living sacrifice*. We should not follow the patterns of the world but be transformed by the renewing of our minds through the reading of the Word and following the Spirit of God who lives in us. We belong to each other in the Body of Christ as much as our body parts make one whole body. We are to love others as we love ourselves. We are to honor each other. What an amazing world it would be if we lived this chapter! At least the Body of Christ should try. Sinners would flock to enter God's kingdom. If we are persecuted, we are blessed; that's kingdom ways. We rejoice when the Body of Christ is rejoicing, and we weep when others weep. Revenge is not ours, so we return our vengeful hearts to God and trust Him to take care of any offense.

My Prayer

Father God, You are awesome in love and deed. You sent Jesus to live here on the earth as an example of how we are to live. Jesus, when you ascended into heaven after Your death and resurrection, You sent the Holy Spirit to live in us and teach us how to fulfill the Word of God. By reading Your Word daily, with the power of the Spirit, we can learn to renew our minds and be transformed into our new life. Thank You for leaving us gifts of the Spirit. Help us know what our gifts are and show us how to utilize them to further your kingdom. Help us to live in unity and to love our enemy. Lord, help us today to live in the newness of what You have for us. Help us live in the *Storybook Fairy-Tale Reality of the Kingdom of God* so that we can live differently from the world. Renew our minds, reform our lives, and revive our hearts today so we can treat our fellow man kindly and graciously, in Jesus Name! Amen.

Write a summary of chapter 12.

Not thinking too highly of ourselves brings us the ability to prefer others over ourselves. Being kind is a character trait of our Lord.
As we hang out with Him in the Word and in prayer, we tend to become kind-hearted.
Brotherly love with kindness is intense love.

Our Worship

Refiner / Chandler Moore & Steffanie Gretzinger
https://www.youtube.com/watch?v=UGFCbmvk0vo

CHAPTER 13

Living Under Authority

Read the complete chapter of *Romans 13*

> *Let every soul be subject to the governing authorities. For there is no authority except from God, and the authorities that exist are appointed by God. (Romans 13:1)*

My Thought

God, our Father, created everything. He is in charge of everything. We know that God, our Father, had given Satan authority over this earth after Adam and Eve gave up their title deed to planet earth through their disobedience to His ways. Still, even the control Satan has is limited and under the strict eyes of our Father, especially after Jesus died and rose again. Jesus conquered death and the grave, so Satan is limited to what he can and cannot do. Remember Job. In *Revelation*, the title deed of the earth goes back to the proper hands, Jesus'. Until that day, we live in a world of sin, temptations, and tragedies, a world with a mixture of good and evil. Nothing happens without our Father knowing about it. So, every leader set in place and taken down is under the appointment of God. Yes, Hitler, the Pharaohs, and all leaders, contrary to God's ways, have been put in authority by God. What does that tell us about our lives? God has a plan more significant than we think. His ways are higher, and His thoughts are not our thoughts.

Your Application

Today, look into the different infamous leaders and see if you can find a higher purpose in their leadership. Check out Hitler. Do you see the favor other countries had on Israel because of the holocaust and what happened? God is not unjust, even if it seems like it. He is Love, He is Good, and He only does what is best! Write out your findings.

> *Therefore whoever resists the authority resists the ordinance of God, and those who resist will bring judgment on themselves. (Romans 13:2)*

My Thought

We are subject to all authority, for God has appointed each one, so we are to obey the laws of the land and to follow our given leader. Does that mean if they are evil leaders like Hitler, we are to give into immorality? No! *But Peter and the other apostles answered and said: "We ought to obey God rather than men (Acts 5:29).* We are to follow our leaders until they forsake the Word of God. They would not bow down to the idol of the king. The Lord had appointed that king, yet the Three Hebrew Boys did not obey him when the king asked them to do something God did not permit. We are to know the Word, so we understand what is permissible and what is a definite law against our Lord.

Your Application

Today, read of the Three Hebrew Boy and look into Daniel's story. What law did Daniel disobey, and what consequence did he suffer? The end days are coming, and you need to be ready to suffer for the Name of the Lord Jesus. Would you, today, be willing to be thrown into a fiery furnace or be thrown into a lion's den? Meditate on this serious subject. If you are not ready, ask your Father God to help you.

> *For rulers are not a terror to good works, but to evil. Do you want to be unafraid of the authority? Do what is good, and you will have praise from the same. (Romans 13:3)*

My Thought

If we obey the laws of the land, we have no reason to worry or be afraid. Given rules and regulations to keep clear boundaries, seems apparent, yet it is in the Word, so our Father God is being a good Father, reminding us to keep the laws and not be afraid of our leaders.

Your Application

What are some ways you may not be keeping the law of the land? Today ask the Lord if you have offended Him by not taking a particular law seriously. Even if everyone else doesn't keep it, what does the Word say?

> *For he is God's minister to you for good. But if you do evil, be afraid; for he does not bear the sword in vain; for he is God's minister, an avenger to execute wrath on him who practices evil. (Romans 13:4)*

My Thought

Most leaders are ministers of God for your good. Let's look at pastors. God has appointed them, and if we don't like everything that goes on in a church, we are to pray for our leaders and not speak against them. We are to pray for God's conviction and strength to be put into them. The Lord is against those who speak evil against one of His leaders, even if that leader is wrong.

Your Application

Today, take a look at *1 Samuel 24*. What did God say to David when he cut the hem of King Saul's garment? Even though King Saul was a carnal king, God had protective boundaries for him. What does that tell us today about our pastors and presidents? Be very careful. Write out what God is saying to you through this verse.

> *Therefore you must be subject, not only because of wrath but also for conscience' sake. (Romans 13:5)*

My Thought

We are God's children, and we must be an example of our Father, so He says don't only obey because we don't want to get in trouble, but do good because we represent our Father, and we should be morally correct even when we do not agree with all the laws.

Your Application

Think about times you have obeyed out of fear and not out of conscience's sake. Allow the Word to tenderize your conscience so you will be more sensitive to His Spirit. Write ways you can become more sensitive to His Spirit and the people around you. Ask the Lord if your spirit needs a bit of adjustment to His Spirit.

> *For because of this you also pay taxes, for they are God's ministers attending continually to this very thing. (Romans 13:6)*

My Thought

The IRS is a pain to everyone who has to pay taxes. We would rather put our money elsewhere. Isn't it funny that our Father had to put this specific law in the Word? He could have put any law here, but God knows our affinity towards money and knows we would have a hard time here. How many honestly don't pay their taxes, cheat on their taxes, or are angry every time April 15th comes around? We can all laugh, but it is an irritation to most. God, our Father, says that the IRS are God's ministers. Ha! We wouldn't call them that; we probably call them our thorns in the flesh! God's Word is God's Word, and even if we don't like it or agree with it, His Word is the final say, and as His children, we must submit.

Your Application

Today, ask God to open your eyes to His ways and ask Him to allow you to pay your taxes without irritation because He has told us to do it. What are other things that annoy you that you can begin to give to God and allow Him to change the way you think about them? Another chance to renew your mind! God is a God of order. Also, pray for the IRS workers to not take personally what so many people think of them.

Render therefore to all their due: taxes to whom taxes are due, customs to whom customs, fear to whom fear, honor to whom honor. (Romans 13:7)

My Thought

God is trying to teach us an important lesson. Money is just that, money. Don't get caught up in money. Render to them what is due. We are to obey and pay our taxes and customs (government fees) when they are due. When we let go of our money to obey the laws of the land, God will take care of us and actually repay us in other ways for our good attitude and obedience. We are to fear (reverence) those over us and honor those put in places of honor, such as our President. We may not like whomever is in office, but we are to honor the title of that office in whom he/she sits.

Your Application

Do you pay taxes? Do you pay your customs? Do you show reverence toward those to whom it is due? Do you honor those in power over you? Ask these questions honestly to yourself because sometimes prayers are not answered, and you wonder, "why"? Could it be that you are walking in disobedience because you are not submitting to God's ways?

Love Your Neighbor

Owe no one anything except to love one another, for he who loves another has fulfilled the law. (Romans 13:8)

My Thought

Speaking of money, the Father is now going to be direct in His ways. He says, owe no one anything— no debts, except that of love to one another. God, our Father, is teaching us a valuable lesson. Don't think too highly of money, and don't use money to obtain things you can't afford. Live within your allowances. If we set our mind to loving God and loving our neighbor, we will fulfill the law and be content.

Your Application

Do you place money as a status quo? Are you important because you have money? Are you walking around in debt? Stop now and allow the Word of God to soak into your spirit. Your Father wants you to be free. If you are in debt, look into ways of paying off each debt and be set free to live in the boundaries of what God has for you. He wants to give you His daily Bread from heaven, and He has lots of resources. Take the time to look up scriptures on the Bible's outlook on money. Write a comparison paper on how well your attitude and behavior of money differs from the scriptures.

For the commandments, "You shall not commit adultery," "You shall not murder," "You shall not steal," "You shall not bear false witness," "You shall not covet," and if there is any other commandment, are all summed up in this saying, namely, "You shall love your neighbor as yourself." (Romans 13:9)

My Thought

If we love, we live within all the commandments. We won't commit adultery if we love, we won't steal if we love the one we would steal from, etc. We would not do this to ourselves, so if we love others as we love ourselves, we will please God. It's that simple in words, but it is tough to love everyone; most people have a hard time. It is not easy for us, but it is easy for our spirit when we connect to God's Spirit. We must learn to connect every day to His Spirit and His ways to live in the complete fullness of His will.

Your Application

Do you love others as you love yourself? Why is it hard to love? Take time to think about this and see if you can't find an answer. Be honest. Now write out how you can change.

> *Love does no harm to a neighbor; therefore love is the fulfillment of the law.* (Romans 13:10)

My Thought

Out of the more than 600 laws from the Old Testament, the 11 laws from *Amos,* and the three laws from *Ecclesiastes,* Jesus narrows it down to 2 in the New Testament when He states that we should love God with all our heart, soul, mind and strength and love our neighbor as our self. In so doing, we have fulfilled the law of Christ. In fulfilling the law of Christ, we are free, happy, content, and understand the laws of our *Storybook Fairy-Tale Kingdom.*

Your Application

Take the time to read *Galatians 6:2.* What does it tell you to do? Jesus knew that if we looked to Him more than ourselves and looked to others above ourselves, we would find true fulfillment. Are you fulfilled? Are you content? Check out who you prefer first, you, Christ, or others?

Put on Christ

> *And do this, knowing the time, that now it is high time to awake out of sleep; for now our salvation is nearer than when we first believed.* (Romans 13:11)

My Thought

Paul is reminding us about the times we live. He was telling the Romans that the time of salvation is closer now than when they first believed. If Paul is warning the Romans about the times, how much more should we understand the times?

Your Application

Read *Matthew 24.* See how many of these things have come to pass or are happening now. You see, the time of the Lord is here, and you must take the Word of the Lord very seriously. Awaken to His

Spirit! Now is not the time to sleep. It is time to get ready for the return of our Lord. Write out the events that have taken place already.

> *The night is far spent, the day is at hand. Therefore let us cast off the works of darkness, and let us put on the armor of light. (Romans 13:12)*

My Thought

There seems to be a time when we can play in the kingdom of God and be lukewarm, but not today. Today is the day to understand we cannot play games in the kingdom. Our *Storybook Fairy-Tale Reality* is real, and we must take our King seriously when He tells us to put away the deeds of darkness and live in the light, His light. Living for Him is not for the weak of heart. It is for those who know His love and who are not ashamed of Jesus or His gospel.

Your Application

Check out where you stand with your Savior. Are you dabbling in the darkness? Do you love Him when it's convenient? Are you ashamed of His gospel, the very act of your salvation? The night is over, and the day is here for you to stand for what you believe. Is it hard for you? Ask your Father, and He will give you the faith and the strength to stand.

> *Let us walk properly, as in the day, not in revelry and drunkenness, not in lewdness and lust, not in strife and envy. (Romans 13:13)*

My Thought

Love overcomes all evil. When we love, we will overcome all the sins that live in us. We cannot live in darkness and light. We must choose to walk in His light and to live in His love. All darkness must leave us as we choose to walk in the light of His love.

Your Application

How often have you used light to dispel your problems? I'm not talking about revealing all your bad to anyone, but have you let the light of God's Word expel the darkness of your life? Today check out His light and ask Him to push away the wrongs in your life. Ask Father to illuminate His truth to you. Write about what you've discovered. Now share it with someone else (not your bad, but how Father can dispel all darkness with His beautiful light).

> *But put on the Lord Jesus Christ, and make no provision for the flesh, to fulfill its lusts. (Romans 13:14)*

My Thought

Oh, what a good Word, but how do we put on Jesus Christ? The answer is in the verse. Who is Jesus Christ? He is LORD in this verse. So to put Jesus Christ on, we must allow Him to be LORD. The meaning of Lord, according to Dictionary.com, *"is a person who has authority, control, or power over others; a master, chief or ruler."* Do we allow Jesus Christ to call the shots? Does He get to have authority over our decisions? Do we allow Jesus Christ to control us and have power over us? Is He our master, our ruler? If any of the answers to those questions are "No," then we have not put on the Lord Jesus Christ. If our answers are "Yes," then we are given the strength to overcome our lusts by making no provisions for our flesh.

Your Application

Is Jesus Christ Lord of your life? How do you know? Do you struggle with lust in your life? By lust, I mean, "I want it now!" That is what lust is, wanting something now without thinking of the consequences. Do you struggle with something in your life? Good, you are human. Do you give in to the temptation of the struggles in your life? Then He is not Lord of your life. Read Joseph's trials in *Genesis 38-50*. He had struggles, but he didn't give in to them. He is a fine example of letting God be Lord over him. Make Him Lord today; you will expel the darkness and live in His wonderful Light!

Romans Thirteen gives us some practical insight into how to live in peace and harmony by obeying the laws of the land, praying for our leaders and paying taxes. God has chosen the leaders we have. Living a peaceful life under their authority is what God asks of us. Don't owe anyone money, but only owe a debt of love. As we remove our dark deeds and walk in His light, we can remember His coming is imminent, so be ready and waiting for Jesus.

My Prayer

God, you have given us leaders to rule over us. You have placed them in their position, help us honor them and pray for our leaders, and submit to the laws of our land. Help us to pay our taxes, even when we don't want to. You are the God of wonder and awe! We love You. Show us how to be debt-free and only owe our neighbors a debt of love, Your love. Create in us a love for our neighbor to "do no harm" as Your commandments state. The time is coming for Your return. Find us watching and waiting for You. What a day that will be when we see You for the first time. Keep us away from the darkness of evil and remind us to stay in Your beautiful light. We choose to make You our Lord today, in Your mighty Name. Amen.

Write a summary of chapter 13.

So, to put on Jesus Christ, we must allow Him to be LORD.
The meaning of Lord is a person who has authority,
control, or power over others, a master, chief, or ruler.
Do we allow Jesus Christ to call the shots? Does He get to have
authority over our decisions?
Do we allow Jesus Christ to control us and have power over us?
Is He our master, our ruler?

Our Worship
Here Again (Extended Version) / Live / Elevation Worship
https://www.youtube.com/watch?v=zfLcdBuB7NY

CHAPTER 14

Living in Freedom

Read the complete chapter of *Romans 14*

The Law of Liberty

Receive one who is weak in the faith, but not to disputes over doubtful things.
(Romans 14:1)

My Thought

This chapter is all about tolerance. Being able to see from others' perspectives and accepting their different ways. When I was younger, I was taught a strict religion; anyone not adhering to this way was "going to hell." As I grew and matured in the Word, I found Jesus speaking a different theme. He said, "Receive the one who is weak in their faith." This means to love on them and don't let their weakness (or our presumed strength) cause disputes. As we listen and love, we can do more good than condemning and excluding others with different opinions.

Your Application

Is there someone who bothers you today because they see Jesus in a different light than you? Sit and listen to them. Accept them even if you do not agree with everything they say. God does not want us to have silly disputes, but Satan does because it can separate us from each other. If the conflicts aren't involving Jesus as King and Lord, they probably aren't that important. Tolerance and openness are the keys as long as you know the Word and where you stand in your relationship with Jesus. Never let anyone influence you into believing a different gospel! Read *Galatians 1*. Paul was adamant about knowing what you believe and sticking with it. Write out what the chapter has taught you.

For one believes he may eat all things, but he who is weak eats only vegetables.
(Romans 14:2)

My Thought

Ah, vegetarians are weak? Not so. Back in Bible times, meat was offered to idols, so vegetables were the safer route for the Jews so as not to offend the law. Jesus fulfilled the law, so the people were no longer under any obligation to the law; any meat was now allowed if they didn't know it was offered to idols. Some didn't believe in Jesus as the Messiah and loved the law more than their freedoms. Their faith was weak. Paul was explaining to receive this person without judgment.

Your Application

You may have been raised with parents who said, "This is the only way." Then, you come across someone who did it differently. It could have been as simple as the way one eats. In America, we use utensils. In the Philippines, they use their hands. You could allow that to bother you or accept the difference with an open mind. Learning from other cultures helps to expand your mind. What is something that is bothering you? Could it be you need to develop your thinking and accept others' differences? Ponder on this today.

> *Let not him who eats despise him who does not eat, and let not him who does not eat judge him who eats; for God has received him. (Romans 14:3)*

My Thought

God loves all cultures, all peoples, and all who come to Him. He loves His children and wants us all to get along. Don't despise your brothers and sisters in Christ. Do not judge them, especially those who are new in Christ. It is not our job to "change them," but it is our job to teach them to be an example of the Word and love them.

Your Application

Today, practice loving someone in the Body of Christ who is different from you. Learn why they are different and accept them as your brother or sister. We do not know the backstory of their past or even their day, maybe something horrible happened to them. If we were to know, we would have compassion instead of judgment.

> *Who are you to judge another's servant? To his own master he stands or falls. Indeed, he will be made to stand, for God is able to make him stand. (Romans 14:4)*

My Thought

God matures His servants (children). God knows what His children need and will put the truth in their lives. Who do we think we are when we judge? God? We are not. Judging is an easy thing to do. It is sad how quickly we can judge without knowing all the facts of a person's life. God help us today to stop judging and to begin accepting. You, God, accepted us.

Your Application

Take note today how many times you start to judge; you may surprise yourself how often you do. Remember *Romans 14:4*, commit to memory. Ask God to help you stop judging and start blessing in its place.

One person esteems one day above another; another esteems every day alike. Let each be fully convinced in his own mind. (Romans 14:5)

My Thought

Worship on Sabbath or Sunday was the argument. Paul is clarifying since Jesus' death and resurrection, the law is fulfilled and now there is freedom. Let each be fully convinced in their minds what is best without judging the other. Now, this comes down to knowing what you believe and standing with what you believe. Another example is Halloween, which most Christian communities do not celebrate, yet some Christians believe that God can redeem any day even if it is a satanic pagan holiday. *"This is the day which the Lord has made, we will rejoice and be glad in it"* (Psalms 118:24). So they allow their children to dress up and express the day for good instead of evil. It is a big difference in each person's mind. This belief does not make one person right and the other wrong. It is just a difference in how they see the holiday. It is not to be judged or argued over. We are to accept each person's belief. God will convict if we or others are wrong; we should enjoy each day, leaving the judging and convicting to our loving Father, who is looking out for our best. He wants us to get along with one another, to walk in unity.

Your Application

What do you find in conflict with the Church? Is it in the Word, but you are rebellious because you disagree, like tithing, or is it a difference of opinion? Stand with the Word and change if you need to. If you are not sure what you believe, figure it out through reading the Word and studying and asking for wisdom from the leaders of God, then be convinced and take a stand. Look up unity scriptures, write them out and ask God to help you live them.

> *He who observes the day, observes it to the Lord; and he who does not observe the day, to the Lord he does not observe it. He who eats, eats to the Lord, for he gives God thanks; and he who does not eat, to the Lord he does not eat, and gives God thanks. (Romans 14:6)*

My Thought

All we do should be unto the Lord. Our observing of days, eating food, and our work should be done as if the Lord were the only one watching. If the Lord does not convict us, then we should stay on course. Convictions from the Lord are right. It is specific and absolutely clear, like a broken bone. Condemnation is from the devil. It is like the flu, causing aches and pains and shame without knowing where exactly we hurt. Condemnation drives us further away from Christ. Conviction leads us closer to Him.

Your Application

Is the Lord convicting you today? Then change your ways according to what He is asking of you. Are you being condemned? Then resist the devil, and he will flee *(James 4:7)*.

For none of us lives to himself, and no one dies to himself. (Romans 14:7)

My Thought

We are not an island to ourselves. We each need one another. Not only that, we all belong to the family of God. God, our Father wants us all to get along. As we mature in Him, we realize the importance of getting along and living in harmony.

Your Application

Who do you depend on today? Thank those people who help you in life today; better yet, write them a card and tell them what you appreciate about them.

> *For if we live, we live to the Lord; and if we die, we die to the Lord. Therefore, whether we live or die, we are the Lord's. (Romans 14:8)*

My Thought

We are servants of the Most High God. What we do in life and death will all come into account before our God. We need to live daily knowing He is watching, and we want to please Him in all we do.

Your Application

Live today, every moment, as though Jesus is right there with you. How will you react differently today? Write out what you learned.

> *For to this end Christ died and rose and lived again, that He might be Lord of both the dead and the living. (Romans 14:9)*

My Thought

Jesus is Lord. He is Lord of our lives here on earth, and He is Lord of our afterlife as we walk through the door of death into our everlasting life. We are accountable to Him. He is the one that we should fear (reverence) and daily please Him.

Your Application

Why is it so easy to become distracted and please yourself or others instead of your Lord? Think about that today. If you could live every day just for you, what would it look like to God? If you could live every day wanting to please others, what would it look like to them? If you lived every day pleasing God, what would it look like to you? Write an essay and conclude who you should prioritize daily.

> *But why do you judge your brother? Or why do you show contempt for your brother? For we shall all stand before the judgment seat of Christ. (Romans 14:10)*

My Thought

It is easy to judge our brothers on sins that are not our own; sins we don't commit. Yet we have all sinned; we all struggle with something. We need to humble ourselves and see that each person, as well as ourselves, have weaknesses. We want to stand before the judgment seat of Christ with a clear conscience that we did not judge others.

Your Application

If today you were to stand before the judgment seat of Christ, how would you rate? Do you walk in the forgiving power of the blood of Christ, or are you walking in your own power? Do something about it if you need to.

> *For it is written: "As I live, says the Lord, Every knee shall bow to Me, And every tongue shall confess to God. (Romans 14:11)*

My Thought

There will be a time in everyone's life when they will acknowledge that Jesus is Lord. That gives us cause for hope! Jesus, our Lord, will be recognized by those who rebuked Him, spit on Him, ignored Him, and denied He existed. All will bow a knee to His Majesty, and all will open their mouths and confess that He is God. Hopefully, it won't be too late for those who are not serving Him now because God is not willing that any should perish.

Your Application

What does it mean to you to confess Jesus Christ as Lord? Write it out. Do your actions speak it? If not, do something about it. The Holy Spirit is a good teacher and helper; ask Him to help you today to walk in your convictions.

> *So then each of us shall give account of himself to God. (Romans 14:12)*

My Thought

We should all know that our account of sins will be covered by the blood of Jesus. He made us righteous and holy. When we stand before the Lord, our righteousness will be His. We are not striving to be good; we are learning to know Jesus and walk with Him. It is two different ways of living. We have all sinned; we are all bad, but Jesus' death and resurrection make us right before Father God. We wear His Robe of Righteousness! We need not be concerned with our righteousness, but we need to be concerned with our walk and how we show off Jesus and His love by our actions of love, peace, and joy. Our account will be how we lived here on earth. Did we accomplish the plans God set out for us, or did we waste our days on trivial and frivolous things, chasing our own agenda?

Your Application

What account of sins holds you hostage? What forgiven sins does Satan use against you? Let it go to Jesus and be covered once and for all by His blood. Jesus washed you clean, so silence accusations, and walk in unity with the Spirit of God. You are righteous, not by your own doings but by Christ. That creates joy in you, and joy is contagious. Let your joy out today, and let others wonder why you are so happy! Read the account of Jesus' parable of the talents (*Matthew 25:14–30*). Who of the three men was doing God's will? Which one was frivolous? That's how we will give an account before God.

> *Therefore let us not judge one another anymore, but rather resolve this, not to put a stumbling block or a cause to fall in our brother's way. (Romans 14:13)*

My Thought

We need to resolve our judging down to only judging our own bad. We need to allow the Lord to show us our sin and, by the power of the Spirit, change our ways. When we see others struggle, we need to share how we struggle and how the Spirit of God has empowered us to change.

Your Application

What is one thing you are struggling with today? Bring it to the Spirit of God and allow Him to change you from the inside out. Take out your journal and write about your struggles like King David did. When we read the *Psalms*, we see he wrote about his struggles but usually ended up with a God solution or praise. Try it.

The Law of Love

> *I know and am convinced by the Lord Jesus that there is nothing unclean of itself; but to him who considers anything to be unclean, to him it is unclean. (Romans 14:14)*

My Thought

Jesus has purified everything to make them clean according to food (read *Acts 10:9–16*). If someone strongly opposes a particular food, don't object. They are loyal to what they believe. The mind is a powerful engine that cannot change easily. It is up to God to enlighten people, not us. We get to love them and pray for them.

Your Application

In situations where someone sees differently than you, or more important than the Word of God, be tolerant when it comes to anything that does not involve the soul's destination. Pray for someone today who adamantly disagrees with you, especially something you think is trivial. Ask God to allow you to see this person from His eyes.

Yet if your brother is grieved because of your food, you are no longer walking in love. Do not destroy with your food the one for whom Christ died. (Romans 14:15)

My Thought

So now it comes down to compassion. If someone is stumbling because of our freedoms, then with compassion for this person, we put down what makes them grieved. This is a sure sign of love. It is a sign of the love of Jesus in us. What is more important? Our freedoms to do anything we want, or the one affected by what we do?

Your Application

Today, die to your freedoms and choose to allow someone to see the love of God in you by making them more important than your wants and desires. This is pure freedom and a selfless act of love.

Therefore do not let your good be spoken of as evil; (Romans 14:16)

My Thought

We all have a belief system that guides our actions. We can walk in grace with so much freedom in our love for God that we can be free to do anything because our gauge is the conviction of the Holy Spirit. Others feel condemnation when they make a few decisions outside of their religious restrictions. If we are free to eat or drink a particular food or beverage because we know it won't affect us, we must not let our good intentions become a source of gossip or causing a brother or sister to stumble because they cannot eat the same food or drink without stumbling. We are to have a good balance of doing the right thing at the right time. As the Holy Spirit leads us, He will guide us. In defense of what is said, we can't go around being fearful of what we eat. We also have to be sensitive to move in compassion and truth. We need to live a life of balance.

Your Application

Today, why don't you look at your heart's intentions. What are some of your selfish and uncaring motives? Even though you have the freedom to do it, is it offending someone else? You will be held accountable for your motives, not just your actions. Read *Ecclesiastes 12:14*. Write about it.

for the kingdom of God is not eating and drinking, but righteousness and peace and joy in the Holy Spirit. (Romans 14:17)

My Thought

The kingdom of this world says eat, drink, and be merry. It says feed your belly, numb your senses, drown your troubles and don't worry, be happy. Our kingdom says do what is right, live in peace, and have joy in the Holy Spirit. Our kingdom says to look out for others as well as yourself. Food and drink are the essence of the world's kingdom, feel good now, and instant gratification. The kingdom of God says, look after your fellow brother and sister, enjoy your food but don't worship your bellies.

There is so much more to life than food and drink. Paul is moving us to the higher standards of the *Storybook Fairy-Tale Reality of the Kingdom of God* and breaking the traps of the kingdom of this world (Satan's snares).

Your Application

How important is food to you? Take a moment and think about the place food has in your life. Do you eat to live or live to eat? In the next few days, fast for a day, three or seven, you will know where food stands in your life. If food is a stronghold, break it. Meditate on these verses: *Matthew 6:25, John 6:27, and Matthew 4:4.*

> *For he who serves Christ in these things is acceptable to God and approved by men. (Romans 14:18)*

My Thought

When we follow scripture, we please God. We also become favored by men, for they see we do not make ourselves more important than others, but we place others as important. The words acceptable and approved are powerful. We can have doors open to us when we are acceptable by God and approved by man. God knows that what He is saying to us is for our good. He knows the path He is directing us to. We need only to give up the need to be right in our own eyes and in the sight of men and be obedient to God's Word and ways.

Your Application

Where do you struggle in serving God? Think about it. Is it a struggle with your flesh or with God? Do you trust Him? Do you have trust issues? Look into your soul to discover your trust level with God. Can it be better? Work on it today by serving God in a place where you struggle. Write about the results.

> *Therefore let us pursue the things which make for peace and the things by which one may edify another. (Romans 14:19)*

My Thought

We all long for peace. We want to lay our heads on our pillows at night and know we are at peace with God and others. This is one thing that distinguishes between our God and other gods. Peace cannot be manufactured. It only comes from the true God. Other gods are not real. Jesus is our Prince of Peace! The more we pursue the things which make for peace and look out for others, the more we have an inner peace no one can take away.

Your Application

Are you living in the peace God has for you? Do you pursue the things of God that promise peace? Do you edify others? Look up peace scriptures and compare them to your life. How's that going for you?

> *Do not destroy the work of God for the sake of food. All things indeed are pure, but it is evil for the man who eats with offense. (Romans 14:20)*

My Thought

Food is not as important as the kingdom of God. To destroy the work of God so we can maintain our ways is caring more about ourselves. God has made all things pure for us, it is clear, but to offend someone knowingly by eating, is evil.

Your Application

Read *Matthew 5*, the Beatitudes of Jesus. What attitude should you have towards your brother and sister? Write it out.

> *It is good neither to eat meat nor drink wine nor do anything by which your brother stumbles or is offended or is made weak. (Romans 14:21)*

My Thought

Paul is summarizing his letter by reiterating his message. It is not acceptable to cause our brothers to stumble, to offend them, or to make them question their faith, making them weak. We are here for one another. No man is an island. Our decisions affect others. We are to live in the freedom of the Spirit. We are to die to our selfish ways. *It is possible to live in joy and to walk in love.* We must learn the difference between following the Spirit correctly without being manipulated by others. A fine balance.

Your Application

It is good to live in harmony with one another. It is good to guide each other in the faith. It is good to strengthen your brothers and sisters. It is good to beware of wolves in sheep clothing trying to take away your joy and peace. Look up scriptures for this.

> *Do you have faith? Have it to yourself before God. Happy is he who does not condemn himself in what he approves. (Romans 14:22)*

My Thought

Do we walk in complete freedom? Great! Keep it with you and God. Happy and approved are we who know what we believe and yet know how to use our faith around others. Freedom is a state of mind; we can be free in our faith and still hold back for the sake of others. We have to understand what living in the *Storybook Fairy-Tale Reality* looks like. The scriptures talk about it over and over. We are to look to others higher than ourselves. We are to follow our kingdom standards; love one for another: "*Therefore if you have any encouragement from being united with Christ, if any comfort from his love, if any common sharing in the Spirit, if any tenderness and compassion, then make my joy complete by being like-minded, having the same love, being one in spirit and of one mind. Do nothing out of selfish ambition or vain conceit. Rather, in humility, value others above yourselves, not looking to your own interests but each of you to the interests of the others" (Philippians 2:1-4).*

Your Application

This is not talking about not taking a stand for your faith in Jesus. It is talking about not offending your fellow Christian brothers and sisters. Today look up *Genesis 13* and write about Abraham's freedom to choose and what he did instead. What did you learn from this?

> *But he who doubts is condemned if he eats, because he does not eat from faith;*
> *for whatever is not from faith is sin. (Romans 14:23)*

My Thought

This chapter is all about our liberty in Christ and tolerance of others. We are liberated to live in freedom and peace. If we use our liberty in selfish motives, we then destroy what freedom was given to us. This chapter is also about our sound faith in what we believe. We are not to waiver in our beliefs but stand firm. Faith is the language of heaven, and we must know what we believe. It takes studying the Word, assimilating it into our soul and spirit, and purposely getting to know God the Father, God the Son, and God the Holy Spirit. If we do not have faith, we sin. Our core being should be one of faith.

Your Application

Think about these things and see what the Spirit wants to show you. Is there a change of heart and mind needed? Does your faith give you freedom, or do you stumble in your faith? Do an in-depth survey of your soul and write about it. Now, go, share this chapter with others.

Romans Fourteen tells us not to argue with others about what they think is right or wrong. Eating and drinking and the importance of days may seem unimportant to some, but others believe it is important. Let each one think as they wish as long as it isn't pertinent to the truth of our salvation. We will all stand before the judgment seat of God. Every knee will bow, and every tongue will declare that Jesus is Lord above all lords! We will each give a personal account of our life's work, so let's be more concerned about our own character rather than pointing out others' flaws. Always looking out for the good in others, not causing others to stumble.

My Prayer

Lord, we need Your help in this chapter's quest. It is so hard to live a life looking out for the other person over ourselves. Without You, we are self-centered. You gave us *Romans 12* to help us see that You understand our weaknesses. Thank You. You have given us the Holy Spirit so we can walk out this chapter. Help us to know the difference between looking out for our fellow man and being manipulated by them. Show us all how to live the way You want us to live, and also that You have already empowered us to live that way. We love You, love Your scriptures, and love this life You have given us. We are so thankful for all the blessings You have poured upon us; let us now give freely. In Your precious Name. Amen.

Write a summary of chapter 14.

Jesus is Lord.

He is Lord of our lives here on earth, and He is Lord of our afterlife as we walk through the door of death into our everlasting home. He is the one we are accountable to. He is the one that we should fear (revere) and daily please. He is the judge; we must leave the judging to Him.

Our Worship
Miracle Little Miracle / Elevation Worship & Maverick City
https://www.youtube.com/watch?v=Viiw6tGimHo

CHAPTER 15

Living in Unity

Read the complete chapter of *Romans 15*

> *We then who are strong ought to bear with the scruples of the weak, and not to please ourselves. (Romans 15:1)*

My Thought

Paul continues writing about the past verses. If there is someone weaker who lives differently from us, we should not get caught up in trivial things they may do. It will only please us and not God to get into an argument over things that don't matter, such as going to church on Saturday or a person smoking or only eating vegetables.

Your Application

Ask yourself, will what I say edify this person and make them a better person, or do I just want to voice my opinion, sound important and win the argument? Whatever the answer, you know which way to go. Try it today, remain silent when it's for your benefit, speak up when it benefits another.

> *Let each of us please his neighbor for his good, leading to edification. (Romans 15:2)*

My Thought

Can we even imagine what life would be like if we lived this out? Let us please our neighbor/family member/friend for their good, leading to their betterment. Let's all try this for a day and see what happens to us—yes us—not them; but what outcome will we receive? If God inspired Paul to write this and if all things work together for our good, can you imagine how good we would feel after we look for the best of someone else and put ourselves last? Aren't we reminded of the last shall be first? What does that mean? If we placed ourselves last in the equation of relationships, honestly looking for the good of others with no hint of getting something out of it, by the end of the day, we would understand what Jesus said, *"It is more blessed to give than to receive"* (Acts 20:35). Don't get this mixed up with being manipulated by others. There is a vast difference.

Your Application

Today, try it. Look at *Philippians 2:3-4*, meditate on it and ask God where you can change in this area of your life, if you are interested in pleasing God, write out how you can change and keep yourself accountable for that change. It is better yet to give it to someone you trust and ask them to keep you accountable in these areas by asking you how you are doing every week. This is the crux of the Christian walk. If you continue reading in *Philippians 2*, you will see Jesus' example to us. He denied his deity during the time on earth to take on the form of a servant.

> *For even Christ did not please Himself; but as it is written, "The reproaches of those who reproached You, fell on Me." (Romans 15:3)*

My Thought

The perfect example for each of us, Jesus Christ, Himself, did not do things for His benefit. He did things that would glorify His Father and edify others. We can learn so much from Jesus. I know that sounds silly—of course we can learn a lot from Jesus, He's God, but how often do we take Jesus' examples to heart? The WWJD (What Would Jesus Do?) is passé now, but in light of what they were trying to get across, why not try it today, as we begin to think on Jesus and the many examples He gives us. He has all the answers, and He gave us His living example here on earth.

Your Application

Study the life of Christ Jesus as often as you can. Is what was most important to Him while on the earth most important to you? What was His destiny? Do you know yours? Who did Jesus hang out with during His three years of ministry? Did Jesus try to find a comfortable life here on earth? There are so many lessons He left you. Be like a detective and search out the clues He left behind. It says in *Hebrews 1:9*, He was the most joyous among His brothers. He gave you the way to a joyful, abundant life (*John 10:10*). Find it today. Better than WWJD would be WWJHYD (What Would Jesus Have You Do?), Jesus requires different actions and behaviors from each of us according to our callings and gifts (*John 21:21–22*).

> *For whatever things were written before were written for our learning, that we through the patience and comfort of the Scriptures might have hope. (Romans 15:4)*

My Thought

The scriptures are here for us. With each new generation, God has the Book of His Words just for us. It's never out of stock, and it's never too old to be relevant to us. *"The Word of God is active and alive, sharper than a two-edged sword, piercing even to the division of soul and spirit, and of joints and marrow, and is a discerner of the thoughts and intents of the heart"* (*Hebrews 4:12*). As we patiently dig through scriptures, we will find comfort and hope.

Your Application

Today, decide to keep the Word of God close to you. Study it, find answers, read it like a novel, and accept it as love letters from a Heavenly Father.

Now may the God of patience and comfort grant you to be like-minded toward one another, according to Christ Jesus, (Romans 15:5)

My Thought

Ah, *unity*! Check out this verse. God has patience towards us and comfort for us. It's hard for us to live in unity because we are selfish and want our own way. The only way we can become like-minded is if we all gaze on the beauty of Jesus, not looking at each other. If we have our focus on Jesus Christ, our Redeemer, we absolutely can become unified. It's easy to write but much harder to do. It only takes one person to turn selfish, and others are offended, and they begin to work things out their way, turning selfish like the first one. Notice it says within the verse, *"may the God of patience..."* We have to be so glad that He is patient with us. The verse says, *"May the God of patience and comfort grant..."* grant you to be like-minded towards one another. It does not come from our ability but from His Holy Spirit. *What is impossible for man is possible with God (Luke 18:27)*!

Your Application

Ask God today to grant you the ability to be like-minded towards your brothers and sisters in the family of God. Ask God our Father to allow others to be like-minded. This does not mean we are cookie-cutter Christians. God has different tasks and purposes for us all. It does mean we are gracious towards others who have different callings, gifts, and thoughts of the Word. *We are not to compare ourselves to others, compete with others, or control others.* We are to accept each other and pray for each other. What a day that will be when we are a unified Bride only interested in bringing glory to our Savior, Jesus Christ, and our Father God. Jesus left His Spirit here with us to do this very thing, to be unified. It can be done, or it would not be written in the pages of His Word. Pray, *"Thy will be done, Thy kingdom come into my life today."* Work at being like-minded as Christ was towards His Father; write the benefits of doing it His way.

that you may with one mind and one mouth glorify the God and Father of our Lord Jesus Christ. (Romans 15:6)

My Thought

Why does God our Father want us to be like-minded? He wants us with one mind and one mouth to glorify Him. People know it is impossible for everyone to agree, right? Ask congress? Ask churches? Checkout playgrounds! How about our own families? The human race can't get along and agree, do you agree? Is God asking the impossible of us? Yes, but God does not request the impossible without making it possible. Paul is saying, we can be on the same page if we look at the scriptures, learn from them, know what Jesus Christ did for us, and focus on giving all the glory to Our Father in heaven. In a sense, this is what humility looks like. If we drop pride, focus on the cross, and give our Father glory, we will be like-minded.

Your Application

Today, look into being like-minded with your fellow Christians and see how hard it is for you. Could this be a sign of pride or humility?

Glorify God Together

> *Therefore receive one another, just as Christ also received us, to the glory of God.* (Romans 15:7)

My Thought

All Christians ought to receive each other. Our Savior has received us, and we have no reason not to accept others. No matter what hindrances may stand in our way. Christ on the cross forgave all our sins and welcomed us as His own. We now get to follow that same example to forgive, forget, and receive. What does receive one another mean? Not to be cliquish and hang out with only those you know. Welcome all into the body of Christ, go out of your way to welcome newcomers. It also means to forgive those who have harmed you.

Your Application

Today, if you are not receiving someone, ask God to show you what you should do about it. He understands the pain and knows whom you should receive, and those you should set good, clear boundaries. We are allowed to protect ourselves from evil people and not receive them, but God does want us to accept people who have harmed us if there can be a reconciliation in the end. God knows who; just open your heart and mind to His still small voice (*1 King 19:11–13, Psalms 46:10*). Go out of your way to welcome those new to the Body of Christ. Treat others the way you want to be treated.

> *Now I say that Jesus Christ has become a servant to the circumcision for the truth of God, to confirm the promises made to the fathers,* (Romans 15:8)

My Thought

Jesus came to serve, not to be served. He went to the Jews first to confirm all the truth of the Old Testament. There are over 300 prophecies of Jesus in the Old Testament, and each one has been fulfilled. That's impossible unless God is real, and His Word is infallible.

Your Application

Check out some more of the Old Testament prophecies and find where they are fulfilled in the New Testament; it's an amazing find. Write it out.

> *and that the Gentiles might glorify God for His mercy, as it is written: "For this reason I will confess to You among the Gentiles, and sing to Your name"* (2 Samuel 22:50; Psalm 18:49). (Romans 15:9)

My Thought

Jesus came as a servant and proved prophecies from the Old Testament's Fathers were correct. Jesus went to the Gentiles (anyone who is not a Jew) to establish His mercies. God grafted us into His family to show His mercy and to be glorified. Paul begins to write out scriptures about the Gentiles' future written way back in the Old Testament. He is setting a truth and backing it up with scripture. We, who are Gentiles, are spoken of in the beginning because God had a plan for us before the world's foundation. We are loved, and God, our Father, proves it.

Your Application

Today, thank God for His mercies towards us; they are new every morning, inexhaustible, and unique! Meditate on *Lamentations 3:22, 23*. It is so important to know the Word. Paul knew it and was able to make his point with the Word. You can learn so much and have so much wisdom if you know your Word. Make a point today to read and study it and hide it in your heart (*Psalms 119:11*). Who are the Fathers of the Old Testament? Write them down and one character trait they each had.

> *And again he says: "Rejoice, O Gentiles, with His people." (Deuteronomy 32:43)!* (*Romans 15:10*)

My Thought

We will be rejoicing with the Jewish nation who God called to be His people. There will be a time when we will all rejoice together over our Father. How exciting for us! Think of God, our Father, and His excitement when His plan from the beginning comes into fulfillment. His Son's broken body and poured out blood made it all possible for Jews and Gentiles to come together and unite to be His big, happy, eternal family!

Your Application

Today, look to the Jewish culture, and try to understand them. You will live with them in eternity, so why not know more about them now. Look up five cultural differences between the Jewish nation and the Christian culture. Write it out.

> *And again: "Praise the LORD, all you Gentiles! Laud Him, all you peoples"* (Psalm 117:1)! (*Romans 15:11*)

My Thought

God, our Father, speaks of us throughout the Old Testament. We are part of the Big Picture of God, so rejoice that we, too, have been chosen to live forever with our Lord. The enemy of our soul will continuously accuse us and make us feel inferior any way he can. These scriptures in *Romans 15* tell us who we are.

Your Application

Use these scriptures next time the enemy tries to tell you you're "less than." Proclaim your confidence in Christ and put the enemy under your feet. Remember we are following Jesus' example: when He came against the enemy, He used the Old Testament's Covenant (*Deuteronomy*) and three times, He said, "*It is written…*". Know your Word, for it is your weapon as well as your comfort.

> *Know your Word, for it is your weapon as well as your comfort.*

> *And again, Isaiah says: "There shall be a root of Jesse; And He who shall rise to reign over the Gentiles, In Him the Gentiles shall hope (Isaiah 11:10)."* (Romans 15:12)

My Thought

The root of Jesse is Jesus, and He now reigns in heaven with our Father; because of this, we have hope for a future (*Jeremiah 29:11*)! The Gentiles are mentioned throughout the Old Testament because we were part of God's miraculous plan from the beginning. We were never an afterthought, we were chosen by God, just like the Jewish nation. Chess is a strategic game of forethought, thinking three to four moves ahead, God in His ability to see the future, maneuvered the Gentiles in to His game of life.

Your Application

How does that make you feel? God thought of you from the beginning of time. Let that settle into your mind and shift down to your heart. You are a loved child of God. Tell someone today.

> *Now may the God of hope fill you with all joy and peace in believing, that you may abound in hope by the power of the Holy Spirit.* (Romans 15:13)

My Thought

Paul is proclaiming joy and peace will be ours as we believe in the God of hope by the power of the Holy Spirit. We cannot believe unless the Holy Spirit draws us to the truth. It is not us that seeks after God, but God through His Spirit seeks after us. As we receive His Spirit, then we are given truth. Joy and peace are possible, even if our past wants to haunt us. The enemy of our soul wants our past to cause anxiety, bitterness, and regrets. God wants us to be in His complete peace. Healing can happen when we let Him take us back to the paths of our hurts and pains to replace them with joy and peace. He will heal our past if we let Him. Only He can heal us.

Your Application

Today, believe that the Spirit can fill you with all joy and peace. Abound in hope by the power of the Holy Spirit. Be courageous enough to be led by the Holy Spirit to the places He wants to heal you. Pray for an understanding of this verse and meditate on it until you get it! Read *Romans 3:11*; what is the verse saying? Write your thoughts.

From Jerusalem to Illyricum

Now I myself am confident concerning you, my brethren, that you also are full of goodness, filled with all knowledge, able also to admonish one another. (Romans 15:14)

My Thought

Paul is edifying the Romans with good words of what he thinks of them. Paul says he is confident that they are full of goodness, filled with the Word, and able to keep each other accountable. What a great confidence that is and what a good church! The people were full of goodness (kindness towards one another), they were full of the Word of God, and because they knew the Word and loved each other, they could give a warning to anyone who wasn't following God's Word and the people accepted it. That's an excellent way to run a church.

Your Application

Are you good? Are you full of the knowledge of the Word? Can you admonish a brother/sister in the Lord with love and correction? If so, great, you are following in Paul's steps. If not, then ask God today to help you come to this place of maturity in Christ. Your goal is to live in the eternal mindset and look for His coming; in so doing, you will be more concerned with your moral character instead of caring what others think of you. You will also be able to admonish others with the insight of the Holy Spirit, absent of selfish motives.

Nevertheless, brethren, I have written more boldly to you on some points, as reminding you, because of the grace given to me by God, (Romans 15:15)

My Thought

God gives grace (God-given talent or gift to reach a specific group) to us in areas we have overcome. Paul was writing boldly to the Romans in some areas because God had given him grace in that area, such as preaching the gospel to the Gentiles. Paul had less grace towards his Jewish family. He longed to minister to his family, but God gave Paul more grace to minister to the Gentiles.

Your Thought

In what area has God given you grace? That is the area where you will be most effective. Stay focused and single-minded, and you will be a powerhouse for the Lord. God has chosen each one of us to be a light in a specific area. If we are all over the place, then we are not shining in the place the Lord has ordained us. Often, Paul went to the Jews with less effect because He was called to be focused on the Gentiles. Stay where God puts you. He will take care of your concerns just as God had His eyes on the concerns of Paul, his Jewish family. Where do you have more grace? What does God want you to do with it? Write it out.

that I might be a minister of Jesus Christ to the Gentiles, ministering the gospel of God, that the offering of the Gentiles might be acceptable, sanctified by the Holy Spirit. (Romans 15:16)

My Thought

God called Paul to the Gentiles first, then to their kings, and then God called Paul to the Jewish nation (*Acts 9:15*). Paul had a grace to speak to the Gentiles, and they listened. Who was Paul a minister of? He was a minister of Jesus Christ. We need to remember that we are not a minister of our denomination or a minister of a certain person, we are ministers of Jesus Christ, and we will give an answer to Him for what we have done according to our calling. We will be accountable for what He says. That doesn't mean we are not to be submissive to those in authority over us; it just means we are all servants of the Highest God.

Your Application

Don't be a person who is easily manipulated; know your Word, know your calling, and especially know your God. Today open your eyes to what the Spirit of God is asking you to do. Who is He calling you to influence? If you don't know, ask a friend or mentor to pray with you for the answer.

Therefore I have reason to glory in Christ Jesus in the things which pertain to God. (Romans 15:17)

My Thought

Paul has reason to glory in whom? In Christ Jesus, he doesn't glory in himself, lift up himself, or brag about himself. Paul brings glory to Christ in the things that pertain to God.

Your Application

Check out who gets the glory when you do things for God. Be careful in this area of your life. Follow Paul's example and let the credit go to Jesus. Memorize *Proverbs 27:2*.

For I will not dare to speak of any of those things which Christ has not accomplished through me, in word and deed, to make the Gentiles obedient—(Romans 15:18)

My Thought

This is such a key verse for all of us. Paul chooses not to discuss his adventures towards his own goals. He is only going to speak of the accomplishments he has in Christ. We all can get caught up in our own world, "this is my world, and you can live in it"! Paul instructs us through his example not to speak of our own accomplishments. He writes and talks about what Christ has done through him to bring the Gentiles into obedience and salvation.

Your Application

Where have you gained victory in your Christian life? This is the area that God wants you to give praise to Him. Your victory is the area that God has given you the grace to help others break out of their bondage and obtain victory. Find scriptures in *Proverbs* that talk about not lifting up yourself but let others praise your good deeds. Write them out and put them to memory.

> *in mighty signs and wonders, by the power of the Spirit of God, so that from Jerusalem and round about to Illyricum I have fully preached the gospel of Christ. (Romans 15:19)*

My Thought

Paul did mighty signs and wonders by the power of the Spirit of God. We, too, can do mighty signs and wonders by the power of the Spirit of God. How? As we fully preach the gospel of Christ. It's not looking for the signs and wonders that bring on the signs and wonders. It is preaching/sharing the full gospel of Christ that brings on the mighty signs and wonders. We get that mixed up because we think the signs and wonders are the main events. The gospel of Christ is, and will always be, the Main Event. Signs and wonders follow those who believe (*Mark 16:17*). Believe what? Those who believe that Jesus is God's Son who came, died, and rose again to bring reconciliation between the Father and His chosen children.

Your Application

An important note to you: look to the gospel of Christ, not the signs and wonders. The signs and wonders are the Holy Spirit's fireworks, but they will fizzle out if sought after. The gospel of Christ is the real thing. Signs and wonders will follow after seeking Christ first. Look up *Luke 10:20*; what did Jesus tell the disciples to rejoice over? Write about it after meditating.

> *And so I have made it my aim to preach the gospel, not where Christ was named, lest I should build on another man's foundation, (Romans 15:20)*

My Thought

Oh, Paul, what a great word to us today! Paul did not preach Christ where there was already a church; he went to the man/woman who had not heard of the gospel. He didn't try to pull people from another man's work; he went to the unreached people.

Your Application

Learn to reach out to those who haven't heard the Word. It's easy for us to talk about Christ amongst our own. Step out of your comfort zone and talk Christ to a college student who doesn't even know who Jesus is. Try it today.

> *but as it is written: "To whom He was not announced, they shall see; and those who have not heard shall understand (Isaiah 52:15)." (Romans 15:21)*

My Thought

Paul uses scripture again to show why he does what he does. It's an essential part of being a believer, to *know what you know, to believe what you know, and to share what you know.* Isaiah is talking about the Gentiles, us! Christ was announced to the Jews. We were not the first to hear about Jesus; the Jews were. They didn't get it because they were looking for a king, not a baby. Those of us who love Jesus and call Him, "Lord" heard and understood. Thank you, Holy Spirit, for revealing the truth to us.

Your Application

Do you know why you believe what you share? If not, why not begin today to commit to reading/studying the Word daily. Be thankful continuously for the Holy Spirit bringing the Good News to you!

Plan to Visit Rome

> *For this reason I also have been much hindered from coming to you. (Romans 15:22)*

My Thought

Because Paul was busy preaching the gospel of Christ to those who haven't heard, he had been hindered in going to Rome. He wanted to go but had been directed by the Holy Spirit to other places.

Your Application

Make sure you know that you are in the place you are supposed to be. Surrender your ideas and agendas to the Holy Spirit, and He will guide you into the right paths. Read *Acts 16:6, Acts 19:21, Acts 20:22–24, Acts 21:4.* In your opinion, was it a mistake for Paul to go to Jerusalem, or was he following the Spirit? Search out other scriptures and thoughts of what other theologians thought. Write it out.

> *But now no longer having a place in these parts, and having a great desire these many years to come to you, (Romans 15:23)*

My Thought

Paul's work in the Holy Spirit seems to be accomplished, and his desires were no longer taken into his own hands but were given over to the Holy Spirit, so although he had desired for many years to go to Rome, he had not gone there yet.

Your Application

You, too, may desire to go somewhere, but God may have other plans for you. Follow Paul's example and listen to the Spirit. Learn to walk in the Spirit by quieting your flesh and listen to His still small voice (*Psalms 46*). Practice right now after reading the *Psalm.*

whenever I journey to Spain, I shall come to you. For I hope to see you on my journey, and to be helped on my way there by you, if first I may enjoy your company for a while. (Romans 15:24)

My Thought

Paul had plans to go to Spain. On his way, he wanted to stop in Rome to visit his brothers and sisters in Christ and hoped to receive financial help to get to Spain. As we read *Acts*, it doesn't say that Paul ever reached Spain. He did make it to Rome, his final place of ministry, before he was killed. Our plans are not our own. We can say we want to do this or go here, but the ultimate plan lies in our Father's hands. He will direct us through the Spirit.

Your Application

Today, you may have plans but be like *James 4:15: Instead, you ought to say, "If the Lord wills, we will live and do this or that."* God's ways, thoughts, and plans for us are better than our plans for ourselves; learn to trust Him. Give your agenda and desires over to Him today. Read *Isaiah 48:17*, hide it in your heart.

But now I am going to Jerusalem to minister to the saints. (Romans 15:25)

My Thought

Paul is heading back to the Jews again; how he loved his people. He will eventually die because of them, but his love for them was from God, and it could not be quenched.

Your Application

Ask God to fill you with such a love today for the people group He has put in your life.

For it pleased those from Macedonia and Achaia to make a certain contribution for the poor among the saints who are in Jerusalem. (Romans 15:26)

My Thought

Paul gathered money for the poor, persecuted saints in Jerusalem while he traveled abroad to minister to the Gentiles. He was always looking for ways to meet the needs of his people. The Macedonians and the Achaians were generous to help out Paul in his quest.

Your Application

When you are out influencing others, look to see what they can do for someone else, as Paul did. It is always more blessed to give than to receive (*Acts 20:35*). It is a good trait to teach others: I am here to minister to you, and it would be great if you could give towards this other need. Who can your friends help today by "collecting a donation"? There are so many great places to share. Try it.

It pleased them indeed, and they are their debtors. For if the Gentiles have been partakers of their spiritual things, their duty is also to minister to them in material things. (Romans 15:27)

My Thought

They were pleased to give to the Jewish saints because through the Jews, Jesus came, and the Gentiles are indebted to the Jewish nation for giving us the spiritual heritage. It remains clear to Paul that since they were brothers and sisters in Christ, they should help them out materially if they had the resources.

Your Application

Whatever your gift is, share it with others. As you each share your gifts, we fulfill the law of Christ (*Galatians 6:2*). We should each be indebted to each other in the debt of love. Give it to someone today.

Therefore, when I have performed this and have sealed to them this fruit, I shall go by way of you to Spain. (Romans 15:28)

My Thought

Paul is going to bring the material gift of the Macedonian Gentiles and the others to the persecuted saints in Jerusalem and then head out to see the Romans on the way to Spain, or so Paul thought was the plan. Again, we should always have our intentions covered with *"thy will be done."* We will never go astray when we allow the Spirit to have the final say.

Your Application

You must fulfill your obligations to what you have promised and then set your plans before the Lord and let Him direct your paths. Write out *Proverbs 16:3* and put it to memory. Every morning set your plans before God and let Him direct them. What an adventurous life you can live!

But I know that when I come to you, I shall come in the fullness of the blessing of the gospel of Christ. (Romans 15:29)

My Thought

Paul has spent many hours writing to the Roman saints. He knows he will see them, and when he does, he will be full of the blessings of the gospel of Christ. Focused on one thing and one thing only, Paul shares the gospel of Jesus Christ. He will be full of Christ and will bring it to the saints. Paul indeed would come to Rome, but not on his own. Paul is brought to Rome by the centurions who kept him in prison waiting for trial. During those years in prison, not once, but four times, Paul took the time to write his fellow brothers and sisters in the churches he established on his missionary journeys, which gave us some of Paul's Epistles.

Your Application

The only way you can come to others in the fullness of the gospel of Christ is to be in the Word, in worship, and share what God has done in your life. Paul was about that, so should you be focused on the same things; it brings abundant life and fullness of heart! Take inventory of your life; are you carrying the fullness of the gospel of Christ? If so, great, keep it up. If not, then work towards that with joy, knowing the Holy Spirit will bring you there as you take the steps He leads you on. What epistles did Paul write while in prison? Read them with the mindset that Paul was in prison. Is he begrudgingly writing them, seeming sorrowful that he was stuck in jail, or did he bring hope and encouragement to the churches? What can you learn from Paul? Write it out.

> *The only way you can come to others in the fullness of the gospel of Christ is to be in the Word, in worship, and sharing what God has done in your life.*

Now I beg you, brethren, through the Lord Jesus Christ, and through the love of the Spirit, that you strive together with me in prayers to God for me, (Romans 15:30)

My Thought

Please pray for me, Paul asks, as he ends his letters to the Romans. He has built a relationship with them, and now he is asking for prayer. Paul is a great example of a leader. It is good to give out, but we must also ask for help. We are in the same boat, worshiping the same God, and we all need each other. No one is better, and we show that by giving of ourselves and asking for help.

Your Application

Are you naturally a giver or a receiver? Think about this question. Ask the Lord to help you balance out by learning to be both.

that I may be delivered from those in Judea who do not believe, and that my service for Jerusalem may be acceptable to the saints, (Romans 15:31)

My Thought

What does Paul ask? That he may be delivered from those Jews who did not believe and brought trouble upon him. He prayed that his service would be acceptable. He was honestly asking prayer for deliverance from the Jewish people who didn't believe. Remember Paul had been persecuted many times by his own people, they had incited riots because of him, and they had whipped him, so when he asked for deliverance, he was seriously asking for that. He also requested that the offering he was bringing from those who had given would be acceptable to the Jewish believers. He wanted the gift to be enough.

Your Application

When you ask for prayer, be specific, and know what you need. Then honestly ask for help. In *Acts 18*, Paul was in Corinth when he wrote the book of *Romans*. How long did he stay, and to whom did he preach?

> *that I may come to you with joy by the will of God, and may be refreshed together with you. (Romans 15:32)*

My Thought

Paul asks the Romans to pray that God would allow him to come to Rome; he had tried so many times before, and now he was hoping it would be God's will that he finally meet them and be refreshed with them in the joy of the Lord. Paul is a great example of one who denied his own agenda and followed God's will.

Your Application

The Lord's will is most important; you must always submit to it, and you will find yourself in the joy of His calling. Go through the whole day today doing His will. What does that look like? Honestly, going about your day with Jesus in mind.

> *Now the God of peace be with you all. Amen. (Romans 15:33)*

My Thought

The peace of God is a wonderful thing, and Paul leaves that as the last thing. He proclaims, *"The God of peace be with you all."* Astonishingly, peace is something many people do not have. The rich may worry about their money. The intellect may ponder on too many things to establish their superior knowledge. The poor may wonder where their next meal will be. The student may search for the next adventure. People all over the world are searching for something that brings peace. Peace only comes from God. He owns it, and He gives it out freely. All they have to do is acknowledge and accept His Son.

Your Application

May you know one of the greatest feelings in the known world, peace. It can't be bought, bribed, or stolen. Peace is a trust that God is in control, and there is nothing good He will leave out of your life. Pursue His peace and see how long you can keep it. You will know the difference. Look up scriptures on peace and write them out. Pray for those you know who are living without it. Share your peace with them.

Romans Fifteen shows us how to live patiently and peacefully for God's promises to be fulfilled. Again, may we live in harmony with each other as it is fitting for us as followers of Christ Jesus. Acceptance is key. Gentiles and Jews are to come together with our differences and unite. As with all races, we are to love each other. Paul is reminding his fellow Romans, as well as us, how to behave in a way that is pleasing to our Father and our Savior. Paul was anxious to tell the Good News to those who had never heard so they would see and understand! Speaking about interceding for himself, Paul encouraged the Roman Christians to pray for him and his struggles because they had a love for Paul given to them by the Holy Spirit.

My Prayer

Our Father, thank You for Jesus coming as a baby, living sinless in our world, dying for our sins and victoriously rising from the dead to show us our sins are forgiven, ascending to the right hand of the Father and sending to us the same Spirit that lived in Jesus so we could live out our lives victoriously as well! We are blessed beyond measure for all You have done for us. We also thank You for Paul; he brings so much truth and is an excellent example of leaving all behind to follow You. Help us look out for each other and ourselves, as the scriptures tell us for our good. Teach us to receive one another as Paul instructed his fellow Romans to do. Thank you, Father, that before the foundation of the world, we, the Gentiles, were thought of, with a plan in place for our salvation! Now may You, the God of patience and comfort, grant us like-mindedness, so we with one mind and one mouth glorify You. May You, the God of hope, fill us with all joy and peace by the power of the Holy Spirit. May we be encouragers, speak words of love to those we meet each day, and accomplish those things You have asked us to do without conceit or glorifying ourselves. Help us share with those around us the gospel of Christ. Please help us to be an influence on those who need to see the love of Christ. Lead our paths to the people we can speak Your truth to. May we pray for others and ask for prayer when needed. May You, the God of peace, be with all of us! In Your magnificent Name. Amen!

Write a summary of chapter 15.

We need to remember that we are not a minister of our denomination or a minister of a certain person. We are ministers of Jesus Christ and will one day give an answer to Him according to our calling. We will be accountable for what He tells us to do. That doesn't mean we are not to be submissive to those in authority over us. It just means we are all servants of the Most High God. Don't be a person who is easily manipulated. Know your Word, know your calling, and especially, know your God.

Our Worship
Used to This / Maverick City Music
https://www.youtube.com/watch?v=pWp8E_Y2Lk4🔗

CHAPTER 16

Living in Community

Read the complete chapter of *Romans 16*

> *I commend to you Phoebe our sister, who is a servant of the church in Cenchrea (Romans 16:1), that you may receive her in the Lord in a manner worthy of the saints, and assist her in whatever business she has need of you; for indeed she has been a helper of many and of myself also (Romans 16: 2).*

My Thought

In the next 17 verses, Paul will greet several fellow workers in Christ, a large number of them women. They were friends of Paul whom he had associated with throughout his missionary travels. Paul met Phoebe in the city of Corinth. Phoebe is bringing Paul's letter (*Romans*) to the Romans. *Proverbs 27:2 "Let another man praise you, and not your own mouth; A stranger, and not your own lips."* Paul is commending Phoebe for using her gifts from God to further the kingdom. It is an excellent example for us to remember to commend others for their good deeds and hard work and let others commend us. Her name will always be remembered by those who read God's Word.

Your Application

Whether your name is ever mentioned, or you remain unknown to your present world, what you do for God is important and life changing. Keep seeking Jesus, a relationship with the Father, and walking daily in the Holy Spirit. God records your actions, and like Phoebe, you will receive your reward.

Greeting Roman Saints

> *Greet Priscilla and Aquila, my fellow workers in Christ Jesus (Romans 16:3), who risked their own necks for my life, to whom not only I give thanks, but also all the churches of the Gentiles (Romans 16:4). Likewise greet the church that is in their house (Romans 16:5).*

My Thought

Oh, the importance of having lifelong friends who support you. Priscilla and Aquila are Paul's fellow workers in Christ Jesus. They were Paul's converts, who became Paul's best allies and friends. Wherever they went they created a church in their home. They were laser-focused on spreading the gospel of Christ. Paul's mission was to be a church planter. Priscilla and Aquila fed and matured the church with their teachings. What a great team they were together. They were willing to lay down their lives for one another; that is the true connection of commitment and love.

Your Application

Find a way to build a church in your home. It is vital that you are sharing the Word of God with others. When I say build a church, I mean share the gospel to others using your gifts. You might have the gift of evangelism, then gather and share. You might have the gift of a teacher, then teach others what you are learning. You might have the gift of a pastor, then comfort others with the word of God. You might have the gift of hospitality, then ask others over to share a dinner. Whatever your talents, use them daily to "build a church." You do not have to be ordained to minister to others. Simply use the gifts God has given you and share it with those the Holy Spirit puts in your path. Also, look out for others. Pricilla and Aquila risked their lives for Paul. They were not only interested in their own lives, but the lives of others. Read *Philippians 2* and write out how the first verses are linked to Pricilla and Aquila. How does it speak to you?

> *Greet my beloved Epaenetus, who is the first fruits of Achaia to Christ (Romans 16:5b). Greet Mary, who labored much for us (Romans 16:6).*

My Thought

Epaenetus is one of Paul's first converts. The joys of leading people to Christ is unforgettable. Paul's friend, Epaenetus, is in Rome. Paul sends his greetings to him with a reminder of who he is. He also greets Mary, a laborer, meaning she looked after the poor, the children, and the younger ladies. In a sense, she was a nurturer. Like Martha in the gospels, she wasn't afraid to get down and dirty to labor in the kingdom. She did what she was gifted to do.

Your Application

There is nothing more thrilling than to lead others to Christ. Who is your first? Write them a letter today. If you have not introduced someone to the Lord yet, then ask God today to give you the chance to do so. Labor like Mary today, see a need, use your gifts to help another fellow man.

> *Greet Andronicus and Junia, my countrymen and my fellow prisoners, who are of note among the apostles, who also were in Christ before me (Romans 16:7). Greet Amplias, my beloved in the Lord (Romans 16:8). Greet Urbanus, our fellow worker in Christ, and Stachys, my beloved (Romans 16:9). Greet Apelles, approved in Christ (Romans 16:10).*

My Thought

Andronicus and Junia are kinsmen of Paul; they were Christians before Paul came to know Jesus. They were known by the 11 apostles of Christ, the Peter, James, and John crew. They could have possibly been in the upper room when the Holy Spirit fell (*Acts 2*). When Stephen was stoned (*Acts 7*), Paul could have seen his kinsman in the midst. They undoubtedly prayed for Paul's salvation. After Paul's conversion, he shared a prison cell with them. A great way to deepen relationships when stuck in one uncomfortable place. Why they were in Rome is unknown; they were probably there as leaders to further the maturity of the Roman saints. Paul knew they were there and greeted them. We know little of Amplias, Urbanus, Stachys, and Apelles. They were beloved in the Lord, beloved of Paul, fellow workers in Christ, and approved by Christ. They sound like many of our dedicated workers of Christ today. They definitely made an impact on Paul's life to encourage him and work with him.

Your Application

Saul/Paul was a tenacious man who wanted to destroy the first fruits of God's new move. He was murdering the new Christians. Part of his family had become saved and supposedly prayed for Paul to understand the good news being spread. He did become a follower. His family is now mentioned in these verses. I am sure no one in your family is as bad as Saul/Paul. Take encouragement that prayer works, and your family will come to believe in Jesus as you pray for their salvation. Paul also loved having loyal friends in Christ. He knew he could trust them, and they helped him in his ministry. Today pray for your family member who does not know the *truth*. Be a trusted friend to someone, serve, and encourage them.

> *Greet those who are of the household of Aristobulus (Romans 16:10b). Greet Herodion, my countryman. Greet those who are of the household of Narcissus who are in the Lord (Romans 16:11).*

My Thought

Paul is sending greetings to the household slaves and servants who live in the Roman Palace. Paul is related to Herodion, who is in the lineage of Herod. Interestingly enough, even though Rome was not a safe place to be a Christian, God planted His Word and His people in the Palace to influence the influential. There is not one place that God's Word will be removed. His Word stands forever, even in darkness! What an encouragement to us today to remember this verse and what it means. God was in charge back then and will remain in charge forever. We need not be ashamed of the gospel or in fear of it being denied in the darkest places, such as the Roman Empire.

Your Application

God calls us to the seven mountains of influence; not all called will be pastors or minister in a church. You may be called to be a "minister" in the arenas of business, arts and entertainment, media, family, education, government, etc.… Be a light wherever God has called you to influence. Where are you called to rule and reign? Write a paper on what you are called to do.

Greet Tryphena and Tryphosa, who have labored in the Lord. Greet the beloved Persis, who labored much in the Lord (Romans 16:12). Greet Rufus, chosen in the Lord, and his mother and mine (Romans 16:13).

My Thought

These precious women, Tryphena and Tryphosa. Their names imply they were aristocrats, their names meant "dainty" and "delicate," which means they did not work for a living, and yet here in verse 12, Paul explains that they labored in the Lord, what a beautiful sight of transformation. Aristocratic, high influential women brought to the level of love. All people were equal. They labored with the other apostles because they came into contact with the truth. Persis is another woman who worked with them. She possibly traveled with Paul on his missionary journeys. These three women who were in Rome had made an impact on Paul's life, and he was greeting them. Rufus and his mother possibly go way back to the days of Paul being Saul. A young Saul sat at the feet of Gamaliel, a great Jewish leader, to learn the Jewish Law. Saul could have possibly stayed with Simon of Cyrene, with his wife and two sons, Alexander and Rufus. Simon was the man who carried Jesus' cross to the hill of Calvary. Simon believed that Jesus was the Son of God and led his family to believe. Here Rufus is being remembered by Paul as well as his mother, whom he adopted as his own.

Your Application

In these scriptures, we see that what we do for the Lord will be remembered. So today, do all that you do as unto the Lord. Make a point to be intentional. At the end of the day, write about how you felt and the reactions you had as you were intentionally doing all you did today for Jesus.

Greet Asyncritus, Phlegon, Hermas, Patrobas, Hermes, and the brethren who are with them. (Romans 16:14)

My Thought

Paul greets a community of Greek men. They were in Rome as possible businessmen; they heard the gospel, believed, formed a group, and had a house church.

Your Application

Again, let every place you go become a church. Not in the literal sense, but speak, read, and act out the Word of God to those around you. Make it fun!

Greet Philologus and Julia, Nereus and his sister, and Olympas, and all the saints who are with them. (Romans 16:15)

My Thought

Philologus means "a lover of the word;" what a great name! We should all be lovers of God's Word! Julia, Nereus, and his sister, Olympus, and all the saints show us a great infiltrating of Christians before Paul came to Rome. *First, I thank my God through Jesus Christ for all of you, because your faith is being reported all over the world (Romans 1:8).* How awesome is that? Nereus could have been a housekeeper to a prominent Roman citizen named Flavius Clemens, who later became Consul of Rome. This was one of the highest political offices in the city. In 95 AD, Flavius Clemens was sentenced to death because he was a Christian. Could it have been the influence and infiltration of Nereus? We will never know until heaven, but we do know that God places His people right where he wants them. Check out Daniel in the book of *Daniel*. Nereus, in his later years, became a martyr for the cause of Christ.

Your Application

Whether young or old, rich or poor, we are all one in Christ. Do not let anyone intimidate you. Share the good news with someone you wouldn't normally talk to.

Greet one another with a holy kiss. The churches of Christ greet you. (Romans 16:16)

My Thought

Paul is good friends with many who are in Rome. Although he has not been there, he does have brothers and sisters there that he has worked with in the past. Paul seems to have quite a few, and he greets them all in the love of the Lord. When he is finished greeting them all, he sends greetings from the many churches he has established throughout his missionary journeys.

Your Application

We are one big family. Paul knows some in Rome but acts like he knows them all because they are all part of God's family. We have brothers and sisters we have never met, isn't that exciting? We will one day meet each other. Until then, we can pray for one another. Today pick a country, learn about it, and pray for your brothers and sisters in Christ. Write out what you have learned and write out your prayers.

Avoid Divisive Persons

Now I urge you, brethren, note those who cause divisions and offenses, contrary to the doctrine which you learned, and avoid them. (Romans 16:17)

My Thought

A good word from our brother Paul, avoid those who cause division and offenses contrary to the gospel of Christ. He said it even stronger in *Galatians* 1. He said even if an angel should preach a different gospel than the one I preach to you, cut him off. We are to know our Word and defend it by not allowing others to bring division or offense to the Word.

Your Application

Keep an open mind to the Spirit of God to not let anyone bring division to God's people. If anyone is bringing offenses to the gospel, deal with it in love, but if the persons don't repent, avoid them. Don't put fuel to their fire; let God work on them and deal with them as He knows best.

> *For those who are such do not serve our Lord Jesus Christ, but their own belly, and by smooth words and flattering speech deceive the hearts of the simple. (Romans 16:18)*

My Thought

These people who try to bring division are not looking to serve God, but their own appetite. They will try to manipulate the weaker among us. We must not let this be. Remember, in the previous chapters, Paul addressed that the stronger of us should look out for the more vulnerable.

Your Application

Read in *Deuteronomy* what happened when the weaker Israelites would lag behind on their trip to the Promised Land (*Deuteronomy 25:17-18*). Write about it.

> *For your obedience has become known to all. Therefore I am glad on your behalf; but I want you to be wise in what is good, and simple concerning evil. (Romans 16:19)*

My Thought

The Romans Christians were known for their obedience. Paul was happy about that, but he wanted them to be wise in what was good and innocent in what was evil. It is easy to become mixed with good and evil in today's society, in what we allow ourselves to listen to and watch. We need to pray to God to be wise and to make good choices in our daily living.

Your Application

You must be strong in the Word and be wise in His goodness. Don't let the evil of this world get into you; be innocent of the things of the world that seem harmless but are worldly and evil in the eyes of God. Be set apart from the world; that is what holiness is. No mixture of evil should be involved in your walk with God. We are to be examples in our world, but we are not to participate in the evil of this world. Are there things today in which you have compromised with evil? Take an inventory of what you watch and listen to, how you speak, and how you treat others. If there is compromise or mixture, take it to the Lord and let the Holy Spirit convict you and judge you so you can change. Write out some goals you can accomplish regarding this verse.

> *And the God of peace will crush Satan under your feet shortly. The grace of our Lord Jesus Christ be with you. Amen. (Romans 16:20)*

My Thought

Satan has a date with the God of peace, and it isn't going to be pretty. We are reminded that shortly the God of peace will crush Satan under our feet. Going back to the *Genesis* story, we see that prophecy spoken of in *Genesis 3:15*; now Paul reminds the Romans to remain holy, that shortly the prophecy will be accomplished, and Satan will be crushed. The Lord Jesus Christ's grace be with you.

Your Application

This is a tool for you to use against Satan. When he accuses you about your past or current struggles, remind him of his date with God!

Greetings from Paul's Friends

> *Timothy, my fellow worker, and Lucius, Jason, and Sosipater, my countrymen, greet you (Romans 16:21). I, Tertius, who wrote this epistle, greet you in the Lord (Romans 16:22). Gaius, my host and the host of the whole church, greets you. Erastus, the treasurer of the city, greets you, and Quartus, a brother (Romans 16:23).*

My Thought

All the brothers with Paul now greet the Roman brothers and sisters. We are again reminded we are one big happy family, and we will finally meet once and for all in heaven with Christ. Paul reminds us to work together so we can remain strong. Paul and his group encouraged and strengthened one another. Tertius was an amanuensis for Paul.

Your Application

You are not alone. You have a big family waiting to meet you. Live your life knowing you are loved not only by a loving Heavenly Father but by your brothers and sisters who have gone before you and those who live with you. Make a point to be connected to others in your sphere of influence. Read *Hebrews 12:1* and then go back and read *Hebrews 11*. Who is this great cloud of witnesses surrounding us? Write your thoughts.

> *The grace of our Lord Jesus Christ be with you all. Amen. (Romans 16:24)*

My Thought

The grace of our Lord Jesus Christ is with all who will readily receive Jesus. GRACE: God's Riches At Christ Expense. His grace is given freely to us. What? Another tremendous gift from our heavenly Father. We deserved death but are given life abundantly because of His death on the cross and His resurrection three days later. We are given grace.

Your Application

Live in grace! You and I don't deserve what Jesus gave us, but Christ freely gives it to us to enjoy. There is always a reason to rejoice. Be happy today for this one verse! Write out five ways you see the grace of God in your life. It's a choice to rejoice! Make a point to do it.

Benediction

> *Now to Him who is able to establish you according to my gospel and the preaching of Jesus Christ, according to the revelation of the mystery kept secret since the world began (Romans 16:25)*

My Thought

To Jesus, who is able to establish you according to Paul's gospel, the preaching of Jesus, to the revelation of the mystery kept since the world began, we are recognized in the kingdom, belonging to the family of God because of Jesus. The secret only revealed by the Holy Spirit. We wonder why some people just do not understand the gift our Father God gave us through the life and death and resurrection and ascension of His Son. This is the greatest faith we can have. Greater than the healing of cancer or an amputated leg replaced. Knowing Jesus and understanding He is the Son of God, our Savior, who came to destroy sin, hell and the grave; to set us free of all our bondages and lead us into eternal life, that is the greatest faith required from us. Others do not have this type of faith and will not desire it, they long to live out their own lives their way, sad to say.

Your Application

Think of the *Storybook Fairy-Tale Reality* world where you live. Jesus has made that possible for you. You rule and reign with Jesus here on earth as you pray His kingdom come, His will be done. Practice that now. Who and what is the mystery kept secret (*1 Timothy 3:16*)?

> *but now made manifest, and by the prophetic Scriptures made known to all nations, according to the commandment of the everlasting God, for obedience to the faith— (Romans 16:26)*

My Thought

The mystery is now evident by the prophetic Scriptures that came to pass because of the obedience of Christ to the faith. What was a mystery to all who lived before Jesus came, died, and rose again, is now known to us. We live in a great generation; we can understand fully what the last generations before Christ only saw partially. We see clearly, yet we still only see a part of what God will do. We wait patiently for Christ's second return; we have read about it and know it will happen. This is what it was like for those in the past who understood the Messiah was coming but didn't know how it would come about.

Your Application

As we study scripture, we must take it seriously and live it actively and intentionally. What scripture is a mystery to you now? Look at it, ponder it and meditate on it. Ask the Holy Spirit to illuminate the meaning to you. Look up scriptures about the second coming of Christ. Write a comparison essay on your thoughts about Jesus' second coming and how you think those who were awaiting the Messiah had similar ideas.

to God, alone wise, be glory through Jesus Christ forever. Amen. (Romans 16:27)

My Thought

There is only one wise God and to Him be glory through Jesus Christ, our Lord forever! We stand in the presence of the only wise God every day, every moment. He is our Father God and alone carries wisdom. May the knowledge of the glory of the Lord cover the earth as the waters cover the sea!

Your Application

Today, be confident in Whom you serve. Be confident in His love for you. Confidence is contagious. *Know who you are in Christ. Know your purpose. Know where you are going.* Write it out in a final essay. Keep it with you to remind you when the evil step-father bombards you with his lies and his taunts. You are an overcomer! Use my mantra next time the enemy speaks to you: "The devil is a liar; Jesus is the Truth!" Say it until you believe it!

Romans Sixteen we see the Kingdom of God is a community, we, like Paul, should remember to connect to those God has placed in our lives. *Romans 16* connects us with Paul's fellow workers in Christ. We get to see how Paul encourages and appreciates his friends. He has a wide variety of brothers and sisters in Christ. He shows the importance of all his friends. He specifically calls out the women who have ministered with him for Christ, placing a stamp of approval for women in ministry today! Then Paul goes on to warn us about those who divide and upset people with false doctrine and manipulation. Watch out for these people. Paul does not work alone (an example to us), he writes greetings from himself and those working with him. He ends the book of *Romans* by giving glory to the only wise God, through Jesus Christ forever. Amen.

My Prayer

To the only wise God, our Savior, may we continue to deep dive into the book of *Romans* so we may mature as followers of You. Lead us to people we can connect with to further the gospel. Help us to be discerning concerning false prophets or manipulative people. Lead us on the right path and continue to keep Satan under our feet. To You Lord, we commit to obey, serve and love forever. In Your saving Name, Jesus. Amen!

My Final Thought

You are the loved child of God, who lives in a *Storybook Fairy-Tale Reality of the Kingdom* that is real. Jesus is your Prince, and He has come to rescue you from the evil villain (Satan), yourself (your sinful nature), and the world. He has a place waiting for you in eternity. Better yet, He has a place for you here and now, in Himself, to be safe from harm and evil. He will teach you through hard times to trust Him, and He will guide you to let go of all things that are not of Him. He has paid the ultimate price for you to be free to live an abundant life in the *Storybook Fairy-Tale Reality of His Kingdom*.

Your Final Application
Keep studying Romans until it becomes a part of you and share it with all who will listen. God Bless your spirit and soul to prosper.

Write a summary of chapter 16.

You must be strong in the Word and be wise in His goodness. Don't let the evil of this world get into you; be innocent of the things of the world that seem harmless but are worldly and evil in the eyes of God. Be set apart from the world; that is what holiness is. No mixture of evil should be involved in your walk with God.

Our Worship
The Blessing / Kari Jobe & Cody Carnes / Live From Elevation Ballantyne / Elevation Worship
https://www.youtube.com/watch?v=Zp6aygmvzM4

EPILOGUE

Your death has given me the keys
In Your resurrection
I have been set free
To my old life
I am no longer bound
In the new life
Your grace
Your love
Your mercy
Is where I am found
No longer a slave to my old mentality
No longer a victim of my own brutality
Destructive words
And harsh criticism
Are the covenant of old
No longer are you timid
Now I call you bold
Fierce and courageous
Trusting humble gracious
Loving lowly and forgiving
Compassionate merciful free
Hope-filled joyous and complete
In Me you no longer lack
In Me you are set free
From negative thought patterns
That seemed so crippling
You Jesus are my righteousness
My covering

My identity
You have cleansed me of my sin
You have poured streams of living water
To create life within
Your love covers a multitude of sin
Your grace showers me
Empowers me to win
In you I have victory
We overcome defeat
You remind me of whose I am
And strengthen me when I am weak
May my heart be humble
May my thoughts be life-giving
May the meditation of my heart
And words of my tongue remind myself
That You have already won
That You are for me
Not against me
May my heart be aligned to You
May every thought purpose and drive
Bring glory and honor for You

Chante Munoz-Medina (July 2017)

AFTERWORD

Now you see why *Romans* is such an important Book of the Bible to read and to meditate on, so we can learn to live in the Spirit of our *Storybook Fairy-Tale Reality of the Kingdom of God*. We do live in two worlds. We are aliens here, just passing through, and yet we are royalty and priests with a purpose. We are to influence as many people as possible. We are to live victoriously in our lives so others may see the light of Jesus. *Romans* helps us see the other side of the coin of life. We are to live here on the physical earth to occupy until Christ comes, but we are to live in the *Storybook Fairy-Tale Reality of the Kingdom of God*. We are to rule and reign here on earth through our prayers, positions, and practical actions.

Living *Romans* is impossible, some say. I agree! Living the way of *Romans* is impossible in our physical bodies and souls, but not impossible in our spirits. His Spirit transforms our spirits that transform our souls (minds and hearts). We must learn to die daily to our ways. His ways are higher. His thoughts are beyond our understanding. His ways are better for us than our ways.

Isaiah 55:8–9 (NIV)
"For my thoughts are not your thoughts,
neither are your ways my ways,"
declares the Lord.
"As the heavens are higher than the earth,
so are my ways higher than your ways
and my thoughts than your thoughts."

We can live on a higher level with purpose, following what the Spirit of God has for us daily. We are not better than others, but we have a greater understanding of why we are here. We see from our higher position, where we are seated with Christ in the heavenly places (*Ephesians 2:6*). What is impossible with man is possible with God (*Matthew 19:26*). We must understand through *Romans* and the rest of God's Word that we are to live victoriously because Jesus won the victory for us. How do we live victoriously? By believing every Word that comes out of the mouth of God (the Bible). We all have lived a tragedy (not unlike our characters in every storybook fairy-tale), and the enemy will use it for his glory, to make us doubt our God and His goodness. We must overcome every hurt and pain of our inner man/woman by appropriating the Word of God, like medicine, into the very places we are hurting. Indeed, we must know that Jesus took that very hurt and pain and shame on Himself at the cross, so we do not have to bear it anymore. It is the truth! It is our reality! It is our victory! You may still feel the hurt; you may even believe that you cannot forgive the perpetrator of that hurt. You can't and I can't, unless we read *Romans* and God's Word over and over again. Then, we will understand, the light will turn on, and we will be set free. The Word is our book of sight! What we cannot see now, as we continue to read it, we become transformed into the reality of the *Storybook Fairy-Tale of the Kingdom of God*. We become stronger in that world than the physical world because the Spirit fashions us into who God says we are. We have the power to break the spell of the enemy, not to become the victim but the hero and heroine of God, not only setting ourselves free but those in our God-given paths, bringing glory and pleasure to God, our real purpose! It truly is an exciting life to live for God! We are only passing through this life, but why waste it when we can live in the very existence of what He has for us now? Why do I believe all of this? The Word of God is more real to me in the past 60 years of my life than any other voice! I believe what it says and live out my beliefs. I am victorious and want that for you as well. You and I are royalty and priests in a world that sees us as normal. We get lost in the love of God, the goodness of God, and the fact that He teaches us what is best! As far as the world knows, it sees us in the shadows, but God shines His Light on us to show us who we really are!

Romans is the foundation of the depth of our perception of what Jesus did for us and the freedom of our walk in Christ. It's actually our play-by-play book of how the Spirit transforms our lives from flesh to spirit. If we get saved and live a life without knowing *Romans*, then we are unable to grow in the understanding of our inheritance, in the great expanse of our destiny, and the fullness of our power and influence here on earth.

It really is a *Storybook Fairy-Tale Reality*. We haven't a clue what is before us in this spiritual life. Paul opened the door for us in *Romans*, and we took a peek of what God has for us. It's up to us to walk through and perceive what is right before our very eyes, not our physical eyes, but the eyes of our spirit. It's up to us, after reading *Romans*, to take action.

May the Lord Jesus, our Savior, Father God, and the Holy Spirit become your best friends. May your relationship with the Trinity become like that of Paul's, may they become more real to you than what is right before your eyes, and may you walk in the Spirit and live a victorious life! May you be blessed with God's favor and power to proclaim the gospel unashamed! Amen.

Thank you for picking up my book and reading it. If it has blessed you, please share with others how it has affected you and encourage them to read Romans Reviewed.

My Prayer for You

"But let all who take refuge in You be glad;
let them ever sing for joy.
Spread Your protection over them,
that those who love Your name may rejoice in You
Surely, Lord, You bless the righteous;
You surround them with Your favor as with a shield.
Psalms 5:11, 12

It's a choice to rejoice!
It's a choice to live in the Spirit
It's a choice to die daily to your agenda
And follow His.
It's a choice to share His good news.
It's a choice to please God.
It's a choice to realize who you are and where you live.

You are a loved Child of God.
You live in a Storybook Fairy-Tale Reality
 In the Kingdom of God!

It's ultimately a choice whom you will serve, and
It's a choice to decide where you will spend eternity.
Choose this day Whom you will serve!

Laurie

ABOUT THE AUTHOR

Laurie Kay Rodriguez has studied the Bible for most of her life. It is her second language. She has brought the book, Romans Reviewed, to life with her knowledge and love for the Word, yet in a very believable and understanding voice. She desires to pull each reader into what the Word is saying specifically to them. Get ready for an amazing ride into the past to open wide your understanding of your present and future.

She is an amazing wife, mother and truly fun grandmother. An American missionary, author, teacher, body sculpting specialist, certified fitness trainer, and accomplished a theology degree. She is an avid reader and a self-taught woman of God.

Early life: Born April 30, 1957, in Medford, Oregon, to Christian parents, Fred and June Nelson. Her father was a "sought after" homebuilder and her mother was a caring childcare provider. Laurie is the youngest of the six children (2 deceased at a young age—Connie and Freddy), Bryan, Randy, (Carla, my sister in law), and Julie. All of whom worked in the construction company with her Dad or helped Momma Nelson. In the Nelson family, Bible devotions came before the start of the day, and at the end of the day. They enjoyed camping, hunting and going to the beach.

Family: Laurie met Samuel Rodriguez at Bethany Bible College in the late 1970s and they were married in 1978. They have three grown children; Natasha, is the oldest, married to Angel Perez. They have four delightful, mischievous children, Tatiana, Josiah, Elijah and Isabella. Ashley, the middle child, is married to Michael Jappe. They have a 2 ½ year old little girl, Penelope Sophia and a 10-month old baby girl, Giselle Margauz! Sammy Rodriguez the youngest, is married to Chandler, they have a baby girl on the way! The three children were home schooled and brought up in the Church. Laurie and Sam enjoy ministering to couples, traveling, days off at the beach, watching the Niners, Warriors and SF Giants, hanging out with good friends and family, playing cards, discussing politics and being grandparents. Laurie is a true and faithful friend to many.

Ministry: Laurie committed her life to Jesus Christ at an early age and has been a Sunday school teacher, she has discipled young men and women, director of Moms groups, taught couples classes with her husband and wrote a Bible curriculum, Surfing the Word. Her love of the Word of God has caused her to dig deeper into that Word to take it to the nations. As a young couple Laurie and Sam, and their children completed a 3 month discipleship training school, Crossroads, with Youth With a Mission in Salem, Oregon, and completed a three months missions trip to Romania. Upon returning from Romania they came back to minister in Sacramento, California, for a five year commitment before going to the Dominican Republic as a missionary family to work at a private school, where she discipled groups of teenage girls and women. Sam and Laurie went to Nicaragua to help stop sex trafficking of minors, one of their greatest passions. She also ministers to her clients at the spa. Laurie is working on her second book, Goodbye Daddy, Hello Father God! Laurie is an encourager and prayer warrior who lives by faith and not by sight. (Written by Friends.)

Portions of Romans Reviewed revenue will be donated to organizations who work towards stopping sex trafficking of children.

Printed in the United States
by Baker & Taylor Publisher Services